SARAH'S STILL LIFE

SARAH'S STILL LIFE

A NOVEL

MATTHEW KOPF

NDP

NEW DEGREE PRESS
COPYRIGHT © 2021 MATTHEW KOPF
All rights reserved.

SARAH'S STILL LIFE
A Novel

ISBN   978-1-63676-892-2   *Paperback*
        978-1-63676-893-9   *Kindle Ebook*
        978-1-63676-894-6   *Ebook*

First Edition: September 2021

Front cover design: *Jason Gierl, Insect Hobby Designs*
Back cover design: *Maria Shtelle*
Layout: *Max Kolpak*
Developmental Editors: *David Kopf, Kristine Nieman*
Acquiring Editor: *Mohan Fitgerald*
Marketing and Revisions Editor: *Joanna Hatzikazakis*
Media and Marketing Consultant: *John Marszalkowski*

This is a work of fiction. Names, characters, places, and incidents either are the product of author's imagination or are used fictitiously. Any resemblance to actual persons, living or dead, business establishments, events, or locales is entirely coincidental.

To my wife, Ani—my love, my liberator, my candle in the dark.

"If a man has no tea in him, he is incapable of understanding truth and beauty."

—JAPANESE PROVERB

"No trumpets sound when the important decisions of our life are made. Destiny is made known silently."

—AGENES DE MILLE

CHAPTER 1

Whenever the phone rang, Sarah Hall held her breath; usually just for a moment, but it caught in her throat like a sip of water gone wrong. In that split second, she wondered what anxiety-made-real lurked on the other end of the receiver. Was her mother finally dead? Maybe just jailed or committed indefinitely. Or was it a boyfriend calling to break it off? No, wait, hadn't had one of those in a long time. Life had taught her that anything was possible, and it was usually bad.

In her dreams, the voice on the other end was a distant lover who spoke in sweetness and security, someone who understood the world and her, but when she awoke, it all evaporated like an alcohol swab before the needle sting of loneliness.

Most of the time, however, it was a telemarketer or a customer asking about hours.

Sarah's thirty-plus years of experience with a human incendiary device as a mother had left her singed and seared and stained. Since the death of her father, Henry—the ghost of a man that he was—her mother's explosive events had been hotter, fiercer, and more erratic. In her mother's rare moments of calm brought on by pill-induced chemical equilibrium, Sarah could live and dream; free to think about a future and bathe in the cool, restorative waters of hope. Otherwise, it was a battle for survival.

For a few years, Sarah had Christopher to lean on, to stabilize the wings of her life. But, over time, the downward strain of her mother proved too much. That, or the pull of his free, young, blonde admin was too tempting. Either way, he was gone, and Sarah was alone in her struggle to contain her mother, get an education, and hold on to what slivers of a future she could grasp.

Tight blue flames licked the bottom of a large stainless-steel pot as Sarah pulled her flowing brown curls into a loose ponytail and waited for it to boil. The early morning rush had kept her busy, but now the Family Kettle tea shop was quiet and still, just how she liked it.

The building sat amongst a row of plucky boutiques in a regenerating part of town in a city, much like the rest of America's Midwest, in a constant struggle to fill the void left by the fall of its industrial sector. The shop itself was small but well-appointed with a café, an area for packaged tea and gourmet snacks, and a corner featuring serving ware and accoutrements. Decorated in a tasteful, if somewhat dainty, style, the store was pleasant and comfortable.

Sarah had learned to take advantage of the gaps in the storm, to spread out like a desert flower after a blitz of rain. In these moments, she liked to visualize her future: blazing new trails in flavor as a budding food scientist; in love with a smart, handsome, cultured, exciting man; and of course, freedom from her mother's endless cycles of turmoil, illness, and misery. It was a fantasy, but one has to live for something.

The pot hit the third boil with large bubbles pushing to the surface, bursting, then immediately replaced with new bubbles. Sarah transferred the water to the waiting leaves and continued her daydream. The smell of rustic earth and berries filled the air and coated her return to fantasyland in a velvety layer of olfactory glory until an icy gust kicked her in the knees, knocking her back to reality.

"Ugh, it's too damn cold out there for this time of year," said Loretta as she closed the door. "How'd it go this morning?"

Loretta was a hard woman with a soft heart for the downtrodden and the elderly. She had clawed her way up the ladder at the finance firm of Smith and Broderick's in an era when people "like her" didn't do that sort of thing. She was the protégé of Anton Smith, Derek Smith's progressive younger brother, who—much to his brother's dismay—was anxious to help shatter glass ceilings and old norms. When Anton died of a stroke at sixty-six, the directors cleaned house, and Loretta was forced into "early retirement" and decided to open the Family Kettle. Over the years, she'd become a second mother to Sarah and the first one of any quality.

"Busy, but I handled it."

"You always do. Though I see from those stacks of papers that you're still procrastinating on that English essay," Loretta chided and smoothed her hair as she pointed to a pile of papers. "You wait any longer and you'll be my age by the time it's finished." Loretta's frame shook with a hearty chuckle.

"Please, no. It's already taking me too long. Not just the paper, all of it. And I'm already too old! Everyone in class is, like, twelve! Why do you think I'm still single? Too young at school, too old here. Unless I want a geriatric sugar daddy or something. Beatrice might be able to drum one of those up for me," Sarah said with a laugh. "Anyway, the essay is just about done; it looks worse than it is."

"Well, good," Loretta exclaimed with a mock scold. "You know, don't write this place off yet; you never know what kind of a handsome, stud of a man might walk through that door."

Sarah rolled her eyes and giggled as an elderly gentleman with bulging, wide-set eyes and a complexion like burled walnut strolled through the door. He blew on his hands and rubbed them together to fight off the chill. In the quiet room, his sandpaper-like palms sounded like a guiro in a pop song. *Exactly what I mean*, Sarah thought to herself with a quiet chortle. *The perfect example at the perfect time.*

"Hi, Rich! What'll you have today?" Sarah asked sweetly. She loved Richard, but he was old enough to be her great-grandfather—not exactly her type.

"Oh, the usual. A package of peppermint for the later and a cup of English Breakfast for the now. Be sure to tie it up nice, now, like you always do," Richard cooed in his age-softened voice.

Richard nearly always ordered the same thing, but Sarah liked asking as much as he liked telling. She wrapped his order in a shiny, imperial blue box (though sometimes she used pink) tied with a pair of the shop's trademark bows. Loretta called the packaging the store's "little extra."

She handed the box to Richard.

"Say, Sarah." His voice creaked like an old cabinet hinge. "When are we going to get another one of your blends? Your Winter Special was really something."

"Aw, thanks." Sarah blushed.

Loretta chimed in. "That one sold fast. We'll have to arrange something."

"I look forward to it," Richard said. Everyone smiled in agreement.

As Richard walked away, the phone rang.

Sarah held her breath.

Out of the corner of her eye, she saw Loretta move toward the tintinnabulating phone and winced as she answered. Sarah exhaled and began to put away the ribbons. With a start, Loretta's voice interrupted her work.

"Sarah, it's for you."

Sarah's shoulders sank as she turned around; she feared she knew what Loretta was about to say.

"It's Ralph at the pharmacy. Sounds like Nancy's had another *incident.*"

The automatic doors hissed open as Sarah rushed toward her mother's register. She rounded the aisle into cosmetics and stopped with a gasp. The floor was covered in heaping mounds of broken plastic boxes and metal display hooks all covered in a fine dusting of technicolor powders as one imagines the snowfall in Oz. Some of the pigments were smeared and ground into the bare spots of the cheap, faded linoleum where customers had walked right through the mess.

Sarah tiptoed between the tussled ruins, careful to avoid a pair of metal shelves that hung by only one side and sagged like a disused diving board with rotten springs. At the end of the aisle, an upturned makeup chair was nearly all that was left of the demonstration area where Nancy and her coworkers gave customers complimentary applications of all of the latest in low-cost fashion. Sarah often wondered who came into a corner pharmacy for makeup advice from minimum wage, past-middle-aged women. She looked up from the carnage and found Karen, shellshocked, waiting for her. Karen was one of Nancy's coworkers—a shy, kind, and sweet woman with the unfortunate fate of looking like a bloodhound with a two-pack-a-day cigarette habit. Today, Karen's wrinkled, disheveled countenance had an added green tinge of worry.

"She's in the back. Sh-she's been like this for… nearly an hour," Karen stammered. "It started when sh-she came back from the Quick Bread and d-didn't look good." Karen took a deep breath and concentrated on slowing her speech. Her stammer yielded. "The next thing we all knew, she was screamin' hysterical-like. Shoutin' and throwin' herself into the product displays; just pushin' everythin' off the shelves and sobbin'."

Sarah shook her head in embarrassment and wished she didn't have to do this again.

"Ralph talked her down enough to get her into the break room. I tell ya, this was sumptin' else, maybe even worse than last time. Jus' yesterday she was tellin' me she was 'gettin' her life back together.' Don't look like it to me."

Karen escorted her through the grey, dimpled, swinging doors that led to the back rooms. The rusty hinges complained as they returned begrudgingly into position behind them. A moist, somber air laid heavy across their shoulders as their footsteps echoed against the bland cinderblock. All was made worse by the harsh flickering glow of banks of buzzy, agitated florescent tubes.

At the door to the break room, Karen withdrew. Sarah took a breath and watched her go before turning her gaze to the narrow window of the stippled plastic door to survey the situation like a scout on a high hill before a battle. The long, narrow room had three folding plastic tables set against the wall. In the far corner sat a pair of blinking, abused vending machines and there, with her back to the door, was Nancy slouched over a rickety table, her head in her hands. Nancy's large, corpulent body spilled onto the surface like an overinflated water balloon sagging over a child's arm.

Sarah held back, behind the door, to compose herself. The adrenalin rush after Ralph's phone call had mostly subsided and had been replaced with a sick lethargy suffused with swirling hotspots of anger and resentment. They'd been through this sort of thing before—too many times—and each event left Sarah's life upended in one way or another. Last time, shortly after Henry died, Sarah was forced to drop her class and take days off from work to smooth out the situation with Ralph and the cops after Nancy snapped on a customer and stormed out of the store in her bra shouting, *"I'm a person, too,"* like some kind of protest. In truth, a small, geeky man in short sleeves and a tie asked her if an item had scanned incorrectly, and she lost it. After a long cascade of cuss words, she removed his glasses and threw them across the store. Then, with a nearby pair of scissors, excised his tie before removing her own shirt and draping it over his head as she marched out the door. With Nancy, it was always something different and, according to her, never her fault.

Another deep breath brought Sarah to a calmer place. She knew she had to get Nancy out of there with as little drama as possible. As she peered through the small window, she could hear her mother sobbing and murmuring softly to herself. Despite her feelings about the situation, Sarah couldn't help but find a well-head of compassion for her mother. After all,

MATTHEW KOPF · 15

she really was a sick woman and, like it or not, she was her mother. With that in mind, Sarah eased into the break room.

"Mom... Mom..." Sarah whispered as she sat down next to her mother and patted her on the shoulder with a gentle tap. "Mom..."

"Sarah! Whadda you doin' here? You know you can't visit me at work; it distracts me. They'll fire my ass," Nancy yelled through her tears.

"Mom, your distraction is not foremost in their minds right now. It's the tore-up makeup department, the whole place in shambles that they're concerned with. What were you thinking? Why did you do that?"

"I didn't! I couldn't handle it. Just too much, the awful customer, the lady at the Quick Bread, and... then... and..."

"It's okay, Mom." Sarah rubbed Nancy's arm in an attempt to calm her.

Nancy cut in, "It's not my fault. It's not my fault! If they hadn't talked to me like that. I'm a person too."

"Who? What did they say?" Sarah beseeched.

"This square old lady who clearly thought she was better than me. We were discussin' a new line of lipsticks that all us girls are excited about. The conversation was goin' real nice. The lady nodded and smiled as I spoke."

Nancy rubbed her arms and began to pick at a red spot on her wrist.

"Then, I suggested a nice shade a red, an' she laughed at me real mean, like a villain or somethin'. She said, 'That color might work where you come from, but where I come from that color only means one thing.' Then she mouthed the word *whore*. You believe that? I mean, that's the shade I wear, for cripes-sake. I was so pissed off, I had to go to lunch."

"So, you stormed off to the Quick Bread?"

"Yeah, I grabbed my things outta the break room and hiked across the parkin' lot to get a sandwich. At the counter, there's this skinny little thing snickerin' at me and poppin' her gum. I order, an' she just stares at me like I'm invisible. I order a ham and cheese, no mustard. When I sit down to eat it, no cheese, and mustard all over it. You know I don't like mustard; scrawny bitch poured it everywhere."

"Did you complain and ask them to make you another one?" asked Sarah, calm as an abandoned shore.

"Yeah, and she just stood there like she ain't never seen no person before. I stormed out of there an' went back to work. I still never got my lunch."

"So, one lady insulted your lipstick and the other, a girl, from the sounds of it, looked at you funny and screwed up your order, so you trashed your own store? Does that make sense to you, Mom?" Sarah asked semi-rhetorically.

"What does it matter?" Nancy snorted.

"What does it matter?" Sarah's tone became incredulous and rebuking. "Mom, you did thousands of dollars' worth of damage, and you scared the hell out of customers and coworkers. You terrified poor sweet Karen." Her grasp on calm and collected began to slip.

"Karen? Bah, an outta place candy bar scares Karen. The customers, the customers! They get what they deserve. Who cares what they think? It's the way they treat me."

"But you can't just destroy things because someone said something you didn't like. A mean customer doesn't give you the right to do what you did." Sarah threw up her arms in exasperation. "You know this isn't acceptable behavior. I mean, come on, I thought you were making progress with that new psychiatrist of yours."

MATTHEW KOPF · 17

"But I am!" Nancy waved her arms as she shouted, her skin flapping like the wings of a bird. "I've been doin' so well; ask the doc. I've gotten my life back together." Nancy shimmied her shoulders and pretended to straighten a necktie.

"No, Mom, you have not '*gotten your life back together*,'" Sarah exclaimed, using air quotes for emphasis. "Are you off of your meds?"

"Ah, I don't need them now. I've got my life back together," replied Nancy, calm and stone-faced.

"Stop saying that, please! You know you need to take your meds; that's what allows you to *get* your life back together. Remember what the doctor said?" Sarah was at a loss.

"The doctors don't know nothin'. They've been tellin' me things all my life. Where has it gotten me? No one listens; no one believes me. I'm the victim here. I was raped as a child."

"Not this again," Sarah said with a groan.

"Well, it's true! It's not my fault; things happen to me."

"Look, you can't keep doing this. You need to get back on your meds and see that shrink."

"Yeah, yeah. Fine, I will," mumbled Nancy.

"You better. Geez, I don't know how they let you come back after last time."

"Ralph's a sweetheart, that's how."

Sarah looked into her mother's bloated, red face. "That may be true, but I'm sure he has his limits. Let's not test it."

Once Nancy was safely deposited at home, medicated and calm, Sarah walked toward her own apartment. The night was chilly and crisp, one of those evenings where it was so clear that, even in the city, the stars shone as bright waypoints in the sky. The cold air kept her pace up, but she felt like crawling. The day had left her drained and empty like a stale battery. There was no power left to focus on any one thing, so her thoughts drifted and darted with abandon. Naturally, her mother's situation was at the forefront, and she found herself hoping against hope that it would blow over and not derail her life. She had only just gotten back on track after Nancy's previous episode.

Sarah let it leave her mind but found herself aching with loneliness and longing, to go home to something other than an empty set of rooms—to go home to *someone*. She wanted a man, not a coarse thing but a complement to her. A smooth, sensitive person who might understand her plight and her dreams. Her thoughts shifted to her future, the goal. To finish school and have a career, to create unique and expressive flavors. The road had been so long and would be longer still; she was years out of high school and nothing to show for it. She didn't want to feel those feelings again, she had no energy for it, so she focused on the stars—their beauty and awe. As she admired them, she thought about how the root of their beauty was a raging inferno of fusion and heat and violence but from this distance cast only a pleasant glow.

CHAPTER 2

Saturday morning, the Kettle was abuzz with customers drifting in for their caffeine fix or to grab a good gift. Loretta was home sick and left Sarah to do the delicate dance between the sales counter and the modest café. Reinforcements were still hours away, and Sarah tended to customers with vigor and dedicated abandon. In truth, Sarah lived for these moments—the constant motion, the blur of time and talk into a cacophonous slurry of activity that, at the end of the day, left tasks accomplished and customers satisfied, with almost no idea on how it all fell into place. Further still, it was a blessed distraction from her worry and woe.

A forty-something woman in red crop pants and an ice-blue blouse flagged Sarah down as she stepped away from the register. The woman had a seven-year-old in tow, and together they looked like a pair of Precious Moments dolls with identical bobs of soft, flaxen hair.

As Sarah approached, an argument over some gourmet caramels concluded with the little girl clutching a few in her hand; several more were in their basket. Clearly, she had won. Sarah assumed that the rest of the decisions would be made likewise.

"Can I be of assistance?" Sarah's voice bounced with a salesperson's lilt. "It looks like you two might need a little help deciding."

"Yes, please. We are having company tomorrow for a dinner party and are trying to decide between the English Breakfast and the Spring Rain Blossoms. I generally like the traditional teas; this other stuff seems a bit too trendy."

"But I think the Spring Rain Blossoms looks pretty and tasty," interjected the small girl.

The entry bell chimed.

"Good morning, welcome to the Family Kettle!" Sarah exclaimed with cheerful routine.

"Thank you very much, lovely," said a man's voice.

Sarah only caught a brief glimpse of his dirty-blond hair and brown blazer but felt a sting of recognition that she couldn't place, something familiar about his easy movements and carefree air. She spun through the archives of her mind: customers, people from class, friends of friends, but with so little to go on, she came up short. *One of the hazards of retail: everyone looks familiar.* Sarah shrugged.

She turned back to the mother and daughter but kept an eye out for the man in the brown blazer. After she recommended the English Breakfast, the pair squabbled amongst themselves, so Sarah took the opportunity to step back and discretely looked for the man to no avail.

As the mother and daughter finished their negotiations, the mother nodded as the little girl squealed with joy and dropped both boxes of tea into their shopping basket.

A line had formed at the register, and Sarah hurried to ring out the waiting customers. In her rush, she looked for

22 · SARAH'S STILL LIFE

the man in the brown blazer but didn't see him. She worked through the line, and while wrapping a delicate, classic British-style tea set into a box, Sarah caught a brief profile of the man in the brown blazer. Only the slightest curvature of his mouth and the bottom edge of his coat were visible behind a rack of greeting cards, but his tiny dimple looked cute even from across the store. She swore she'd seen him before.

Next in line was Beatrice Bisset, an old busybody with a sing-song voice and a penchant for flamboyant hats and unsolicited opinions. Today, Bea, as she preferred to be called, wore a felt, broad-trimmed hat in two-toned purple with a large bow. The rich fabric sat in stark contrast to her rice-paper skin.

"Good morning, Sarah," she sang, the sharp point of her nose skyward. "Did you change your Earl Grey blend? Because my Daniel, you know Daniel—the chemist for Dow—he said it tastes like you're using a bergamot flavoring instead of actual oil of bergamot." Her disdain for such shortcuts was clearly evidenced by her tone.

"Bea, it's the same blend we've been using for years; nothing has changed. It's the same high-quality tea you've always bought from us." Sarah's voice was thick with a cheerful varnish.

"Well, I don't know, it tastes a little funny to Daniel and me. Maybe I ought to talk to Loretta."

"She's at home today, but you have my word; it's the same," Sarah said in a placative but pleasant tone.

A brown blur flitted in the corner of Sarah's eye. She turned but saw nothing but a stocked shelf. Her mind reeled; she wanted nothing more than to surge down the aisles and solve her mystery. But Bea… and the line. After a quiet sigh of resignation, Sarah turned her attention back to Beatrice.

"I guess it's okay. I trust you, dear. Maybe not some of those other sorts Loretta has in here, but you... You know what's what. Say, whatever happened to Christopher?"

The line behind Bea shuffled anxiously. She didn't seem to notice.

"Um, we broke up. He was spending too much time in the office." The thought of her ex and, as Sarah liked to call her, *that little bitch* started a blaze in back of her mind as she handed Bea her change and box of wrapped tea.

"That's too bad, dear. You deserve a nice man. Like my grand-niece, Stacy; she netted herself a stockbroker and moved to New York. Anyway, deary. We'll talk next time. Tell Loretta I said hello."

Sarah nodded and waited as Bea carefully placed her change and receipt in her purple Louis Vuitton purse, each item in its spot, slow and measured. The line fidgeted with impatience, but Bea paid it no mind. The door rang, and both glanced up in time to see the back of the man with the brown jacket as he walked away. His coat was well-tailored and tight-fitting. Very stylish, probably expensive: Ralph Lauren, Hilfiger, or some other fashionable brand. Sarah never had the money to pay much attention to brands, so she couldn't be sure. Even from behind, his hair appeared wind-blown but well-groomed. Her heart beat a little faster, and a half-smile scurried across her face as he moved out of view. She still couldn't place him but couldn't shrug it off—her curiosity bit at her like an angry Bichon.

"Bea, wait, before you go," whispered Sarah. A groan emanated from somewhere behind Bea. "You know everybody. Does that man who just left—the one with the brown jacket— did he look familiar to you? I couldn't get a good look at him, but what I saw seemed so familiar."

"Can't say so." Bea craned her ancient neck to get one look at the figure from behind, now almost out of view. "I don't think I've seen him before." Bea's voice was quiet and serious. "But that keister looks good from where I'm standing." She winked as she turned and shuffled out the door.

Sarah laughed to herself and nodded in agreement as she turned back to the line.

A while later, the crowd had diminished, and Sarah took the spare moment to clean the café tables. After a few, she found herself staring out into the world beyond the little tea shop and wondering how much of it she'd ever get to know.

"A penny for your thoughts," came a gentle voice. "At least, that's what they used to say when I was your age. I suppose with inflation, it ought to be more; can't get much for a penny these days." It was Bernard, a regular who spent most days hunkered down at his favorite table, cane dangling off the side, watching the world go by. He always said the Kettle was a much-needed escape from his ugly, dull senior apartment. He spent so much time at the Kettle that he was practically a fixture himself. In his working years, he'd been a construction foreman. Age had made him quiet and introspective. He walked with a slight limp on his right side after a run-in with some rebar and a rogue shovel. The steel rod had torn through his thigh and nicked his femoral artery. Had the construction site not been next door to a hospital, he surely would have died.

"Yeah, a few thousand more and maybe I can scrape up bus fare out of here." Sarah's voice was saturated with tones of longing, like a wolf to the moon or an ancient incantation on a deserted plain echoing through the night. "Pssh, where would I go anyway? I'd still be me." She shook herself out of her daze and wiped the table in front of her. As she swept the crumbs into her hand, she turned to Bernie. "Will it always be like this?"

"Like what, sweetheart?" Bernie's voice was patient and kind, like what Sarah imagined a grandfather's would be. She never knew her grandparents; Bernie was the closest thing.

"Chasing, always chasing. Do I ever get to catch anything? It always feels like what I want is just around the corner, but then I turn and it's just more road and empty space."

"I know what you mean, Sarah. I'm on the other side; it has passed me by and all I can do is watch it move to the horizon." Bernie's bright eyes squinted and then turned sullen.

"Oh, Bernie, I'm sorry." She put her hand on Bernie's shoulder. "I guess we're both on the outside looking in. I guess it's all about one's perspective?"

He laughed a little, mostly to himself. "I suppose so. The older I get, the more perspective I seem to have, but the less of everything else. Getting old isn't easy, sweetheart, but I suppose it's better than the alternative. At least most days." His laugh turned hearty, and his eyes regained their usual brilliance.

"You think there's a balancing point somewhere? You know, a moment in life where it all kinda breaks even?" Sarah asked and leaned against a chair near Bernie. The cleaning could wait.

"Hard to say. I don't feel like I ever found one, but maybe I just didn't see it. Most people aren't really present most of the time, you know? I certainly wasn't back in my younger days. It's funny, what people have and what they think they have aren't always the same thing." Bernie opened his hands as he spoke. "Life just sort of unfolds and changes. Tough to pin much of anything down."

Sarah nodded and sat down across from Bernie. "I think I know what you mean. Like, I had a man once and thought we were going to build something together, but he decided otherwise." She picked at the rag on the table in front of her. "Or school: How long can it take one person to get a chemistry degree? Seriously! I just want to finish and move on, get into development or something. I study, I cook, I taste; I have a notebook full of ideas, but every time I think I'm getting somewhere, something pops up. Mom has a breakdown, Dad got sick, I get dumped."

Sarah pushed the rag aside and looked right at Bernie. "Loretta's been great to me, but I need a career; a real future. Most days, I don't know what to do. At least when all else fails, I have my books. That's one thing I know; a good book and a little music go a long way."

Bernie nodded in agreement. "It's not easy, sweetheart, that much is for sure. We all have our hills to climb, I suppose. Me, I never went to college. I don't have all those smarts like you do."

Sarah's face reddened at the compliment, and she smiled.

"But," Bernie continued. "One thing I can tell you is that the world is full of barriers: some are self-induced, some are circumstance, and others are people who want to stop you because someone stopped them." Bernie squinted and looked Sarah in the face. "Sometimes when you find yourself with nowhere else to turn, you just have to push."

"Push?"

"Yes, push. Head down, shoulder to the wheel, and push. Imagine you're in Egypt, in the pharaoh days, and you have to get your block to the top of the pyramid. The path is full of ruts and stones and people who won't get out of the way;

the ramp is steep and there are no guard rails. It's just you and the block. So you do the only thing you can: push."

Before Sarah could answer, the chime on the door rang and an onslaught of customers descended into the store. Sarah thanked Bernie and shook herself out of it. She had work to do.

CHAPTER 3

The rough bristles scraped against the plastic shower walls, and the air reeked of bleach and bathroom cleanser. Sarah was doing her best to keep Nancy's essentials livable, but Nancy wouldn't let her touch the filthy kitchen or overflowing bedroom. With Nancy's large size, any meaningful cleaning of the tiny bathroom was beyond her capabilities.

After a busy day of customers and the thrill of her mystery man, Sarah was exhausted. Regardless, Nancy, and her bathroom, needed Sarah's attention. Back on her meds, Nancy was compliant but out of it. When Sarah arrived, Nancy was at the kitchen table staring vaguely through a months-old issue of *Redbook* and eating an over-sized bowl of Cheerios. As Sarah scrubbed the small patch of flooring between the back of the toilet and the wall, she thought about all her mother had put her through.

Her mind flashed to how the constant undulations of Nancy's health had rippled across her life. How waves of crises would roll over her like the periodic flooding of the Nile, or some great river, that crippled the inhabitants of surrounding villages and choked everything in its path, then receded just long enough for the victims to repair their broken lives and lull themselves into the belief that it would not happen again. Sarah shook her head at all of the false rainbows in the parable of Nancy's life.

Sarah remembered coming home from school to find Nancy still in pajamas and in bed. The exact same place as when she'd left that morning. Sarah would listen as Nancy moaned about the weight in her limbs leaded down by depression and hopelessness, as if she lived on Jupiter and gravity pushed harder on her than everyone else.

Each scrub reminded her of something she'd endured.

Scratch.

The two-and-a-half months of seventh grade missed due to Nancy's drug-addled tango with some stairs.

Scrape.

Finished that school year by flashlight because the electric bill sat unpaid on the counter, buried in beer cans and debris until the power company pulled the plug.

Ssshhhkk.

The coup de grâce for that year: making up three tests and two projects while Nancy and Henry engaged in a three-day battle and binge session. They screamed and cried then sulked and numbed themselves—Henry in his chair with a case of Old Milwaukee, Nancy on her bed with a box of pills. Sarah hid in her room, too scared to leave.

Psssht. She sprayed the sink, and more recent memories swarmed.

Six weeks into her first college semester, after "a few too many" T3s, Nancy and her wood-sided station wagon veered into a playground and lost a fight with the jungle gym.

Squeak.

After weeks in the hospital, Nancy needed significant physical therapy and around-the-clock care. Henry was useless and left Sarah to manage the nurses and take up the slack. Grades fell, A's turned into C's.

Throughout Sarah's life, from grade school to college, any long-term commitment like a semester or school year was challenged by the constant interference of Nancy's misadventures. Rarely did a day go by that she didn't wonder, *What's next?*

Despite it all, here she was, worn out and elbow deep in tub ring and Scrubbing Bubbles. Sarah recollected a recent conversation with a classmate who'd asked her why she continued to help her mother when she treated her so poorly. Sarah's response: "Because you play the hand you're dealt, and I was dealt her." Even weeks later, the answer startled her. It sounded too much like something Henry would've said.

As Sarah turned her attention to the toilet, she thought about Nancy's life and how it was a constant series of repeating cycles of depression, anxiety, low-grade paranoia, and moderate schizophrenia. Nothing was ever static; if one illness was under control, another would soon falter and reemerge—crests and falls. Sarah felt like a helpless surfer permanently trapped on the waves of the oceans of Nancy's madness.

This is what I do. Her mind replayed more highlights from Nancy's "incidents" and all of the endless rehabs and therapies and chores she'd done over the years. *This is what I do instead of having a life. Instead of finishing school or going on dates, I scrub toilets and save my mother from oblivion. Instead of having a real social life and hobbies, I have this. This is my life.*

MATTHEW KOPF · 31

Though to Sarah, Nancy's illnesses were simply the result of cosmic bad luck. One event seemed to shape Nancy's response to what the Fates had cast her way. Sarah had heard the story many, many times and seemed to be the spring from which Nancy's grievances leapt.

The story, as Sarah recalled it, went something like this: At seventeen, plagued by fragments and episodes of illnesses she didn't understand, Nancy either fell under the sway of a powerful hallucination or was the victim of a sinister act of violence.

In those days, not unlike the present-day, Nancy often looked for escape. But rather than having a cabinet full of prescription everythings, she turned to whatever she could find. Pot, booze, ludes, pills, powders; it didn't matter, as long as it worked.

Imagining her mother as a teenager, when her life's hardships were still in their infancy, was something Sarah struggled to do. She felt that looking backward through the lens of time seem to offer more distortion than clarity. The one exception was this story of Nancy's purported sexual assault by her father's friend, Dan Nelson.

As it had been told to Sarah, on that night, Nancy had found her way into her dad's bottle of Top Shelf Brand whisky and consumed half of it along with a small handful of little brown mushrooms she'd received from her friend, Adrian. Nancy passed out under a blanket on the family's orange floral couch while watching the *Beverley Hillbillies*. To this day, the show still put Nancy into mania.

Nancy's descriptions of what went on in her head that night told of a twisted blend of lucid, exotic, and reality-defying dreams. One detail that always stuck in Sarah's mind was how Nancy described a cool breeze that entered through the patio doors and swayed the curtains. She said it looked like the house was breathing. Sarah imagined some decrepit old house wheezing and gasping for air under the strain of a young Nancy and her dysfunctional parents.

The story continued that sometime later, Nancy faded in to discover a man standing over her with his pants around his ankles and his dick in his hand. She talked about the sharp curve of the man's smile and how his upper lip shook like a third-rate Elvis impersonator.

"Nancy, Nancy, how did you like that? I've got a lot more for you before I'm done. You'll love it!" Nancy emphasized how the man's voice cracked with a baleful laughter; the thought sent shivers down Sarah's spine.

As Sarah finished cleaning the mirror, she recollected the end of the story. Nancy awoke on that orange sofa and the man was gone. Only a warm, slippery sensation between her thighs remained—her hands, underwear, and the couch were covered in dark, thick, red blood.

The doctor diagnosed her with female hysteria brought on by the hormonal changes of her period. The assessment made Sarah chuckle every time. With her science background, she knew that "hysteria" was used as a catchall term from the olden days for a long litany of problems presented by women that male doctors didn't want to deal with.

Sarah remembered how Nancy would crescendo the story to a climactic finale. After weeks of worry and apprehension, she finally gathered the courage to tell her parents. In exchange, she received a beating for taking her father's whisky. Later, her father talked to Dan, who insisted he fell asleep in front of his TV that night, just himself, Jay Leno, and a six-pack of Buds.

As an adult, Nancy was never shy about relating this story to anyone, at nearly any time. Sarah was often embarrassed as her mother recounted the details to Sarah's teachers, bosses, or boyfriends. It had been the subject of family lore for years, with the consensus being that it never happened and was a figment of Nancy's delusions. Possibly a side effect of her drug intake. On the facts, Sarah had little choice but to agree but not without feelings of regret and betrayal.

She finished the bathroom and headed back to the kitchen to check on Nancy. She had just taken her latest dose and seemed contented. After a few minor errands, Sarah said goodbye and headed home.

On her way to the bus stop, Sarah thought about her mother's state and her complicated relationship with medicine. At times, she would take everything as prescribed, all of her doses balanced just right, and life would be smooth for a while. Other times, the goal was only to escape, and Nancy would plunge headfirst into whatever pills she had on hand. In those dark periods, a doctor's instructions meant nothing. Staring at the TV, zonked out of her mind, was commonplace. However, no matter how long or deep the plunge into self-destruction, eventually the cycle would turn, and Nancy would be in recovery mode.

Sarah had lost track of how many times she'd heard Nancy declare she was "gettin' her life back together." Sarah joked that when Nancy died, it should be emblazoned on her tombstone. If she were a sitcom mom, it would have been her catchphrase. No matter how many times the cycle swung back, it was clear that if Nancy said it, she believed it. It didn't matter if any normal, reasonable person could see that her life was a mess. Nancy meant it, even if it was preposterous, but it never lasted. After the recent incident, Sarah hoped Nancy was on an upswing, but that seemed uncertain at best.

CHAPTER 4

Exhausted, Sarah cruised on autopilot through the last hours of a slow Tuesday evening at the Kettle. Her morning's chemistry labs kept her moving, but the afternoon's Art History and English classes had sapped her energy. She was keen to recover the shelves, tidy up the displays, and close down for the night.

A tired sigh rushed from her lips as she knelt to align boxes of tea sachets in a frontward-backward formation. The boxes formed an intricate vine and leaf pattern that continued the entire length of the shelf. At the sound of the entry chime, Sarah uttered her cheery but rote greeting and continued to work.

Heavy footsteps clicked behind her and stopped. A polite but noticeable throat clearing brought Sarah to her feet but not to attention.

"Good evening, lovely," the voice said and startled her as she moved her gaze from the shelf. "I hope it's not too late to get some of that English Breakfast. I heard you recommend it the other day, and I'd love to try some."

Sarah's stomach knotted as she realized she was face-to-face with the mystery man in the brown jacket. His face was square-jawed perfection and his hair a dirty blond wave both immaculate and nonchalant. His crystal-blue eyes, the color of the summer sky at noon, set her memory wheels into overdrive like a turbine in a waterfall. Then it clicked—Michael Kensington.

A surge of shock and silliness hit her. *Why didn't I see it earlier?* She tried to act cool.

"Er, hello! Yes, we have it, um, right here." She pointed to a red box with gold accents a few feet to her left.

Not a great start. Keep calm, you can do this. The knots in her stomach were now massive, ten-pound butterflies that had just discovered a trampoline.

"Ah, great! Do you recommend the twenty pack or the family pack?"

"Well, um, do you have a family?" Sarah asked with a blush, then silently chastised herself for being so forward.

"Me?" He laughed, unfazed by her directness. "No. I'm as single as a rhino on the savannah, but I love a good cup of tea. I'll take the big one." A broad smile exploded on his face and showed off his perfect teeth. "Does it work well iced? It's going to be hot soon, and I want to make sure it can cool me down as well as warm me up." He seemed amused.

"Yeah, of course. It works great either way. Add a little lemon and a pinch of cinnamon and you'll be ready for the hot summer days."

"And nights," he said with a wide smile and deadpan tone.

Sarah's heart jumped a beat as she stifled a devious grin. Was he flirting or just making conversation? *God, let it be flirting*! She had always struggled to distinguish between a flirt and what was casual conversation she wished was a flirt.

Before her stood *the* Michael Kensington. Back in high school, he had been untouchable; the girls practically fell at his feet. Now, was it finally her turn?

"Good choice! I can ring you up over there," Sarah said in her salesperson's voice. The initial shock had subsided somewhat, and she'd slipped into a failsafe customer service mode. As she started the ring-out process, her regular self came back online, and she decided to try her hand at boldness.

"You know, you look familiar. I know this might sound strange, but I've been wondering, do we know each other from somewhere?" Sarah asked, playing dumb.

"You don't remember me? Well, I remember you," he said, playful but taunting. "I remember you were always shy and would sit in the middle of class with your head low, like you wanted to be a ghost or disappear."

"Well, you know, some people like the spotlight. I prefer to keep to myself and... just sort of absorb the world, I guess," Sarah said.

Yep, back to normal. Pathetic normal.

The phone rang. For a moment, Sarah froze and held her breath. She begged the cosmos to let it be a customer about hours, a wrong number, something quick and easy.

"Thanks for calling the Family Kettle; how can I help you?"

"Sarah, is that you?" bleated the voice on the other end. It was Nancy.

"This is she, how may I help you?" Sarah hoped her formal tone would help Nancy catch the drift; she was busy.

"Sarah, you gotta help me. Ralph said corporate is thinkin' about callin' the cops and firin' my ass."

Sarah smiled across the counter at the handsome, visibly bored, man. "I'm sorry we no longer stock that brand. I suggest you try elsewhere."

Sarah hung up the phone and took a breath before she turned back to Michael with the best smile she could muster. She hoped her mother had gotten the hint.

"So, you really don't remember me?" asked Michael.

She pretended to grasp for a name, her face contorted with a credible look of confusion, and followed with a feeble shrug.

"Michael Kensington," he said with a self-satisfied grin.

Sarah paused and tilted her head. "Oh, wow!" She let it click. "I certainly never thought I'd see you again. What are you doing here? Didn't you end up at Princeton or Harvard or something?"

"Cornell, actually, but it wasn't for me. I finished up at Georgetown. I've been abroad lately, but I came home to help my uncle." His voice sneered with contempt at the mention of his education but softened at his uncle.

"That's great. Congratulations. I'm working my way through school now. Chemistry; food science, really."

The phone rang again, and Sarah froze with horror. *Ring.* Michael looked at her with confusion. *Ring.* Again, the phone had shattered the moment. Finally, Sarah signaled to him that she'd be right back as she ducked into the back room and answered the call.

"Sarah! What are you doin'? Why did we get disconnected? I wasn't callin' about no product. The corps are tryin' to fire me!"

"Mom." Sarah's voice was quiet but stern. "I'm sorry, I can't talk right now. I have a customer. They probably should fire you after what you pulled. They should probably throw you in jail too. What do you want me to do about it?"

"Can you try callin' Ralph? He's helped me before."

"You're a grown woman. You can call him yourself. You should apologize anyway. He deserves that much."

"I did! I don't think it's gonna work. Can you try?"

"I don't know, maybe." Sarah tiptoed to the curtain and peered out. Michael was still at the counter, fidgeting with a decorative mini tea set. "I'll see what I can do. But I have to go now. Please do not call back."

She hung up the phone and hurried to the cash register. Relieved that Michael hadn't lost interest and left, Sarah flashed a smile and apologized for the delay.

"You're in the spotlight now, aren't you?"

"Huh?" Sarah intoned, confused.

"All those customers the other day, the phone now. No more hiding. You're a regular mover and shaker." He shook his head and pointed at the phone. He seemed impressed by her transformation.

"Ha, thanks. A little, I guess," Sarah responded tepidly.

"So, you're into the hard sciences, then?"

Sarah nodded.

"That's good. Too difficult for me. I'm more of an arts and languages type of guy."

"Yeah, I remember we were in French class together for, like, two days. You showed up, showed off, and then you were gone."

Michael ran his fingers through his hair and smiled; he appeared charmed by the memory.

"It's funny, you were better at it than the teacher. What happened with that?" Sarah asked.

"Well, my obnoxiousness, and my fluency, got me noticed. They decided I 'wasn't right' for that class. I guess I can't say I blame them; I wouldn't have wanted seventeen-year-old me in there either." His smile was unceasing; he paused a moment and touched his hand to his chin. "Hmm, I had forgotten we were the same year; so you've been doing this school thing for a while, then?"

Sarah found his self-deprecating charm enticing. "Yes, you know, still pushing through. I take a couple of classes at a time and work here as much as I can; it pays the bills." She shrugged and brightened. "Plus, I get to work on my palate. Who knew one little species could produce so much variety?" She gestured toward the wall of teas. The last of her nervousness was felled by her enthusiasm.

Sarah placed his English Breakfast in a blue box and tied it with a large yellow bow, accented with a smaller one in silver.

"That looks great, very pretty. Look, I'm going to be in town for a while, so I hope I'll see you around." His blue eyes sparkled.

"I'll be here," Sarah said with a little smile she'd hoped would camouflage her somewhat desperate tone. "Next time, try our fresh tea from the café; different flavors every day."

Michael smiled as he turned and left. It was a tight, contented smile as if he'd found what he was looking for—like a cat poised to play with a cornered mouse.

Sarah arrived home spiraling through old memories and old feelings. Her encounter with Michael had churned up the still, cold waters of her high school self, complete with the mud of her family life and the silt of personal insecurities.

She poured herself a bath and a glass of wine, and she slipped into the soapy abyss. It was impossible to think of those days without recalling the fear and instability of her youth. Sarah remembered a time in junior year, the Friday before the SATs, when she came home to find a trail of beer cans out the front door and Nancy nearly comatose on the living room floor with *Oprah* on full blast. Though confused, experience had taught Sarah to be a keen observer of her environment; the smallest things could be clues, or warnings, about her parents' mood or temperament. She walked through in search of her father or to figure out what had happened. Some days, she'd think of herself as a mini Sherlock Holmes, only her nemesis was not Professor Moriarty but her parents.

That day, clues were not forthcoming; Henry had taken the day off for a long weekend but was nowhere to be found. As she swept the house, Sarah heard gurgling coughs in the living room and rushed to her mother's side. A green sludge trailed out of Nancy's mouth and down her cheek. The coughs became worse and turned into a gag and then a choke. Without panic, Sarah rolled her mother on her side and slapped her back, hard. Again and again, she smashed her open palm into Nancy's fatty back. Finally, the choking yielded, and vomit spewed forth into a pile on the worn brown carpet. Nancy's breathing returned to normal, and Sarah hurried to the kitchen to call 911.

Within minutes the familiar red and white lights were in the driveway; men and women in white, scrub-like coveralls hurried into the house. In moments, they recognized Nancy's situation as an overdose of trazodone and spirited her away to the hospital.

The SATs loomed, and Sarah searched for her father as best she could, calling the Backwater Saloon and the Drop 10 bowling alley, but it was no use. After hours at the hospital, and little sleep, Sarah found her own way to the test.

Her father returned home the following day. Turned out that after a fight with Nancy, he'd retreated to a friend's northern cottage to drink away the weekend.

A silky sip of pinot noir flooded her tongue with the rich, earthy tones and hints of white pepper followed by a bright acidity that segued her thoughts to Michael. In high school, he was always cool, aloof, and way out of her league; the guy everyone knew, either in fact or by reputation—a friend of all but of no particular clique. He had been famous for his silver tongue, flashy smile, and always on the edge of heartbreaking or heartbreak.

Oh, how the rumors and stories flew and circulated like newspapers in the wind about who went where and how far. Like the story of Kelly Launderhen, who, they said, went with Michael to the Museum of Natural History's exhibit on Native American habitations and slipped off into a waginogan for a make-out session—or more, depending on who you believed. Or, Julie Olsenstein, who went to a Salvador Dali exhibit and Michael spent an entire afternoon making little comments and explaining the paintings to her, in French. *Viens voir ce que ce crâne a fait à ce piano*, he would say; or *Je peux voir pourquoi il a peint ça.* By the time they got to the *Horns of Chastity*, she couldn't take it anymore and pulled him into the family bathroom. Of course, the rumor mill never successfully parsed the facts and fictions of these stories. Nevertheless, reputations were set and actions assumed.

None of this stopped girls—including Sarah—from wanting Michael. If anything, it fueled their teenage fantasies and placed Michael as the preeminent object of their desires. Naturally, Michael was delighted to accept such a position and took great advantage of it wherever possible.

Sarah's high school experience with Michael was far less dramatic. Fall of junior year, the dry, golden-brown leaves pressed against the glass walls of the quad as she hurried to the social science wing. Her arms laden with books and her pack on her back, she climbed the stairs to the second floor with only half a minute until the bell; she had to cross campus, so it was a close call every time. To her surprise, the door was held open. In her rush, she'd mumbled a meager "thanks" out of the side of her mouth.

A voice said, as casual as a summer day at the beach, "And where is someone like *you* going in such a hurry?"

She glanced up to see a bright white smile and a winking blue eye looking back at her. Only later, at her desk, did it fully dawned on her who the voice belonged to. She hoped he had set his sights on her, but after a couple of weeks of nothing, she left off the notion. Nonetheless, throughout high school in her quiet moments, like those just before sleep, she would dream about coming under the sway of his cunning tongue and practiced hands.

Most of Sarah's interactions with boys came in the form of fantasy as she huddled beneath her blankets in the still before sleep. She would pick a boy from class and imagine him under the covers with her, utilizing his standout features for her benefit. His arms, his lips, his tongue. Some nights, she'd imagine the strong arms of a jock, like Jose Wharton, and others the delicate lips of a gentle soul, like Rodney Clark or other smart kids with good parents. In her mind, she had dated dozens of boys, playing over the conversations they would have before sneaking off for a free-spirited exchange of fluids. Engrossed in the warm cocoon of her bed, her hands would wander and propel her dreams forward with soft, tender strokes.

Real life was less exciting: movie dates with Paul Albright, or holding hands while pacing the midway at the Fourth of July festival with Eric Ferguson, or that time Andrew Larson slipped her the tongue while slow dancing to *I Swear* at the homecoming dance freshman year. They were all mild and friendly but lacked the passion and panache of someone like Michael Kensington.

More serious affairs came with age, but few were prospective lifers. Sarah hoped that one day she'd meet a guy, and it would all click into place like a caboose that had found its engine—perfect synchronicity. It just took the right guy. She longed for an antidote to the ever-present gnawing ache of loneliness. Despite being surrounded by people every day, she still felt like an island. The more people in her midst, the lonelier she felt. Of course, she had other dreams too—a good career, a comfortable life, and so on—but an end to the static pain of being alone seemed paramount.

With Christopher, Sarah thought she'd found it. He was fit and charming. Not like Michael, but still, he knew how to use a joke or a sweet word to steer a moment. He was pursuing his MBA and on the rise at Mason State Bank, and it seemed it was all set. Then, Nancy had a meltdown or two; Dad's belly bloated, and his constant pain began. Sarah cut back dates and classes to handle it all, and Christopher just started to disappear like a castle in the sand. Before she knew it, he was gone, escaped to a less complicated life with the assistant who had been a high schooler just the year before.

Her thoughts had now bittered, and her skin wrinkled as if aged sixty years as she emptied the rest of the glass and then the bath. She dried herself and hung her towel on the chromed steel rack that glistened with condensation and was warm to the touch. After a quick brush of her teeth, she pulled on a faded The Cure T-shirt and a pair of white cotton panties and crawled into bed. That night, in that phantom zone between wake and sleep, just as she faded into dreamscape, her last thought was of Michael.

CHAPTER 5

Alive, Sarah's father, Henry Hall, had cut a sharp figure. He was tall and slender framed with a muscular, no-nonsense build and deep-set green eyes that looked like marbles trapped in a jar of smoke. A supervisor at Treadco, a tire factory on the edge of town where Route 8 meets the Calawisca Highway, he worked long hours that consisted mostly of hiding in his office until circumstances demanded his attention.

To Sarah, he was more a placeholder than a father. Always present in her memories but sheen-less and flat; a cardboard-cut-out in a La-Z-Boy with a can of Old Milwaukee on one side and a remote on the other. What stuck out in her mind were his little sayings that came at her expense: "Welcome to the real world," or "Life is hard, wear a helmet."

Spring gloom had remade everything into a sopping landscape encased in water and warped into stark monochrome like a moonscape or an impressionistic painting drained of color.

Dark, grey clouds and rain conspired to oppress the masses as they scurried about their day. The drops fell like skinny, pointed needles; the only consolation was that it was a warm rain, spring's way of telling the denizens that despite their suffering, summer was on the way and their hardships would soon be over.

Inside the Family Kettle, Loretta and Sarah staved off the weather's onslaught with spring cleaning, rearranging displays and filling new multi-colored glass vases with upbeat floral arrangements—bright yellow daffodils for cheeriness, light and dainty purple tulips to lend an air of calm and introspection. The rich fragrance of fresh-cut blooms added zest to the ubiquitous earthy scents of dried tea leaves and the variegated aromas of steeping tisanes.

The usual pink curtains were swapped for bright, baby blue ones lined in a gold, rectangular border. Each panel was lovingly made of rich, luxuriant fabrics that would not have been out of place at Versailles and added opulence and regal charm to the small shop.

Sarah stood back and admired their work. "You know, I like these curtains. They add a nice dose of sophistication and a touch of masculine allure."

"Masculine allure. I like that," chuckled Loretta with a sideways smile before she paused in thought. Loretta pursed her lips for a moment. "Speaking of masculine, I was talking with Beatrice and heard that a very mysterious man came in the other day. She referred to him as *hunky*."

The pair retreated to behind the café counter.

"Hunky? What did you put in her tea? What's next? Is she going to be talking about 'ripped abs' and 'hard bodies'? What would her children, grandchildren, or some other relative of hers have to say about talk like that?" Sarah laughed.

"I don't know, but she said you knew him and were looking a bit... lost when he came in. Said your face looked like an old cartoon character—eyes bulging, heart pumping out of your chest, steam from your ears, the whole works." Loretta pumped her arm in front of her chest, imitating the cartoon.

"She did not!" Sarah giggled and waved off Loretta's clowning. "We—both of us—barely saw him, and mostly from behind. Plus, she liked his ass! Called it a *keister*," Sarah scoffed playfully. "We went to high school together." Sarah's tone tightened. "He barely knew I existed. He's come in here since; we've flirted a little, I think. Nothing else."

"Hmm." Loretta took a pen from behind her ear and shook it gently at Sarah. "Sounds like you have a thing. Think he'll come in again? Will I get to meet him?"

"Ugh, I hope so," Sarah said with a sigh. "I'd love to sink myself into some of that! In school, he was the one everyone wanted. Way out of my league. Like, up here, and I was down here." Sarah held out her flattened hand above her head and then down to her waist to emphasize her point. She smoothed out her apron and continued. "Back then, he'd never have given me the time of day. Maybe age has mellowed him out and brought him around to normal women?" She shook her head, not sure if she believed what she was saying. "Well, whatever, if I get a shot at him, I'm going to take it. He's cute, mysterious, and by reputation, a little naughty. After all, he's *Michael Kensington!*"

"Sounds like someone to stay away from." Loretta's pen wagged. "It also sounds like you've got it bad. And as the song says, 'that ain't good.' I mean, I want you to have a new beau and all, but you've got to pick the right kind of man. After what you went through with Christopher and all your mom's... incidents, you don't need any more trouble in your life; that quota is filled."

Sarah could tell Loretta was trying not to sound like an old person giving advice. She was not successful. Sarah nodded. Loretta was probably right; she didn't need any more trouble but wasn't sure that it applied to someone like Michael Kensington.

"You don't even know, Loretta. I dreamed about him in high school; this could be my chance to live those dreams."

"Or, this could be a train wreck. Guys like that are usually not what they appear. Especially the ones who've gotten to pick all of the freshest flowers, if you know what I mean. They get a little too comfortable being the head gardener." Loretta put the pen back behind her ear and tapped the counter. "They usually end up not being the kind of person you'd hope they'd be because they're too busy being themselves, *for* themselves."

Sarah shrugged and went over to the boxed teas to straighten the display. Part of her wondered if Loretta wasn't right. Maybe he was trouble, but was it a good kind of trouble? Would he live up to her imagination? Would he, could he, really be the one to cure her loneliness and salve her battered life? *He's only a man, after all.*

She admitted to herself that she didn't know but switched to what she did know. He was handsome, smart, and had been around the world. He was sensitive enough to care about languages and arts, but was he sensitive enough to care about her? He'd certainly alleviate her loneliness—oh, wouldn't she revel in that—but would he put up with Mother? Sarah resolved to cross that bridge if she came to it, because really, this could all be an exercise in hypotheticals. Maybe he wasn't even interested; maybe it was junior year all over again.

As morning faded into afternoon, the rain slowed and then stopped. The sky lightened as the sun broke through the stratus and cumulus defensive lines. With the arrival of the sun, so too came the customers. As if on cue, the whole cast of regulars came in to make their rounds, all at once. Each with something to say about the new look.

"These new vases are beautiful," Bernard said as he sat down at his usual table. "I like how they're each a little different."

"You know, Bern, the green swirl in that vase goes with your eyes." Loretta pointed to the handmade glass on the table in front of him.

The others nodded in agreement as Bernie smiled and blushed, unused to the extra attention.

"Well, ladies, the place looks great, like a million bucks," Richard commented in his soft, sweet voice. "It looks like a whole new store. I can't believe you two did all this today." He patted Loretta and Sarah on their shoulders and smiled broadly.

"These bluebells and corydalises are exquisite," said Bea loudly as she walked over to the café counter and pointed to an arrangement. "Where did you find them this time of year?"

"I've got a deal with the florist down the street," replied Loretta.

"Looks like you made a good bargain. They couldn't look lovelier if I'd had them flown in myself." Bea's voice danced in choral pitches. "Though if my great-niece Stephanie were here, she could have made them a real treat. She's a botanist with the Boston Botanical Society, you know."

Loretta and Sarah replied with placating words and courteous smiles. They both had enough experience with Bea to know she meant well. She was just Bea.

A few hours later, the regulars had gone, and the Kettle was quiet again. Loretta poured over paperwork in the back office as Sarah prepared to close. She felt calm and satisfied with the day's work. The store looked great, and she had a real sense of accomplishment. The residual stillness after such a day and her proximity to a reliable friend like Loretta brought her a certain peace, something about the familiarity and immediacy of it all.

The door chime interrupted the placid quiet with its sharp clang. Sarah looked from her work and was startled to see Michael as he walked casually toward the café counter. In an instant, like a deer disrupted, she was tense, nervous, and excited. The hair on the back of her neck stood up and danced. Time stood still, his each approaching step in slow-motion, as Sarah's head ran circles around itself attempting to prepare for any number of possible contingencies. The shift from ease to alert was almost dizzying.

"Good evening, lovely! I hope I'm not too late to get a fresh cup of tea. What's the special today?" Michael was casual and at ease; his brown jacket draped over his arm and his white, lightly starched, DKNY shirt open at the collar with sleeves rolled.

Sarah quietly cleared her throat and summoned whatever courage she could find. "No, we don't close for another hour. We've got lots of time for you." She cringed at herself. "Our features today are French Parisian Special and Buckwheat. The French Parisian Special is a black tea blend with hints of vanilla and blackcurrant. While the Buckwheat is, well, wheaty with a subtle, nutty flavor."

"Hmm, both sound good. *Je vais avoir la spéciale parisienne, s'il vous plait,*" Michael said with a smile.

"It has been a long time since French class," Sarah said with embarrassment. "Which is that, then?"

"Lovely, you disappoint. We'll have to work on that." Michael shook his head in feigned admonishment. "I'll have the Parisian Special, with milk and a side of your number, please."

"Oh. I'll see what I can do." Sarah tried to stifle a giggle, and she began to steep the tea and excused herself under the pretense of needing more milk.

"Loretta! Loretta!" Sarah said in a whisper-shout. "He's here, he's here. I took his order—he ordered in French—and he asked for my number. It's finally happening." Whatever thoughts, feelings, or worries she'd had earlier on the subject of Michael Kensington were gone and had been replaced with unbridled excitement.

"Girl, you better be careful," Loretta said as she got up from the desk. "Let me take a look at him." She peeked through the curtains that separated the back office from the café and then turned to Sarah. "He *is* cute but looks devious." She extended the "e" as she spoke. "I don't like it."

"Oh, don't be so negative; this is going to be great. I have to get back; I only told him I needed to get milk." Sarah grabbed a quart from the refrigerator and smoothed her work-frizzed hair in the reflection before heading back.

Sarah slid a blue cardboard to-go cup on a cocktail napkin toward Michael. He lifted his drink and noticed in neat, loopy script a phone number and little smiley face hidden underneath. A broad, smug smile bloomed on his lips.

"You free Saturday?"

Sarah nodded; her shy face slow to crack a smile.

"Great, let's get together then. I'll call you."

"I look forward to it."

With that, Michael walked out the door and left Sarah relieved and excited. The tension of the encounter receded, and a tide of amazement washed over her. It carried her away like a newly dropped twig on an ocean beach.

Loretta snapped the curtain open, looking concerned. "From the look on your face, I know what just happened here, and I hope you're ready for it."

"I've been ready for twelve years! Did you see the look on his face when he asked for my number? So cool, so confident, so… cute! God, I can't wait for Saturday!" exclaimed Sarah, almost breathless. Gone was the sober, serious adult, and in her place was an infatuated, lovesick fifteen-year-old girl.

"Pull it together." Loretta's seriousness broke into a laugh. "If you start making friendship bracelets, we're going to have a problem."

"Oh, c'mon, Loretta. I'm not that bad, am I? Can't you just be happy for me? After all of these years, I finally get to go on a date with Michael Kensington."

"Okay, okay, I'm happy for you. But please, please, be careful. As your friend, I will try to be supportive, come what may. But I've been around men—*men*, hear me—longer than you've been alive, and I usually know what I'm looking at. That man looks like a lot of fun and a lot of heartbreak."

Sarah nodded in agreement, like a child given permission to play on the jungle-gym, and ignored the look on Loretta's face that seemed to say, *I hope I've misjudged this situation, all I can do is watch and wait.*

CHAPTER 6

The wall outside of Burt's Brothers Coffee Company was warm to the touch as Sarah leaned against it and tried to read her tattered copy of *Solaris*. It was seven o'clock, and Michael was late. A gnawing nervousness nearly overcame her; her insides felt as if they were filled with oatmeal and being cinched by an ever-tightening rope.

Unable to concentrate, Sarah shoved the book back into her bag and adjusted it on her shoulder. She paced with nervous excitement, anxious to get the date going and release her pent-up jitters. She took a deep breath and heard her dad's voice echo in her mind: *Toughen up, get a helmet.* Just then, Michael appeared at the top of the hill and descended toward her like Jesus entering Jerusalem. *At least he's actually coming; one hurdle down.* She took several more deep breaths as he got closer.

They greeted each other with a light, awkward hug and small smiles. Their date was to be a simple affair: coffee and a walk in the park. Wafts of roasted beans emanated from the shop behind them. Its soothing scent enveloped them and calmed Sarah. They picked up their coffee and headed down Third Street to the vine-encrusted iron arch that led to Esquire Park.

The park was built in the late nineteenth century and had always been a popular place for couples and lovers. A newly paved pathway guided them through the park as they discussed little bits of nothing. Slowly, Sarah's nerves began to settle. Something about the way Michael smiled and tilted his head as he spoke and his warm, reassuring presence all calmed her. She still wondered if it was all real and not just a dream.

The sun sat low in the sky and streaked the clouds with gentle strokes of pinks, oranges, and scarlets. Their slow saunter led them to the crown jewel of the park—Swan Pond. It had been a haven for the city's residents for generations; its large distorted hourglass shape, as well as its oak and willow-lined shores, made it the perfect getaway from the hustle of the city. The pond took its name from the white, pedal-powered swan boats that gently eased across its calm waters. The magnificently crafted vessels were carved from hardwood with intricate scrollwork and painted in bright whitewash. It was a romantic imperative that any couple who visited the park for the first time had to ride the boats.

Basking in the still, rose-hued light, they strolled hand-in-hand toward the wooden dock. A loud bell-tone emitted from Sarah's handbag, loud enough for both to hear—a brief but unwelcome interruption. Sarah held her breath for a moment but ignored the tone and climbed aboard a tiny vessel. The little white boat bounced in the water as they fumbled to find their balance. After a few awkward moments, they settled into their seats and floated gently across the glass-like water.

They peddled to the middle of the pond and then sat back and relaxed. Sarah alternated her gaze between the broad, streaked sky and Michael's pleasant, sculpted face.

"It's all so beautiful; I'm not sure I ever want to leave," Sarah remarked lazily.

"It looks like some kind of painting, the gentle curves and the weeping trees. It feels so romantic and free." Michael turned his gaze across the pond. "I love the way the paths wind away from the water and how the trees glow under the street lamps." They let the boat lull them. The soft ripples from the undulating boat made hypnotic patterns in the water. Suddenly, the tranquility was broken by another sharp bell-tone from Sarah's bag. She sat up straight with a start. Embarrassed, she fished out her phone and glanced at the screen; it was from Nancy.

ralph says you call

letten me come back

During her time with Michael, she had almost forgotten about her mother. She shook her head and buried the device in the bottom of her bag and attempted to resume their pleasant voyage.

Silence settled over them again. At ease, they listened to the quiet, near motionless water. Until Michael spoke, almost in a whisper.

"I've been wondering something, lovely: Why food science? It just seems so clinical and, maybe even, a little boring."

"Not at all." Sarah became excited; her voice was quiet but articulate. "For me, it's all about perfecting tastes and how we experience flavors. Well, that and how to recreate those flavors consistently. One of my obsessions is tea. The variety of flavors, aromas, and mouthfeels are vast, but they're all the same species." Sarah's face glowed as she spoke.

"Fascinating..." replied Michael, astonished. "I never knew that. I guess I never thought about it, but still. So, Darjeeling and Assam and that English Breakfast are all the same?"

"They all taste different but are all the same species, yes." In the span of a few seconds, a cascade of bell-tones cut into the conversation. Sarah's shoulders sank and the excitement that, moments earlier, had animated her being faded into a frown. Begrudgingly, she checked the messages, all from Nancy:

cant belief theyd come afterme

peopl always after me

bastards

In haste, Sarah replied: *Good, you're lucky. But, please, not right now.* Again, she buried her phone. Afraid of missing a true emergency, she left the ringer on. Michael looked on, contented, until Sarah began again, picking up where she'd left off.

"Anyway, *Camellia sinensis*. It's all the same leaves, but by utilizing different sizes and times of harvesting, they can make dramatic changes in the end result."

Michael nodded with an amused smile as she spoke.

"Black, green, white, and oolong all start the same, but the differences come in how the leaves are fermented and processed. They can create so many flavors with little changes. Oh, boy, so much variety. Smoky or vegetal or delicate or brisk. It's almost endless."

"I love your enthusiasm," Michael said. "You really sparkle."

"Thanks, that's nice of you to say." Sarah smiled. "Did you know the oldest type is Pu-erh? Traditionally, it is fermented, sometimes for years, with environmental yeasts, like lambic beers…" Sarah stopped and blushed. "I'm running on here. Tell me about your time in Spain." She was eager to divert attention away from her nerdiness and back to him.

"Man, I love Spain. Beautiful weather, friendly, passionate people. That little town of mine was perfect, just the nicest place. In fact, there's a little park in my village that's a lot like this one. I never realized that until now. Much smaller, of course, but cute and from the same era."

Sarah listened, leaning back in her seat and closing her eyes as Michael continued about the little park. She concentrated on that very second; she wanted to hold on to it—to her feelings—forever. She wanted to stop time, just for a few moments until the celestial clock of the universe wrested back control. In a way, she felt she had. A large moon rose in the sky as they finished their voyage. Sarah felt new and clean, washed free of the taint of loneliness that had clung to her clothing and skin like cigarette smoke. For the first time in years, Sarah felt real.

Could this be how it begins? Is this the opening of a new chapter in my life?

They disembarked and left the dock. Down the path a short distance, hidden in a tight alcove of large boxwood hedges, was an ice cream stand. The small building looked like a charming shed; a high, A-framed roof with rustic shake siding and a little collapsible chalkboard with the flavors vanilla, chocolate, and blue moon written in a loopy, decorative script. Sarah ordered chocolate in a cup; Michael, vanilla in a cone. They sat at a small metal latticed table that had cooled in the moist, evening air and enjoyed the frozen treats.

Sarah took a spoonful of ice cream into her mouth and savored it as she rolled it on her tongue. "It's funny." Her voice was smooth and casual. "I haven't been to this park in at least fifteen years. This was a good choice; thanks for bringing me here."

"I'm glad you said yes; it has been a lot of fun. Things have been so drab since I got back; this is definitely a bright spot." He took a mouthful of ice cream and thought for a moment then turned to her with a start. "Wait, did you say fifteen years? Really?" Michael looked surprised, as if he'd been told he had a rabbit on his head. "Most people come down for a Shakespeare in the park, the occasional string quartet, the annual arts and crafts show, or something. I mean, I've visited at least a dozen times in the last fifteen years and haven't even been living here."

"Nope, I've never made it to any of those—not a lot of extra time in my world. I'm usually working, studying, or at school." Sarah purposely omitted any mention of her mother.

"Hmm," said Michael, with a little frown as he took another spoonful of iced cream. "We'll have to change that. Study is important—you need to finish your degree and move on—but you have to make time to live." His voice was encouraging but adamant. "The world of science may be huge and beautiful," Michael continued. "But, without art, music, poetry, all of that knowledge would just be perpetuating a blank race. You haven't lived until you've wrestled with Shakespeare, lost yourself in a van Gogh, or sat in front of a superb orchestra playing the 'Ninth.'"

Sarah screwed up her face as she thought about what he was saying.

"Fortunately for you, I can help." He smirked and tittered.

"The 'Ninth'? Whose?" Sarah asked earnestly.

"Really? Beethoven's 'Ninth,' the masterpiece of the Western world. Sure, you can argue Mahler's Ninth or maybe even

Bruckner's if you try hard enough, but to me, *the* 'Ninth' means only one thing."

Sarah was surprised by his sudden passion. "I never knew that. I don't really *know* anything about it. I've been to a museum or two and a concert in, like, eighth grade, but that's it. I guess you'll have to show me." Her voice slid into a silky tease.

In a shrill lament, Sarah's phone shrieked its bell-tone in a fast series of messages. With an apologetic look, Sarah stole a hurried glance at her phone.

What? lucky

Big corp commin after me

no time for your sick mother?

Sarah tried to hide her frustration and typed back in a flurry of thumbs:

not now, mom!

"Boyfriend?" Michael asked with a comic shrug. Sarah didn't answer. "Girlfriend?"

"Trust me, if I wasn't single, I wouldn't be here. It's just my..." Sarah's voice trailed off. She wanted to be forthright and say, "It's just my crazy mom," but she didn't want to scare him off. She was straightforward with Christopher, and, well, look how that turned out. Her mind see-sawed. She knew she'd have to tell him eventually, but not now. "It's just something I needed to take care of."

"Okay," Michael said, unfazed. He took a bite of his cone and swallowed. "This ice cream is pretty good. I didn't have much hope for it, being straight out of a food service container, but surprisingly good. How come I can't make ice cream like this at home?"

"Do you really want to know?" asked Sarah, excited to flex her knowledge and move the conversation away from her mother, even if he didn't know it was about Nancy.

"I was being rhetorical, but sure. Enlighten me."

"Gumming agents. I know it sounds gross, but it's not. It's usually Guar Gum or Carrageenan, but sometimes Xanthan Gum or Locust Bean Gum, depending on what you're going for. At home, it's just sugar and cream, basically, but these gums thicken and bolster and really make the product."

"Huh. What other secrets of this wizardry do you know?" asked Michael, clearly impressed.

"Oh, a little here and there," responded Sarah being coy.

"So, out of curiosity," Michael's eyes gleamed and his words dripped with attentiveness, "have you ever been able to put all this knowledge to use? Have you had a chance to make anything yet?"

"I have a little." Sarah hesitated.

"Go on. Please tell," Michael encouraged.

"Well, I had a class project last year where I developed a vanilla glaze."

"Oh? How did that turn out?"

"Um, well, I got an 'A.'" The words came out just above a whisper.

"That's great! You should be proud. Shout it out loud. Don't hide it."

Her face flushed. "Honestly, I'm not one to flaunt my achievements. I'm really more of a stuff-it-into-a-shoe-box-and-forget-it kind of girl."

Michael looked at her in disbelief. "You should work on that. I'm sure you've got more. What else?"

"Well, it's not technically food science, but I've blended a few flavors at the Kettle. All, except the first one, were big hits. People weren't quite ready for my tamarind-shiitake-chamomile blend." Sarah laughed.

"That's fantastic. Okay, so, other than all of this chemistry stuff, do you like to try new restaurants? You know, go out?" asked Michael, excited.

"I like to go out when I can, but usually it's whatever is around when I'm hungry. It's not usually a planned thing."

Michael looked at her with pity as if watching a documentary on lost children.

"What?" Sarah shrugged in confusion.

"Nothing, it's just surprising that someone so into flavors doesn't dine out with regularity."

"I typically cook. I like to find recipes and explore varieties and variations. At some point, I'm going to deep dive into umami, especially mushrooms, so you better be prepared."

"Don't worry, I can handle it." He grinned. "I love mushrooms. *You* need to prepare to experience the world of culinary delights right here in our old town." It was clear he was trying to up the ante.

"Oh, I'm ready," Sarah giggled and gave him a gentle poke in the chest.

They both laughed and headed down the path. As they strolled toward the east end of the park, Michael took her hand and said in a soft voice, "You know, you're really smart."

Sarah blushed but let him continue.

"I never quite realized. I mean, all that about this tea and chemistry stuff. Such a different world than the one I inhabit." Michael stopped and turned to her, looking directly at her.

"Honestly, I still just thought of you as that little girl huddled in her chair waiting for the world to pass by. But, boy, was I wrong. You're something else entirely." His expression was soft and gentle.

Sarah looked into Michael's face. His smile loomed large above his chiseled jaw, and his words oozed authenticity. She was charmed. "Thanks, Michael. I appreciate that. Most people just tune out when I talk about that stuff."

"I like the counterbalance—your world and my world." He squeezed her hand tenderly and they continued to walk.

The night was full, and the park closed, and with it, their date. It ended where it began, outside a now-empty Burt's Brothers. The streets were mostly deserted. When it came time to say goodbye, Michael put his arms around Sarah and embraced her for a few moments. With a quick motion, he laid a single kiss on her eager lips. The pair said their goodbyes, and then it was over. Sarah hurried to catch the late bus, and Michael walked off into the night.

The next few days, Sarah positively glowed with excitement. Everything she saw, everything she touched had a new meaning and depth, as if she had suddenly awakened from a long sleep. Michael gave her art books, music, and even poetry; it all caught her mind and imagination like never before. Michael's intelligence, wit, and depth of knowledge impressed her. His love for the arts seeped from his pores, like Jack Daniels after a long night of drinking. Sarah treasured the fact that he was completely daft at anything close to science; she loved that his weaknesses were her strengths.

CHAPTER 7

The golden sun dipped into the horizon and announced the arrival of evening with brilliant hues of pinks, oranges, and fuchsias as if someone had tipped rainbow sherbet across the sky. Spring had finally decided to show its soft side, and, after a few weeks of dating, Michael decided it was time to introduce Sarah to his favorite place in the entire city: the al fresco dining terrace at *L'Espérance*.

The smooth, white tablecloths and delicate blue and white French crockery stood in stark contrast with the urban landscape in which they sat. The cracked sidewalk, bermed concrete, and the boarded-up building across the street with graffiti for windows still waiting for its turn at *urban renewal* spoiled the illusion of exoticism but not their meal. They had dined on flounder and prawn in Dijon caper sauce, rack of lamb with mint jelly, and sides of risotto and calamari. Marcel, their waiter, had been attentive and now stood, hands folded behind his back, as he inquired about their dessert plans.

"A proper French meal *must* include a dessert and digestif," exclaimed Michael. The dining experience was a very serious matter for him, especially with a lady.

"Um, sure. Why not? But what do I order?" Sarah asked, feeling unusually timid as Marcel stared at her in silent deference. "Just order for me; get whatever you think I should have."

"As you wish," replied Michael with delight. "I will have a *Oeufs a la Neige* with a *Tariquet Bas Armagnac*, and the lady will have the *Creme Brûlée* with a *Gabriel Boudier Dijon Créme de Cassis*, please."

"Excellent choices, sir. I think you'll love the *Armagnac*," said the waiter earnestly before disappearing into the wall like a wraith.

Sarah was unused to full-service dining. She generally kept her meals out simple and affordable, just as prudence and budget would prefer. Her usual rule was to avoid desserts and more than one drink. By contrast, Michael spared no expense. It was clear that, for Michael, dining was an art, and he was an artist.

After a moment of pleasant silence, Mozart's "Violin Sonata Number 21" danced through the open-air seating.

"Ah, Mozart! A man who knew how to live!" Michael threw his head back and grinned. "Probably the best composer who ever lived and, unlike most of the masters, he wasn't a miserable sod." His voice became vigorous. "Loved to eat, drink, smoke, and play billiards. I've heard that he once went on a binge and played pool for eighteen hours, drank fourteen bottles of wine, smoked seven pipes, ate nine servings of liver and dumplings, and won all of his friends' money. Then, to celebrate, he sat down and wrote an aria."

"Sounds like a wild man. Is any of that true?" Sarah asked, captivated less by the story than by Michael's enthusiasm.

"Don't know, but it's fun to think about—the adventures of a genius. Can't you just picture it?"

They both chuckled and fell into quiet pleasantness. Sarah took a sip of her water and ran her fingers over the ridges of Michael's hand. It seemed to pulse with energy, his passion pumping. She loved the way he seemed helpless to contain his overflow of excitement. But amidst it all, Sarah wanted to know more about him. What she knew from their school days didn't count. What was his family like? What helped create this handsome, passionate man?

"Michael, we've talked about your uncle before, but what about your parents? Do you have any siblings?"

"Whoa, okay." The change in subject matter seemed to catch him by surprise. His countenance shifted, and his fervor retreated. His voice turned dry and stiff, like cardboard. "Siblings, no. In the tempestuous snarl that was my parents' relationship, they only had time for one kid, and hardly that. And the rest is a bit of a tale. Are you sure you're ready for it?"

"Yeah, of course." Sarah leaned closer and waited for him to begin.

Michael took a breath and a drink and then began. "Uncle Geoffrey raised me and cared for me like his own. But I'm getting ahead of myself. See, my parents were a match made in, if not hell, then some kind of soulless purgatory. My dad, bless his heart, was a man of high ambition and low success. Mom wanted the high life and didn't care how she got it."

Sarah grimaced and squeezed his hand.

"Dad tried a number of schemes to get rich and please Mom. The most memorable being a hare-brained line of men's products with little built-in gadgets, like shoes with a heel that slid out to store a wallet or cufflinks that contained a toothpick—it folded, the damned fool."

Sarah tried to imagine it but could only laugh. Michael joined her. "Everything was like something out of a bad James Bond film or a *Skymall* catalog. Needless to say, they all failed."

"Yikes! Sounds like he was a creative guy, though. Seems a shame your mom didn't appreciate that."

"She didn't. None of his ventures were Mother's idea of 'making good money.' She hounded him day and night to 'get off his ass and make some money,' and he tried. Damn, how he tried." Michael shook his head as it came to rest on the palm of his hand. "Eventually, he just gave up and took a job as an insurance salesman. Somewhere in the middle of all of this, I was born. By the time I was four, my mom had had enough and divorced my dad." He took another drink and leaned back awkwardly in his chair. "Dad didn't take it well because, despite her nagging and admonishments, he loved her. After his inventions failed and his marriage fell apart, he was a broken man and turned to drink."

"Geez, that's pretty rough. I'm sorry. Where is he now?" asked Sarah, her tone soft.

"Well, the story doesn't get any better, I'm afraid. He became a regular at a bar down the street from his house. One night in a winter snow event—as they called it—Dad decided to walk home and wandered out into the street. According to witnesses, he trundled through the foot and a half of snow for about a block. Then, he paused and stepped into the street. A moment later, he was hit by a late-night bus on its usual route; he was killed instantly."

"Oh, my god! That's terrible!" Sarah exclaimed, her eyes wide. When she had wondered what lurked beneath, she hadn't imagined such a story. Her heart tore a little as she looked at Michael's normally beautiful face deformed by the memory. It then slackened into resignation.

Seemingly from nowhere, the waiter interrupted with their drinks. After they settled in again, Michael continued.

"It has never been clear whether he stepped off the curb on purpose or if it was just a terrible accident. Honestly, I think he meant to do it; he just couldn't take life anymore. Uncle Geoffrey, my dad's older brother, disagrees. He insists that Dad would never have taken his own life." Michael leaned back in his chair and shook his head, as if disagreeing with his uncle. "We'll just never know for sure."

"Wow, that's intense. How old were you when all of this happened?"

"Almost seven; it was two weeks before my birthday."

"Michael, that's terrible. I'm so sorry. I mean, I've had my share of parental drama, but that is pretty bad. Makes sense that you and your uncle are pretty close." Sarah took a long sip of her *Créme de Cassis*.

"We're close, but we've clashed at times. He's never really understood how I feel about this place, why I had to leave. When I went away for school, he knew I'd be back. When I left for Spain, he was irate, but when it became permanent, he was positively distraught. He just wants me near him."

"So, what happened to bring you all the way back home?" Sarah took another sip.

"Last winter, Uncle Geoffrey had pneumonia and was headed to his doctor. He slipped down the steps outside of his house and banged himself up pretty bad—broken hip, ankle, and damaged his knee on one side."

Sarah winced as Michael detailed the extent of Geoffrey's injuries. "Ouch, that sounds terrible. I'm sorry."

"Yeah, thanks. The good news is he recovered from the pneumonia shortly thereafter. The bad news is that he is going to need a whole panoply of surgeries and a lot of rehab." Michael brought the *Armagnac* to his lips and inhaled the nutty, toffee notes. "That's why I'm here."

While Sarah felt terrible about Uncle Geoffrey's injuries, she couldn't help but be glad Michael had come back.

"He had hip surgery before I even got here, and they shipped him off to some shitty rehab facility. That place saw only dollar signs, not people. I got that straightened out. For now, he's at home, and we're getting the PTs to come to him, but with more surgeries come more rehab. He'll probably have to bounce back and forth between rehab and home. At least I've now found a good place for him when he can't be at home."

"Poor guy," Sarah sighed then pursed her lips.

"He's doing well under the circumstances—he's a tough old guy—but he has a long way to go. I'm amazed that such a sweet man is also such true grit." Admiration rang in his voice. "It's going to be a long recovery process, and he needs my help. I'm all he has, so I took a break from teaching and came home." His words had turned hard and sober, as if made of brick.

Michael lost himself in thought. Sarah fidgeted in her chair while she unconsciously wound her brown curls around her finger.

"Forgive me, all this just churned up a lot of old sediment. I'm worried about him, but at the same time, I resent being pulled back here."

"Oh? Why?" Sarah asked, surprised.

"You really want to know?" His voice turned loud and sharp.

Sarah nodded meekly.

"Truth be told, I can't stand this place. All of my life, I've hated it and couldn't wait to get away. First, there's the goddamn Midwestern winters—months and months of snow—monotonous grey topped off with bitter cold. Of course, eventually when we get a little warm weather, we're plagued by bugs and humidity. As if nature wants to punish us for almost enjoying ourselves."

The depths of Michael's venom for their hometown startled Sarah as he continued.

"Lastly, look at the atmosphere around here. We've created drab, uninspired surroundings." His agitation increased by the word. "Ugly buildings surrounded by ugly people, and no one seems to care. No one celebrates life. It is all about 'just getting by.' Everyone is all, 'I'm cold and I'm miserable, but I'm getting through it.' As if life awards you points for taking shit, being miserable, and trudging on. It doesn't!"

Michael's words stabbed at her. She couldn't help but feel included with those he disparaged. Her life was the epitome of "just getting by." It was the air she breathed and the currency she traded. What choice did she have? She was born in this place, to these parents, at this time, and she tried to make the best of it. While not a direct hit, his words pierced her bubble about what Michael Kensington was and was supposed to be; air escaped as he continued.

"In Spain—all over southern Europe, in fact—there is a zest for life. It is in the food they eat, the songs they sing, the dances they dance. There is a hot-blooded zeal for experience! They know there is more to life than money and drudgery. Even if they're poor, they dance and sing and eat and make love like it all means something. The day I left this place was the happiest day of my life!"

Michael grew quiet again. Sarah could tell he had not meant to get so animated or as irascible as he did, but she still felt wounded.

"But what about me? Am I all of those things to you too?"

"No. Of course not," said Michael, the anger on his face cooling rapidly. "I'm glad I found you. You are my bright spot in all of this."

Sarah perked up and blushed. A little smile bloomed on her lips like a marigold. She started to feel a little better.

"I'm sorry. I just lost my temper; it doesn't happen often. Uncle Geoff always said I got that from my mother."

Again, the conversation fell into silence.

A few moments later, a sly smile came across Michael's face. "Perhaps it is time that I ask you a question or two." His anger was gone and had slid into a playful tease. "What about your dad? Do you guys get along?"

I should have seen this coming; after all, turnabout is fair play. But damn, I don't want to talk about Dad; it'll lead to Mom. It always does. For fleeting moments, Sarah contemplated a lie—they died in a fire; they shipped out to Africa; they moved to Oklahoma and joined a cult. But it wasn't in her nature. She studied his face as she searched herself for a reply; it was compassionate and soft, despite his recent outburst. The seconds clicked by like hours.

Sarah cleared her throat. "My dad and I were never close. He existed. He was a physical presence in my life but not a particularly meaningful one."

"Was?"

"Yeah, he died a couple of years ago."

"I'm sorry."

"Thanks, but it's not necessary." Sarah's lips creased into a tight frown.

"So, how about your..." Before he could finish, Marcel arrived with two plates and another round of drinks. "... Dessert!"

With a flash, the mood was enlivened. The stories of death and family were pushed aside in the name of good dining. *Bless French gastronomy.*

"Nothing like a fine dessert to turn things around! I love *oeufs a la neige*. This place adds a house-made raspberry sauce. Amazing!" Michael scooped up a generous chunk of the floating meringue; he seemed back to his usual self.

Sarah smiled, relieved the conversation about her family had halted. She was happy to be his bright spot. Proud, in fact. The hole in her bubble had been sealed, but the escaped air was gone. She turned to her dessert, eager to savor her *creme brûlée*. Though a rare treat, she adored the first moment when the back of the spoon hit the *brûlée* and gave against the violence with an audible crunch.

With a quick hit, she broke the crystalized layer and took a spoonful of the creamy custard. Eyes closed, she reveled in the smooth, silky texture. The richness of the egg and cream overran her palate with a deep satisfaction that comes only from decadent desserts. She offered Michael a taste, and he accepted with glee. The mood lightened.

To keep the conversation away from her family, Sarah cautiously flipped the tables back to Michael.

"So, how often do you see your mom?" Sarah asked slowly in hopes of avoiding another blowup. "You haven't said much about her. How does she fit into all of this?"

"Mom? Ugh! I suppose we might as well round this out. The quick version is that she doesn't. After the divorce, she ran off with a conman to swindle old rich people out of their retirement money."

"Yikes! That's awful. Do you ever hear from her?"

"No, never. The last time was when I was six years old. Hopefully, she's in jail somewhere with that asshole she hitched herself to, but who knows." This time, he attempted to muffle his anger. "I'd rather not talk about this right now."

Sarah nodded, and with a warm smile she placed her hand over his and gave it a gentle squeeze. His eyes turned to her with a look of kindness and appreciation.

The rest of the evening passed in pleasant conversation and dull uneventfulness. They discussed Godard and the finer points of French New Wave, something of which Sarah knew nothing.

CHAPTER 8

Always a curious child, Sarah loved school and longed for the escape from her lugubrious and demanding home life. The thrill of learning new things and the workings of the natural world held her enthralled, captivated by the mysteries unraveled before her eyes.

The summer between seventh and eighth grades set the course for the next fifteen years of Sarah's life. Thanks to the urging and support of her middle school science teacher, Mr. Wundervoll, she enrolled in a program to prepare children for the future through science. Sarah remembered in vivid detail how the class of twelve-year-olds donned safety glasses and gloves and entered a real science lab.

It all seemed like something out of a crime scene TV show or a monster movie. Sarah was confused and intrigued by the strange, shiny, angular pieces of metal and chrome, mysterious apparatuses with rings, clamps, and platforms upon which clung bizarre glassware. Some were tall and skinny like glass candles, others were stout at the bottom and thin at the top, and another set was strange and bubbly.

That day, the class made charcoal by putting little pieces of wood into test tubes and applying heat from the narrow blue flame of a Bunsen burner. Sarah was shocked that the wood didn't ignite and just blackened into a charred lump. That was it; she was hooked and knew the science lab was somewhere she belonged.

An early summer thunderstorm had taken the city by surprise. The warm winds, lingering daylight, and the soft sun of the season had lulled the town into complacency. The storm was a reminder that summer, too, has its own kind of rage.

Water crashed from the sky in flat sheets that subdued the city. All but the best prepared were caught off guard and defenseless against the pouring advance. People scurried into any shelter they could find—parking garages, awnings, or a lovely teashop.

Before the storm arrived, it had been a slow Tuesday afternoon full of sameness and routine. The Kettle's regulars had come and gone. But the storm corralled random passersby in need of shelter and a warm cup of tea. The stranded customers seemed charmed by the decor and atmosphere of sophisticated whimsy. Sarah and Loretta relished in the unexpected hustle and were proud of the deluge of compliments and feedback from their unexpected guests.

As the afternoon wore on, the storm grew worse; the sky darkened to the blackest grey Sarah had ever seen, but most of the customers had already worked up the courage to continue their journeys. The little shop returned to gentle quiet as Loretta and Sarah chatted amongst themselves.

A short time passed, and the calm was disrupted by the bleating tones of the telephone. Sarah held her breath for a split second before she answered.

"Sarah, Sarah, come quick, I need you!" Her heart sank. It was Ralph again, his voice frantic, out of breath, and desperate. "It's your mother; she's sat herself down in the middle of aisle six and won't move. She's just sitting there with a glazed look in her eyes. Whenever anyone tries to talk to her or move her, she howls something fierce. I've never seen her like this before. I'm at a total loss. Sorry to bother you at work, but can you help? Please?"

Sarah clutched the phone with both hands and squeezed the receiver as Ralph spoke. Her grip got tighter and tighter until her hands were white against the brown Bakelite handset and her face contorted with horror and embarrassment.

Loretta recognized the look. She leaned close to Sarah's other ear and whispered gently, "Go on, take care of your mama. I've got this covered."

Sarah nodded to Loretta with slight relief and informed Ralph that she was on her way. He thanked her profusely until she hung up the phone.

Sarah hustled to gather her things and braced herself for the storm's onslaught. As she set foot outside, she noticed the sky had lightened and the rain had slowed. Nature had granted her a reprieve, as if it were catching its breath. Little did she know that the break in the rain was the last favor nature was going to grant her that day as she dashed down the street in search of a cab.

The wailing inside the Great Midwestern Pharmacy could be heard from the street. It was a loud and shrill screeching, like Yoko Ono through a wood-chipper. Sarah lowered her head and entered through the sliding glass doors.

Sarah followed the noise and found a crowd gathered around Nancy. As she pushed through the horde, she noticed their faces were distorted; their malleable mouths betrayed their thoughts. Some were agape, shocked, and aghast at what they were witnessing, while others grimaced, apparently worried about their own skin but seemed to harbor a modicum of concern for Nancy, though not enough to walk away, of course. Another set seemed excited, even titillated, their half-smirks and shining eyes ablaze as they reveled in the destruction and pain before them. The misfortune of others was irrelevant as long as they were entertained.

Sarah, though disgusted by people spectating her mother's illness, had no time for them. She made her way to the center of the crowd and found Nancy seated on the floor with her eyes closed, encircled with a thick line of smeared cosmetics and broken casings as if she were performing some kind of ritual to the makeup gods. So far, the damage seemed minimal.

"Mom! What's going on?"

"Sarah!" Nancy exclaimed, opening her eyes. "You have to get outta here or they'll get you too. I've managed to protect myself so far, but they're comin' for me. You need to go now!"

"What are you talking about? Who will get me? You're not well; let's get you home and away from these awful people. Come on." Sarah reached for her mother's hand, but Nancy recoiled with a shriek.

"No! The men with the orange eyes will get me. The hideous beasts. I can see them now with their ashen grey faces and black coats; they grin and taunt me and threaten me."

Nancy closed her eyes and raised her arms in front of her face as if expecting to be struck by an invisible hand. A look of imminent pain rippled across her face and was quickly replaced by a distraught look of terror and confusion.

"Mom, they're not real. They can't hurt you. Enough damage has been done tonight. You've upset people and humiliated yourself. We really need to go now!"

Sarah's words were stern but saturated with compassion. She knew her mother was suffering and wouldn't be safe until extricated from the situation. In a long, slow, continuous movement, Sarah again tried to ease toward her mother, reaching for her hand. The moment Sarah made contact, the screeching resumed.

"Yeeeeh! Yeeeeeh! Yeeeeh!" screamed Nancy. Her pitch climbed as she yelled. Her body shook side-to-side as she raised her open hands, palms up, over her head, as if she held an invisible globe like Atlas.

Sarah stepped back to regroup, uncertain how to proceed. The crowd had grown, and it murmured and waved like some kind of kraken or other deep-sea creature. The occasional arm with a phone attached would raise in the air as if a tentacle of the beast. Sarah hated them. All of them. The horrid, disgusting vultures were present only to prey on her mother's anguish. They sickened her.

Sarah looked at her mother covered in smudged lipstick and splotches of mascara and facial powders like an abused prostitute or a junkie. She was a pathetic specimen. At that moment, Sarah resented her, the weak and selfish woman who had always put herself first. Always the aggrieved, always the victim. But she was her mother, so Sarah packed away the anger and hurt and continued to do what she could.

Nancy stood up and began to move in a circle, the volume of her shrieks like a tornado siren that swelled and receded as she moved through her orbit. Her feet now stamped and pounded the ever-battered floor. Her body jerked and jutted like an old-time movie.

Sarah felt a tap on her right shoulder and gasped. She held her breath as she turned around. It was Ralph; he looked concerned and distressed. He was about to speak but hesitated, his mind willing but his tongue failing.

After a moment, he found his courage and whispered in Sarah's ear, "I'm grateful to you for trying to help. I really am, but this has got to end. I'm afraid she may hurt someone, or herself, this time. If you can't get her under control soon, I may have to…" Ralph paused, "…call the police. I don't want to put you or her in that situation, but…"

Ralph's voice faded out before he finished. Sarah gave a slight nod of understanding and returned her gaze to Nancy, whose arms were now flailing as her squealing shrieks rose to nearly unbearable levels. Many in the crowd covered their ears but continued to look on with shock and excitement.

Ralph was right, Nancy was a time bomb. Sarah knew she had to do something. The noise and flailing made it hard to think; it pounded in her head like a steam shovel.

Sarah fought back against the tumult in her head and tried to come up with a plan. Nancy's thick arms moved faster, more erratic, as the crowd cinched the perimeter tighter and stared at them from all directions like zombies. In despair and desperation, and with no coherent plan other than to stop the surreal scene, Sarah pulled Nancy's arms to her sides and encapsulated Nancy's shaking body in the biggest, tightest, hug she could manage. It was like trying to cover a bear with a shopping bag, and that bag was Sarah. Tears streamed down her face as Sarah approached the limits of her ability to contain Nancy against her will.

Through her tear-blurred vision, over the shoulders of gathered assemblage, Sarah saw the pharmacy doors slide open and a tall, familiar man stepped through and paused. Sarah seized with terror and wished, prayed in her own way to the cosmos and the universe, for it not to be true. She could not have felt more vulnerable at that moment if she'd been stark naked with a gun to her head.

Michael surveyed the scene with detached curiosity and sauntered to the periphery of the huddled mass. His face looked concerned and confused as he peered toward the center of the seething gawkers. Moments later, his eyes connected with Sarah's, and a look of recognition clicked on his face, followed swiftly by disgust. His gaze shifted and floated into a dumbstruck stare.

Sarah's thoughts and emotions tore at themselves like rats in a fire, tangled in a web of uncertainty and inaction. She was trapped between the reality of her mother's condition and her fear of Michael's judgment. Nancy calmed down. Her screams devolved into mutters and mumbles and gave Sarah's over-exerted arms a small reprieve. All Sarah wanted to do was disappear, make the whole situation—the crowd, her mother, Michael—vanish like a Criss Angel illusion, but it was not to be. Instead, she was frozen where she stood, locked in place by shame, mortification, and care for her mother.

Shame overcame and suffused her to the very core of her being. Ashamed of the pathetic state of her mother. Ashamed that she wanted to impress a man so much that she wanted her own mother to disappear. Ashamed that all of these people wouldn't just leave her and her sick mother alone. Ashamed that, even now, as an adult, she could not shake the wish to be invisible or just wink out of existence, as she'd wished so many times as a child.

Her wallow in self-pity was cut short by a sudden outburst as Nancy broke free from Sarah's grasp and threw her to the floor. Shards of broken plastic scraped against Sarah's face and powdered chunks of beige gunk stuck to her wounds, forming darkened cakes of blood, tears, and cosmetics. She looked like Emmett Kelly caught in the rain. Her head hit the dirty linoleum floor with a hard, dull thud.

Freed from bondage, Nancy began to scream and run in a circle as if she were being chased by phantoms, hell hounds, or other snarling beasts. Nancy only now realized she was trapped at the center of a crowd and screamed at Sarah.

"You bitch! You brat! How could you betray me like that! Now the men with the orange eyes will get me for sure, and it's all your fault," Nancy shouted and turned to her observers. "They will get all you too!"

This outburst finally pushed the crowd over the edge. They began to mock her mercilessly as they pointed and laughed and waved their arms in the air, a sick parody of a sick woman. The ridicule of her distress was pitiless. They howled in her face while Nancy's shrieks continued in unrelenting cacophony.

Nancy shouted to the crowd and lurched in frantic, panic-stricken movements. A young girl, probably sixteen, moved in to get a better view with her phone as Nancy waved her arms in broad, exaggerated gestures and screamed, "The men with the orange eyes will come for you all! They feast on your mind and laugh at your pain. You will suffer!"

In a spasmodic jilt, Nancy knocked the girl to the ground, and she landed on the opposite side of the circle from Sarah. The crowd gasped then stirred. The shouts and curses came fast: "You hit a little girl, you crazy bitch!" The voices from the crowd managed to drown out Nancy's ranting. A wave of commotion rippled toward the center of the circle. In an instant, the glass doors, walls, and reflective fixtures of the store pulsated in red and blue as a dozen or more police officers encircled the crowd while a pair pushed their way to the front.

The presence of the police broke the spell on the crowd, and it began to dissipate. The stern, authoritative air of the officers perforated the wall of their collective brain and allowed their consciences to seep through the gaps. One by one, the mob became individuals again and wandered off into the wider world. As they did, they looked at each other in seeming discomfort and awkward realization of what they had witnessed and what they had been a part of. It seemed unlikely that many would think too deeply about their experiences that evening, except Michael.

Nancy, her voice hoarse, shouted with the smug wail of the persecuted as another group of officers moved with caution and confidence toward her. An additional officer moved off to help the girl Nancy had struck but paid Sarah no mind.

"Ma'am, we are going to have to ask you to come with us," the first officer said.

"We're here to help you; we just need you to calm down so we can talk about this," added the second.

"The men with the orange eyes... the orange eyes..." Nancy faded to a whisper. Her eyes glossed and arms slackened as they fell to her sides. Catatonia was setting in, and Nancy was oblivious to the officers and their commands. Not even the flashing lights that strobed like a police rave appeared to register.

The officers looked at each other, shrugged, then moved in. The first placed a gentle hand on Nancy's shoulder, and she was reignited; her primal ire awakened, and her arms flew into the air. Nancy's sudden movement knocked the second off balance, and he tumbled to the floor. The other officers reacted. Within seconds, Nancy was in a submission grip—her elbow and arm squeezed toward her shoulder blades as they bent her wrist upward and lowered her to the floor. The cold, blunt edge of the handcuffs cut into her wrists. Nancy howled and railed against the restraints with all of the force she had left. Her body contorted in waves before it gave out and was still. Incoherent, nearly unintelligible words dribbled out of her mouth with an occasional utterance clear through the static: *orange... eyes... men.*

Sarah laid on the floor and tried to process what had transpired. The swirls of colored lights made her head spin, and she closed her eyes to get her bearings. She wondered why the crowd and the officers had ignored her. As she breathed in deep lungfuls of air, she could hear mother's faint whimpers. Nancy laid only a few feet away face down, an officer's knee in her back.

As her mind cleared, Sarah remembered Michael and got to her feet. She saw him, still lingering at the far end of the room, where the crowd had stood, his face a nauseous mix of trepidation and revulsion. It was clear that he did not like what he saw. Before she could catch his eye, he turned and left. Sarah tried to call to him, but nothing came out.

The police read Nancy her Miranda rights and lifted her from the floor. She alternated between kicking outward toward the officers and dragging her feet. When neither action freed her, she went limp, and the officers had to call over three more guys to drag her to the squad car.

Sarah stood helpless as they drove away. The last view of Michael stuck in her mind, his face confused and twisted like a car into a safety barricade. *Where did he go? Why didn't he help? How could he just leave me here... alone?* Her body ached and longed for someone to comfort her to make it all seem okay; to feel the safety and reassurance of strong arms around her. She needed Michael but instead felt the cold, empty embrace of loneliness.

CHAPTER 9

Welcome to the real world. It's tough out there. Life is hard, get a helmet. Some days you're the dog, others the hydrant—usually the hydrant. These were some of Henry's favorite sayings, and Sarah hated them all. The sanctimony and self-righteousness of his little phrases, his quasi-aphorisms, cut straight to her nerves. But sometimes, at times of stress or frustrations, they'd come back to haunt her and heap irritation upon injury but also to bring guidance and warning.

Sarah stepped off the bus onto Commerce Street and eyed up the short blocks of boutiques that led to the Family Kettle. The scene of her mother's breakdown replayed in her mind moment by moment, detail by detail, and every time, she circled back to the same set of questions: *Why didn't I tell him about Mother earlier? If I had, would he have reacted differently? How could he just walk away? Why didn't he help me?*

The last three days had been spent in self-isolation. Sarah had holed herself in her small apartment obsessively scrutinizing every detail of the pharmacy incident. She took no calls and made no calls, just the walls and her thoughts. Now, with the warm sun and fresh air on her face, she felt a slight rejuvenation. Each step closer to the Kettle improved Sarah's mood.

It was quiet when she arrived, with only Loretta and Bernard murmuring in the café.

She looked up as Sarah entered and hurried toward her. "Where have you been? I've been worried. I called. I left messages. Why are you ghosting me?"

"Loretta, please," said Bernard warmly, giving her a pleading look from his booth. "I doubt she needs that right now."

"You're right. Sorry, you know how I get worked up sometimes. You just do your thing. We can talk about it when you're ready."

Sarah nodded and went to work. She was able to keep herself occupied and distracted by brewing samples, as well as restocking the shelves and merchandising the food cases. It was all bland, thoughtless, and reassuring—just what she needed.

After some time, Sarah made her way to Bernard's table and sat down. Bernie put aside his newspaper and steadied the pearlescent handle of his cane which swayed, balanced on the edge of the wooden table. The white handle matched his white oxford and ivy cap. He had spent his working life in jeans and flannel but in his retirement dressed with the utmost care and style. Loretta came over and leaned against the booth.

"Well, sweetheart, how are you feeling?" Bernie asked with an affectionate smile. "You seem to have had quite the ordeal."

"I'm beginning to feel a little better. But I'm so confused and angry."

As the story about the pharmacy unfolded, Bernie and Loretta's faces morphed from friendly, patient smiles to scowls of worry and disapproval. They withheld their comments with visible restraint.

Loretta struggled to hide her feelings. She twitched and grimaced; the creases on her face appearing to darken and deepen as her emotions swayed with Sarah's story.

Bernard was clearly concerned but took the story in stride. At his age, it didn't pay to be hot-blooded.

Sarah finished her story saying, "I still can't believe he did nothing. He just... left."

"It all comes down to this: What are you going to do about it?" asked Loretta abruptly.

"I think that you deserve someone better, someone who will treat you right. Take care of you. Look after your interests, despite your mother," Bernard added.

"Should I have told him about Mom already? I didn't on purpose, trying to avoid another Christopher. I knew he'd find out eventually, but I never imagined it'd be like this!" Sarah's voice frayed as she spoke. "Maybe he was just freaked out? He probably just walked in to buy... whatever... not knowing some crazy lady, who happened to be my mother, was having a massive breakdown. Maybe his reaction is understandable?"

"Understandable, yes. Acceptable, no. At least, that's my opinion." Bernie was calm, a byproduct of his age and wisdom. "I'm sure he was surprised, but that's no excuse for not coming to your aid. If he loves you—maybe you're not at that stage yet—if he even 'likes' you, he should have come running instead of standing there like a fool." Bernie squinted as he spoke, his cadence slow and his tone soft. He was trying to keep the conversation from getting too hot, but Loretta was ready to burst.

"Listen, Sarah. I told you from the beginning to be wary of him, but I know everyone hates an 'I told you so,' so I'm not going to say any more." Her words came rapid-fire. "You did nothing wrong; you deserve better. He should have helped you, plain and simple. Now you know what kind of a man he really is. Get out of this thing while you can."

"Maybe you're right, Loretta. Maybe I should just end it... I don't know."

"You need to talk to him." Bernie's voice was relaxed but authoritative. "Get it all out in the open. Straight and clear. If, after that, you decide to ditch this guy, that's up to you. But you can't hide from this."

"You're right, guys." Sarah pursed her lips in thought. "I'll go talk to him after work, face to face. See what he has to say for himself."

"Do that; you won't regret it," Bernie advised and tapped his finger against the tabletop. "How is your mom doing after all of this? Is she okay?"

"Seems like she might luck out again. I heard from her lawyer this morning. The judge was very lenient, said she lacked 'requisite intent.' Then he sent her to Ruther's for evaluation and rehabilitation pending further proceedings. It should be a good thing for her to have professional care twenty-four seven."

The air was thick and still as Sarah ascended the concrete steps and stood before Uncle Geoffrey's large townhouse. It was a three-story cream and brown brick building, roughly in the Georgian style. The porch was framed in black iron, which focused one's attention on the massive oak door. Sarah landed a series of percussive thuds against the behemoth and waited. The dark hue and deep grain of the door meant it was likely nineteenth century with a quality not seen in the twenty-first. It was late, but Sarah knew Geoffrey was on a steady dose of nighttime meds and wouldn't be disrupted. She didn't care if she disrupted Michael; she wanted answers and wanted them now.

The thought of simply calling him or just sending a message had crossed her mind, but she needed the truth uncut and unedited. Over the past several months, she'd fallen in love, but the truth was paramount. If reality led to the end of their relationship, so be it; better to live a hard truth than a comfortable lie. *Wear a helmet.*

The heavy door creaked open, and there stood Michael in bare feet and tousled hair. He'd certainly been asleep. A worn-out cotton T-shirt, faded to yellow, hung loose on his slender frame, and a pair of pilled blue and green flannel pants hugged his lanky waist. Despite his half-awake state, his eyes still sparkled.

Sarah could almost see the sleep clear from his mind, and he seemed to know why she was there.

"Hi ya, lovely. What are you doing here at this time of night?" Michael leaned against the door frame with a look that was both cheerful and casual but rough around the edges. His good-humored demeanor seemed more the product of his will than of a natural state.

"Michael, we need to talk." His playful smile receded into a grimace. "After what went down at the pharmacy the other day, I have some explaining to do, and so do you." Sarah was no-nonsense and controlled but not angry.

"Then you should come in. I'll put on some tea." Michael's voice was flat, untinged by worry but void of his usual gaiety. They went inside, the heavy oak door closing behind them with a dull thud.

"I've had your tea, better make it coffee." Sarah wanted to grin at her quip and lighten the mood, but she knew she couldn't relent, though he did make terrible tea.

Sarah headed to the living room and plopped down on the blue and grey striped couch. The room had a beautiful oak parquet floor and was lined in painted wainscoting. At the center of the room was a large, rough-stone fireplace. It was rustic but civilized, and Sarah had always felt immediately comfortable in the house, except for today. She settled into the familiar, well-worn cushions that reminded her of the good times she'd had there; how not long ago she was in the same spot with nervous anticipation of Michael's touches, his hands on her for the first time. That echo of a memory reminded her that there was something worth saving.

After a few long minutes, Michael brought in a tray of coffee and snacks and sat on the couch beside her. He had smoothed over his hair and straightened up his appearance to his usual suave but in night clothes. His charming smile was back but seemed cautious.

"So, my lovely, what's on your mind?"

"Well… you. You were at the pharmacy. Where an aging lady had a meltdown, a psychotic break. She was my mother. She has mental health problems. You didn't help me."

Sarah's words fell in stilted steps. Each one tripped and stumbled out of her mouth all at once. Nothing came out properly. She almost panicked but then remembered something Loretta always said. It reminded her to take it easy: *tender wounds ache with even the slightest movement.* After a deep breath, she collected her thoughts, and she started again, slower.

Sarah explained her mom's long battle with schizophrenia and mental illness as well as the toll it had taken on their lives. As she spoke, she watched him—searched him—for signs of understanding or remorse. "What you saw was the worst she's been in years, if not ever. She had been making progress, but she'd backslid a bit, lately."

"A bit? That's an understatement," Michael's voice lilted with an edge of sarcasm. "From the looks of it, it seems to be more of a back-avalanche. I gathered there was something very wrong with her, that much seemed evident." Sarah noticed his cheek pinched slightly, as if he were squeezing it against his teeth.

"This isn't funny, Michael."

"I know, I know; I'm sorry. It's a coping mechanism. I get stressed."

"Yes, well, that isn't going to fly here!"

"Sorry, you're right."

Sarah continued about Nancy's illness, her tendency to play the victim, but also her successes. "When she manages to progress, I'm proud of her. But, more often than not, I'm just ashamed. I shouldn't be, she can't help it, but sometimes I am." Sarah's voice was thin and delicate.

Michael's coping giddiness was replaced with a sympathetic gaze.

She continued. "Worse still, I'm often ashamed of myself for being ashamed. I didn't tell you about her because of that shame. I'm sorry. I didn't want to scare you away."

Sarah paused, her face sad and a moment from tears. She was filled with shame and regret, but an undercurrent of anger wound below the surface like a wild river. She was angry at her mother for creating this situation, angry at Michael for his inaction and ambivalence, and angry at herself for not just letting go and having a normal life.

"I understand why you didn't tell me about her." His tone was empathetic, but the words dribbled out in an awkward fashion. "It's hard being different, or 'not normal.' That I can understand, if nothing else. Maybe her mental illness is like my being raised by my uncle. I mean, I was always the weird one because I had an *uncle* instead of a mom or dad." Michael's words were earnest but slick. "I remember the whispers in school and the rumors spread around about my parents. So, in that way at least, I can understand. How you hide those *secrets* from everyone for as long as you can so you're not seen as 'the weird one.'"

"Yes, it is sort of like that. I can only imagine what you were thinking when you walked in and saw my mom ranting on about 'the men with orange eyes' and that horrible crowd jeering around her."

"It was all pretty shocking, actually." Michael nodded and raised his eyebrows a little. "I didn't know she was your mother; I just came in to get some mixers and saw this huge crowd of people. I've never seen anything quite like it. All I could do was stare and wonder about what I was seeing. I mean, I'm an English teacher, not a shrink."

"And that's kind of the problem here, Michael. All you did was stare, just like one of the crowd." Sarah leaned in, anger rising in her throat. "Even after you knew it was me, you just stood there as if turned to stone. I was on the floor, knocked down by my own mother, and you did nothing. Why? Why didn't you rush to my side, check on me, or something? You're my boyfriend, you're supposed to help me, hold me, soothe me. But you did nothing!" Anger boiled over;

her face was mere inches from his. She looked at him with hard eyes. "You just... walked away. Do you even realize how much you hurt me?"

Michael leaned back, surprised by her sudden fierceness. "Sarah, lovely, I..." He couldn't get the words out.

Sarah closed the small gap between them even further. "Do you even care? That is the question I've been asking myself for days now; endlessly, day and night. It seems to have been asked and answered, but tell me I'm wrong, Michael. Tell me I'm wrong!" She poked him in the shoulder and paused, staring him in the face.

Michael tried to back away as he grasped for something to say. His eyes were wide, and his mouth moved but nothing came out.

Sarah deflated and leaned back in resignation. "Never mind." Sarah sighed. "Just tell me the truth. Do you even care or has all of this only been a lark, a game? Something to pass the time while you're in town?"

"Um, of course I care." Michael shook his head as his face contorted with indignation. "I... I was just shocked. I didn't know what to do. I lost sight of you. I..." Michael clawed for words.

They sat on the couch and stared at each other in silence. Only two feet apart, close enough to feel one another's breath, almost each other's heartbeats, but neither spoke.

Sarah peered into Michael's sparkling eyes and wondered what he was thinking. Was she just a stopover while Uncle Geoffrey healed, a fling? As she gazed deeper, she saw two paths diverging. One, a beautiful future of them together and happy with a life full of love, art, and good living. The other was a dark path of loneliness and empty space like a desert highway at night. Just Sarah, forsaken and alone; a return to singlehood.

The first path began to crumble before her eyes. She did not want to lose it, but she couldn't be with someone who did not really care. Someone who would just sit there rather than answer a basic fucking question. She wanted that life *so* badly but wanted it for real. Unlike her parents, Sarah prided herself on being realistic, on her willingness to live hard truths rather than hide in comfortable lies or fantasies. Michael would not change that. *Wear a helmet.*

"Michael, it is getting late. Say something." Sarah's voice was calm. This was his final chance to redeem himself and save their relationship. The threads that bound them together were bare and slender, like a loose shirt button dangling, likely to break and fall with even the lightest touch.

"Look," Michael said, meeting her eyes. "If you had told me about her, I could have been prepared. Maybe I would have even known what to do. Nevertheless, I'm sorry I didn't do more. I'm sorry I wasn't there for you the way I should have been. I was just shocked. Stunned. I care about you, I do. I don't know what else to tell you."

His tone was deflecting and a little defensive. As he spoke, he squirmed like a worm pinned between a child's finger and the sidewalk.

"I see your lips moving and hear what you're saying, but I don't know if it's enough. I was face down in a pile of broken glass and plastic and whatever the fuck else, and you left me there! You just disappeared!" Sarah was almost shouting, but once the words escaped her lips, she reverted to a state of calm. "What am I supposed to think?"

The thread was pulling and the fray spitting off of the last remnants of the fringe.

"Sarah, I'm sorry," Michael retorted. "I don't know how many times I can say it. I fucked up, I should have done it all differently, but I can't change it now."

"I'm not sure that's good enough. I really don't know if we can continue seeing each other. I hate the sound of that, but I'm not sure there's another way."

The thread had snapped, and the button crashed to the floor.

With wells of tears building in her eyes, Sarah rose from the couch and moved toward the door.

"Sarah! C'mon, let's talk about this; it doesn't have to end." Michael was almost pleading.

Sarah turned around, her face a mixture of frustration and acquiescence. "Michael, I'm sorry. I need someone I can count on, who will be there for me, and I don't feel you can do that." She wiped away tears.

"But..." he interrupted. Sarah could tell he was trying to hold her attention. His face looked long and sallow, as if stalked by a dreaded conclusion or trapped like a rat in its own nest. "Sarah..." Michael gently tugged her arm and squared her to him. He looked her in the eyes and said, "Sarah, I love you."

Sarah had hoped to hear those words from him for so long but could not believe they would come now, like this. Two seconds ago, it was over—she was nearly out the door—and now this. Now that he had seen her mother. Now that he had seen her cry. Now that he had seen her bleed and done nothing. Her mind reeled, at a loss for what to do next. She wanted it so badly, but was it real? Now, it was her turn at silent inaction.

Stillness hung in the room like the moment before an avalanche. Michael stood, a look of bewildered astonishment on his face, like a man whose slot-machine had returned all sevens but with no jackpot.

Michael began to fidget as he looked at Sarah, still drenched in quiet and shock. A look of slow-motion panic and confusion washed across his face. He glanced left to right and bit his lower lip. The silence continued. Stare into stare. After another moment, Michael leaned toward Sarah and wrapped his fingers around the back of her neck. While he looked deep into her eyes, he kissed her. Long, deep, a kiss full of passion and fire. Sarah imagined them on screen in the movie of her life. Even the best of Hollywood paled in comparison to that moment. It was a masterclass. Grant, DiCaprio, and Pitt all could have learned something.

Electricity flew, and Sarah's mind went blank as she melted to nothing, like a snowflake in the sun. He'd touched her before, but this was something different, another level. For that moment, the outside world meant nothing and she was free. All of it, her mother, the pharmacy, the crowd, the pain, and the indecision, were all held at bay by a forcefield of carnal desire.

Sarah wrapped her arms around Michael and slid her hands up the back of his T-shirt. She clutched at him; his warm, firm body invited her to envelop him further. She leaned into him on the striped couch, and they became one.

CHAPTER 10

Reset.

To begin again. From the beginning. Sarah recognized an opportunity to reset her relationship with Michael, to reboot and start anew, to do it differently this time, not so wide-eyed like before.

Caution.

Michael approached Sarah with the caution and grace of a swatted dog. She loved how he brought her flowers, asked her opinion with over-the-top deference, and catered to her desires. It lasted for a time.

Eventually, this premium treatment receded, and things dissolved into a sense of routine and normalcy.

The rolling path of smooth sidewalk splayed out before Sarah and Michael as they strolled together toward City Art Center. Sarah's smile shone like a spotlight; her chestnut hair pulled into a half ponytail with her curls hanging in ringlets, caressing her shoulders and the top of her loose-fitting white dress. With their relationship reset, Sarah felt renewed and reinvigorated.

Michael, always dressed to impress, wore a pair of perfect fitting navy slacks, well-pressed, and a white collared shirt, partially buttoned. With a classic brown leather belt and a brown pair of Allen Edmonds loafers, he was a picture of casual elegance. Over his arm laid the matching navy jacket, and on his wrist gleamed his Oris Aquis.

Sarah could tell that Michael was happy to be back in her good graces, and she was excited about their future. It felt like good things were possible. But sometimes, when she looked closely at him, she swore there was a tinge of uneasiness in his face, as if he felt enclosed or caged in.

They climbed to the hilly peak of Eighth Street, and the front columns of the museum came into view. The tall, proud, neoclassical structure proclaimed itself to the world. Its long rows of large Ionic columns, with the tallest set clustered in the center, guarded the entrance like sentinels before an ancient temple. A long, expansive staircase flowed out from the opening like an angular carpet of marble.

As they neared the building, the shine withdrew, and the cracks in the sentinel's armor, as well as the rest of the facade, became apparent. Years of budget cuts and triage maintenance had taken their toll. The museum was like an aging showgirl who looked twenty years younger from the back of the room, but in the front row, the truth was undeniable: it was just makeup and plastic surgery—a parody of youth. Neither the showgirl, nor the building, could hide the years of hard living and the unceasing march of time. The marble, once gleaming white, was now soiled and full of soot, coated in a layer of black film, a reminder of the city's past industrial might.

In an effort to brighten the greying building, colorful banners were hung between the columns. Bold hues and slick graphics advertised the ongoing exhibits. In this case, works by Joan Miró set against a red background in honor of the special retrospective. The works included the rare and the famous assembled together for the first time.

By the time they reached the bottom of the steps, Sarah felt playful and gave Michael a little shove on the shoulder.

"You're it!" Sarah shouted and squeaked like a schoolchild as she ran up the stairs in a fit of joyful giggles. Michael was amused but shook his head with evident embarrassment and mild disapproval. He continued his moderate march up the stairs. His face seemed to say, *Playfulness is fine for you, but I'm not going to break a sweat.*

Halfway up the steep stone steps, Sarah pivoted around to look down at Michael as he marched up in a measured fashion. She grinned despite her disappointment. His angular jaw and precise movements made him look like a general climbing a stage to address his troops.

"C'mon, you slow-poke," Sarah said with a mock sigh. "Had I known you were such a lethargic fuddy-duddy, I would have grabbed a coffee from the shop we passed and still been able to beat you up these stairs." Sarah shook with a playful laugh.

"If I had known you were so interested in childish games, I could have stopped by that playground we passed and brought along someone a little more mature."

With that, they chuckled together, linked arms, and walked up the remaining stairs. At the top, they paused to take in the view. It was Michael's first time back since his return home, and Sarah hadn't been there since a high school field trip, a fact she was ashamed to admit and simply said it had been "a while."

"I forgot just how spectacular this view is," said Michael. "It's not exceptionally high, but I love the perspective. It's so unique. The distance adds a comfortable layer between us and that world out there. Just a couple dozen yards of marble between us and the chaos of the city. The best part is..." Michael leaned toward the city in vituperative defiance, "...from here, you almost can't see the filth."

The smile avalanched off Sarah's face. "Why would you let anything ugly into this moment? All I see is a beautiful view, the shining sun, and you. What else do I need?"

"How can you help it? It's encapsulating," Michael said with a sneer. "The drab, lifeless people, soullessly shuffling about their dull lives. The black tinge on the buildings from the carelessness of a society that puts greed before common sense and the public good. Sometimes I think the only thing worse than the weather is the utter contempt for decent living." Michael screwed up his face in a huff.

Sarah sighed and her shoulders sank. She hated when his passions turned negative.

"Seriously, take this museum, for example." He waved his arm toward the massive columns. "The collection is excellent. It's respectable, thorough, and varied. A great sampling of Western culture, but how many people visit it each year? What percentage of the city?"

"I don't have any idea. Let's just go enjoy it for ourselves," Sarah said, getting annoyed.

"Almost no one. A handful of percent." His arms shook. "People don't appreciate what they have or even understand why it's important. They stagger on endlessly, anxiously, more concerned with sports scores, celebrity gossip, or some shiny new gadget. They are blind to the riches available to them for just a few dollars." Michael grew louder, his face red. "The culturally impoverished are feet away from a feast for the soul, yet they don't come, and this temple to man's creativity languishes."

"You're ranting like my mother or something. Knock it off; let's just go inside." She made no attempt to hide her frustration but was afraid it could backfire.

"These days, everything is about being a victim, who has been more aggrieved by 'the system,' however they choose to define it. To many, none of this has value because the people and societies that created it were imperfect; in their minds, it's impure and irredeemable. I worry for the future of humanity when it is more concerned with grievances than accomplishments. Humanity can soar, but like fools, we choose to crawl." Michael sulked and looked downward with a frown.

Dammit, Michael. I'm not going to let you ruin this with your moody, ranty shit. Sarah paced a moment and shook off her own irritation. She knew it would only compound with his gloom. With a pivot, she turned back to Michael and spoke softly.

"Michael, everything you've said is correct, but I don't want to hear any more about it. Because, right now, none of that matters. You've overlooked something significant."

"Oh, yeah? What's that?" He was quiet, sullen, and morose.

"That *we* are here together, and we're going to enjoy ourselves. The artistic buffet is on offer for us. Let's feast. If others refuse to see it, that's their loss. No reason to dwell on something you can't change. Let's focus on what we can control—ourselves and our experience. It's a beautiful day,

MATTHEW KOPF · 103

the sun is shining, and we are together. Let's have a good time and leave everything else at the door."

Michael sighed. His foot picked at the ground like a horse. After a few deep breaths, his complexion reverted to its regular shade. He paced awhile in thought and then spoke.

"Okay, Sarah. You win." Sincerity rang through his words. "You're right. We're going to have a good time." A smile returned to his face as he held the door for her, and they headed into the museum.

Ten minutes in the City Arts Center, and Michael was back to his usual self, returned to vigor by drinking greedily from the fountain of culture. He was like a wilted flower gulping in water from a thunderstorm to save itself from the brink. His zest for life had been rejuvenated in more ways than one.

Despite Michael's lamentations, the museum had undergone a recent renovation and remodel. Nothing was where it once was. As Sarah went to the toilet, Michael went to ask about the featured exhibit at the information desk.

Sarah dried her hands and adjusted herself before the mirror as she exited the women's room. The new, glossy white marble tile caught her eye, something about the deep cobalt-grey veins, and she took a moment to admire it. As she headed toward the desk, Michael chatted with the hostess behind the counter. Though too far to hear their words, smiles abounded. The hostess, probably around nineteen, scarcely more than a girl, with a petite frame and young face, wore a tight-fitting navy-blue dress with sparkly gold highlights that matched her large-framed glasses. Sarah thought she looked like an artsy flight attendant.

As she got closer, she saw Michael pointing at the hostess's dress. The girl beamed and giggled as she leaned over the counter and pulled her lapel toward him. He, too, leaned in with a ravenous smile. Both chuckled. As Sarah approached, Michael ducked his head and appeared to say something to the girl who slid him a pamphlet. Then he turned and walked away from the counter and toward Sarah.

"Was she any help?" Sarah asked. "Did she tell you how to get to the Miró exhibit?"

"You know, it's funny. I forgot to ask. She was wearing the most fascinating pin, and I had to ask her about it. It was by some local artist, a Favio, apparently, who makes jewelry out of copper pipes..." Sarah tossed him a jagged look. "I did, however," he continued, "get this brochure; I'm sure we can figure it out." He smiled as he handed the pamphlet to Sarah.

Sarah perused the booklet as she walked a few feet ahead of Michael, her gait plain. Sarah turned around and looked at him. His face was a devilish smirk, his eyes fixed on her.

Sarah blushed. "What are you up to, mister?"

"Oh, nothing at all, my lovely. I'm just enjoying your dress." He grinned and chirped a soft whistle for effect.

"You little perv!" Sarah shook her head and feigned offense. "I'm glad you like it. I picked it out with you in mind."

They entered the Miró retrospective; the display space was a large rectangular room with oak floors, thirty-foot high ceilings, and clerestory windows along the top edge. The floors were stained a light, natural, hue, and the walls were typical museum white—stark sheetrock, no trim. It was a Wednesday afternoon, and their footsteps clacked on the floors and reverberated off walls as they walked through the near-empty exhibit. The only other visitors they saw were a middle-aged couple and an older woman with a cane.

Sarah felt charmed and weightless. The earlier sour mood seemed to have faded, and Michael was in good spirits. She was glad for it.

"God, I love Miró," Michael said with exuberance. "I've been looking forward to this for weeks now. I'm glad we're finally here. Thanks for bringing me."

They looked at the first few paintings, and Michael turned to Sarah. "It all feels like Spain. I get the same feeling when I look at all of this as I do when I'm there. Miró's work speaks to me as if we share a secret of the heart. I can't explain it; it's just uncanny that a painting, or a set of paintings, can make me feel like this. Man, do I miss it."

Sarah nodded. When Michael talked like that, it put her on edge; she felt less important, secondary. As if he had an untouchable place within him that he saved for his precious Spain, or his memory thereof, anyway, and she wasn't good enough to enter. She put it out of her mind and stopped in front of a large painting of a tree surrounded by farm buildings and tools. The stylization and detail drew her attention.

"Michael, what is this one? It is a little weird, but I kinda like it. Though I don't really know what to make of it."

"Oh! *The Farm*! I was hoping they'd have it!" Michael wagged his finger at the painting and overflowed with delight. "This is my favorite piece; I never thought I'd see it in person. It is supposed to encapsulate life on a Catalan farm. There's so much going on; I can't keep it all in my head at once."

Michael smiled ear-to-ear as he examined the huge canvas; his nose almost touched it as he poured over detail after detail working left to right. Sarah watched both amused and impressed as he stood back and took it all in before digging his face back into its finer points. His smile never ceased.

From the countless birds to the distant trees, he studied it all and then turned to Sarah.

"It's as if he crammed in everything one has or does on a farm into one view. This is what I think of when I think of Miró. Some people prefer *Blue II* or the *Constellation Series*, but for me, this is the one. Did you know it was once owned by Ernest Hemingway? He said that 'it has in it all that you feel about Spain when you are there and all that you feel when you are away and cannot go there...' And for me, that rings true. It is precisely how I feel when I look at it. It's like homesickness."

"But this is your home, Michael."

"Yes, this is where I'm living, but that does not make it my home."

Michael's words poked at her skin like a hungry mosquito. She could hear how much he missed Spain and the power it still had over him. Frustration bubbled inside her, because she couldn't compete with what it was to him or how its memory held him. For a moment, she was back on the striped couch with him slipping away, just a little. She pushed it aside. After a deep breath, she smiled to herself and continued.

Michael was ahead of her, and she hurried to catch up until a small painting in a far corner caught her eye.

Sarah stood before the painting, and an unusual sense of calm swept over her. Slowly, from somewhere inside, she felt a small burst of joy. *The Farm* and *The Escape Ladder* were stars of the show, but this one spoke to *her*. It was a colorful impressionistic painting of a vase of flowers on a table. To Sarah, it looked like the table was covered in a striped tablecloth of bright colors. She noticed, thanks to Michael's teaching, distinct nods to cubism and fauvism, but it was not fully in either. The flower arrangement was a mixture of white gardenias, calla lily, jasmine, and a red rose arranged inside a painted vase. The vase had an Asian—perhaps Japanese—feel to it and was adorned with a pair of birds and a folding fan decorated with flowers. Sarah adored how the colors played off one another, the blues and greens of the flowers with the decorations on the vase. How it was all tied together by the broad bands of colors on the tablecloth. The orange, yellow, black, white, and blue streaks alternated across the bottom of the painting, echoing the colors of the flowers in interstate-like ribbons. To Sarah's untrained eye, the work felt like a bridge between Miró's earlier creations and the more surrealist later works that he was so well known for.

Something about the image mesmerized her. The simple subject handled stylistically resonated—connected—with her in a way she'd never felt with a painting. It felt as if it knew something about her, something deep inside that even she had yet to discover.

Sarah had to have it and glanced at the placard: *Still Life with Flowers*. She stood close to it and absorbed the warmth of the colors and the gentle feelings it brought her.

Michael stood before a pedestal and gazed at a small sculpture made of rock and bone. Sarah came up behind him and lingered for a moment to take him all in. As she watched, she realized he was looking past it. As she traced his eye line, she was startled to see a young woman. Like a cheetah, she was tall and lean with piercing blue eyes; her frame was lithe and feline with bleached blonde hair and bright red lipstick. Her lips curved into a sly half-smile as if she were about to pounce. The girl looked up and noticed Sarah and then quickly averted her gaze and hurried away. Michael, oblivious to Sarah behind him, was startled by the sound of her voice.

"I didn't see *her* come in. Do you know her? She looks like she knows *you*."

"Oh, um, Sarah. Hi." Surprised, he searched for a response.

"Her? No, I don't know her. I was just being polite. She was all by herself and smiled at me, so I smiled back. Nothing more, lovely." He smiled and slid his arm around her waist with a gentle squeeze.

Unconvinced but disinterested in spoiling the day with a big argument, she let the cheetah girl drop and put her arm around him. *Still, probably best to extricate ourselves from this situation.*

"I'm getting a little hungry. Want to grab a snack? Let's finish the last bit and take a break. I've read the café was renovated and is something to see."

"Sure thing, my lovely. I could use a drink. A snack sounds good too," said Michael, sounding somewhat relieved.

They exited through a pair of large wooden doors and walked toward the main lobby.

"Let's stop in here real quick." Sarah pointed to the gift shop. "I want to see if I can get a print of that still life."

"What still life?"

"Oh, while you were, um, looking at the... *sculpture,* I came across a wonderful painting called *Still Life with Flowers.*" Sarah turned into the gift shop and thumbed through the prints. "Here it is! But only in an eight by ten?" She gave a small frown. "Oh, well, I'll take what I can get."

"I don't think I saw that one." Michael looked at the print over her shoulder and shrugged. Her fascination with it was lost on him.

The elevator soared to the new café relocated to the top floor. For all practical purposes, it was a large, enclosed balcony with expansive panes of glass and an elaborate, eco-friendly glass roof—modern, fashionable, and state-of-the-art. Like a glass tree house, it gave the sensation of being outdoors while still shielding its patrons from the elements.

They settled into a tall café table near the west side of the room. Michael ordered a scotch on the rocks and Sarah a flute of champagne. From their table, they could see the silhouette of the city as the sun began to merge with the horizon and threw huge streaks of pink through the sky. The room took on a pink blush. Even their drinks had a slight coral tint. Sarah imagined that this must be what it's like to bathe in a cloud.

"Were you happy with the exhibit?" Sarah asked, sipping her champagne.

Michael stared into his drink for a moment and watched the ice crack and spit as the cold pushed its way into the scotch. "You know, I liked it a lot. Miró is not only one of my favorite artists, but the whole thing really took me back to Spain. It reminded me of the dusty, loose soil, the endless sunshine, and the bright, friendly people."

"I noticed you've been pretty distracted today," Sarah interjected. "Too many thoughts of the past? Pretty girls and Spanish sun?" She chuckled but immediately admonished herself for being too on the nose.

"It sounds bad, but yes." He sighed and ran his hands through his hair. After a sip of scotch, he continued. "I've been thinking about it a lot today—everything seems to remind me of Spain. I keep going back to my days in that little village. The main square, not far from my apartment, held pretty much everything—the shopping, the restaurants, any special events. I loved going down there, talking with the people, grabbing great food, and just enjoying life." Sarah watched his features soften, his eyes downcast as he spoke, and knew it came from his heart. "I really miss that place. Strangely, even the light in here reminds me of an adventure."

Sarah appreciated how open Michael was being with his feelings and wondered how it felt to be so connected to a place. As much as she tried to be sensitive to his love of Spain because it was clear what it meant to him, it still grated on her nerves. She resented how it competed with her for his love. That said, she loved listening to his stories but wished they were more firmly rooted in the past. It always felt like Michael's tales were a wave, a large tsunami, of memories that progressed from the past to the future and that all she could do was be washed over in the present.

"One day," Michael continued, "I was out for a walk in the countryside. As I paced through the rolling hills, the wind picked up and blew the dust from the fields into my face; it coated the edges of my sleeves and pant legs. Despite this, the sun was so warm and pleasant that I couldn't be deterred."

Sarah alternated between Michael and the sunset. She felt like she could see him, covered in dust in the Spanish countryside. But she saw him there alone.

"I trekked and wandered through the dry landscape until the sun began to set. I stumbled upon a small hill that looked down on a lush valley edged on three sides by a small mountain range." He gestured with his hands, illustrating mountains with his fingers. "In the distance, the peaks stared at me, like eyes." He leaned in, eyes intense. "I crested the hill and looked down; I was overcome by what I saw."

Michael paused, took a breath, and finished his drink before continuing.

"At the bottom of the valley was a large peach farm with the trees in full bloom. There must have been hundreds. Have you ever seen a flowering peach tree?"

"No." Sarah was slow to respond. She'd been listening but the cheetah girl had crept back into her mind. *I'm sure cheetah girl has seen peach trees.*

"One of the most stunning things you'll ever see!" He quickly became bouncy and animated. "The radiant pink trees fell together into neat rows, flanked by green-brown paths. The alternation of hues made vast streaks of color. Pink, green, brown. Pink, green, brown."

As Michael got excited, Sarah's thoughts moved closer to his story. She enjoyed the ebullient flow of his arms and the crescendo of his cadence.

"The flowering trees ranged from one end of the valley to the other, as far as I could see. I've never seen anything else like it. As I looked out, the wind had stopped, and all became calm. The evening light pulsated, and I felt the greatest sense of calm and peace that I have ever known. It was as if everything was in its correct place. As if *I* was in the correct place. I have never felt like that before or since…" Michael trailed off as he gazed out the window.

"Michael? You okay? You just sort of drifted off there."

"Um, yeah, my lovely." He appeared to shake himself loose from his thoughts. "I'm going to hit the loo and grab another drink. I'll be right back."

Sarah watched as Michael sauntered toward the restrooms and disappeared down the hall. She took a sip of her champagne. It was dry and pleasant with a hint of minerality and green apple that lingered. After another sip, she felt good but hindered. Michael's words and actions had worked under her skin like a series of splinters. She tried to ignore it, but the irritation persisted. She reached for her bag and distracted herself with Asimov's *The Gods Themselves.*

A couple of minutes later, she looked up to see Michael reappear from the darkened hallway and head to the bar. He ordered from the cheerful-looking bartender dressed in a waistcoat and bowtie.

She tried to get back into her book, but Plutonium-186 was insufficient to hold her attention against Michael and the barkeep's grinning and chatting. Sarah watched as they laughed and gestured. *What the hell could they be talking about?* The bartender stood with a bottle of Macallan 18 in his hand as his eyebrows arched. A look of surprise spread across his face as Michael thumbed in her direction. *What is that about? Just pour the drink, it's just a scotch—glass, ice, pour, that's it.*

A few moments later, Sarah's thoughts were willed into fruition as the bartender measured out a double and sent Michael on his way.

"Welcome back." Annoyance skated on the edge of her voice. The splinter wound festered a little. "What were you talking with that bartender about for so long?"

"Nothing, really, just a little Spain talk. He said it's on his bucket list." Michael's face turned to a frown under Sarah's questioning. He took a deep breath and closed his eyes.

"Sorry, not trying to give you the third degree, but you've either been lost in thought or moody and flighty all day. What's going on?" Sarah's tone was inquiring but not prosecutorial. "Plus, I've noticed you being a little flirty with a couple of the girls around here. I mean, between the way you looked at them and the way you talk about Spain, is there any room left in there for me?" Sarah pointed to his chest as she got louder. She calmed herself, but her face betrayed her, and a single tear snuck down her cheek. She wiped it away in hopes that Michael didn't notice.

"What *are* you talking about?" Michael snapped, snide and condescending. "We are having a perfectly good time, and you're on about me looking at women? What women? Is that champagne making you paranoid? That's an unusual side effect for alcohol."

"Michael, you know damn well what I'm talking about," Sarah snapped back. She may not have wanted to cause a scene, but she wasn't going to be patronized. "Have you already forgotten the cute little artsy stewardess girl and the bleached-blonde with the lipstick? I'm sure they haven't forgotten you."

"Wait a minute," Michael responded, getting angry. "What are you getting at? There aren't any girls. I asked a museum employee, who happens to be a woman, for assistance and smiled at someone who did not have the luxury of company. How does that make me wrong?"

Was he being obtuse? Or was she being paranoid? Or was he being defensive because she'd hit a little too close to home?

"I'm not blind," responded Sarah, looking a little deflated. "I may not be a great master of it like you, but I know flirting when I see it."

"I wasn't flirting; I was being nice. Don't you like to be nice to people too? You are nice to people at the Kettle; I don't run around accusing you of things."

"That's my job. I help them find tea. What do you think, I'm going to shack up with the folks who shop there? I'm not big on dating the geriatric."

"You shacked up with me," Michael said with a half-smile, half-sneer.

"You're not eighty years old. You're missing the point." She ignored his smile. "Why do you have to flirt with girls when you have me? Why do I have to hear about Spain all the time and feel like this place where we live is so terrible? We're here, now, together; why is that so bad?" Her anger softened. "Why do I always have to feel like this—this here—isn't enough?" Sarah pointed to her heart.

"Oh, Sarah," he said dismissively. "Why do you have to be so melodramatic? You're seeing things that aren't there. I was just being nice to those ladies. I'm sorry if all my talk about Spain went too far." He drifted into sympathetic. "The retrospective, maybe the alcohol, just took me away a little bit. If you were going to get so upset about all of this, why did you bring me here?"

"I brought you here because I wanted to spend time with you. You!" She pointed at him with a delicate finger, her face like a jagged line. "I know you love Miró, I know you have great memories of Spain, so I thought this would be a good opportunity to spend time together. I hoped that putting all of these pieces together—Miró, Spain, and me—could bring us closer together, maybe build a bridge across all of it." Her face slackened and turned sad. "It didn't work that way. You've been somewhere else all day, and we're farther apart than when we walked through the door."

"Oh," Michael said in quiet realization. "I see." His head drooped, and he pursed his lips in thought. His right hand tapped gently on the table. "You know what? Let's reset and start again from here. Let's sit here, together, and enjoy the beautiful evening and each other's company."

"Okay," Sarah said, easing away from her frustration. "Let's give it a try."

Michael reached across the table and grasped Sarah's hand. She let out a little sigh and smiled with a shrug as Michael gently kissed the back of her palm. They sat in silence and watched the sunlight fade away.

CHAPTER 11

Sarah stepped off the bus onto the cracked sidewalk and shuddered as she looked up at Ruther's Rehabilitation Center. She was there to visit her mother, a prospect she dreaded. Nancy had been checked-in for weeks, since the incident at the pharmacy, and Sarah had not been to see her. They'd spoken on the phone, but face-to-face was always different.

Ruther's had always given Sarah the creeps: a converted nineteenth-century mansion with whitewashed clapboard siding, black shutters, and a slate roof. The building was perched on a hill looking down on the neighborhood below, like Mother at the Bates Motel.

As Sarah walked amongst the once-prosperous neighborhood, she thought about the rises and falls of fortune. How this part of town, where wealthy merchants built monuments to their success and power, used to be the gleaming jewel of the city. Now, it was practically a derelict and overflowed with tenement housing, its former glory all but forgotten.

The grounds were surrounded by a black, ten-foot-high palisade fencing with pointed spikes atop each bar. The gate itself was intricate ironwork that culminated with a central coat of arms, presumably from the original captain of industry who built the place, and a lion's head in the center that held the latch in its mouth. She walked up the path and entered through a set of mammoth doors, like a castle or a giant crypt.

The door to Nancy's room was slightly ajar, and Sarah could hear the TV's low murmur as she knocked on the heavy metal entryway and let herself in.

Although Nancy's crimes had features of violence, the doctors determined she was not a threat to other patients and moved her to the low-security wing. Everything about the room was small: a small window parallel to the door, a small rocking chair, and a small television. Squeezed into the opposite corner was a single bed and nightstand. Nancy barely fit in the room and kept the door open.

When Sarah entered, Nancy sat on a well-worn rocking chair and stared out the window. A gameshow was on the television, but in her vague, semi-drug-induced-haze, Nancy didn't notice.

"Knock, knock. Hi, Mom," Sarah said in an upbeat voice. The familiarity of Sarah's voice flinched Nancy out of her daze.

"Oh, Sarah, I didn't hear you. It's good to see you. Sit down."

Sarah nestled herself down onto the tiny bed and faced her mother, who looked three sizes too large for her accommodations. "How are you feeling?"

"I'm doin' fine. The doctors say I'm makin' real progress. I mean, I haven't been seein' no orange eyes or nothin'. Maybe they'll finally let me outta here."

"Glad to hear it, but remember the judge will decide when, or if, you get out of here. Just focus on doing what the doctor says and getting healthy."

A hard rap came on the door, and the doctor entered. He was in his early fifties with a tall, lean frame and a pointed jaw. He spoke directly at Sarah. "Ms. Hall, can you come with me for a few minutes?"

Sarah followed the doctor to a nearby office. It was a tight closet with a simple desk, computer, and two chairs likely only used for these types of conferences.

The doctor closed the door and sat opposite Sarah. "I want to talk with you about some concerns regarding your mother." His voice was even and flat.

"Concerns? She was just telling me that she's doing great."

"She has a tendency to emphasize what she likes and ignore what she doesn't. It's another sign she isn't ready yet. However," he paused in slight hesitation, "that isn't my main concern. You see, while most of her delusions have subsided and her depression is mostly under control, she has one persistent delusion about your father, Henry. Says he talks to her and compliments her progress."

"Well, she does have a history of schizophrenia," Sarah said casually and felt like she was stating the obvious.

"Yes, we thought we had that under control, but evidently not as well as we had hoped." He paused again and cleared his throat. "There is another thing."

"Oh? What now?" Sarah could feel her face crease with concern.

"She reports pain that we can't source. It doesn't appear to be real."

"That's a new one. Usually her pain is her back or something related to her weight or terrible diet."

"Yes, we've changed her diet, but she complains of thigh pain that our scans and tests can't find. It is possible that it is all just lingering parts of her breakdown manifesting

MATTHEW KOPF · 119

themselves in a different manner. For the time being, we'll make some adjustments to her medications and see how things go."

"I'm glad she's in here so you can keep an eye on her. When she's home, I do the best I can, but I can only do so much."

The doctor nodded in understanding as they stood and exited the small office.

When she reentered Nancy's room, it was exactly as when she'd left. Nancy staring out the window, the TV still making noise.

"Hi, Mom. The doctor had some good things to say about you."

"The doctor, huh? I've been tellin' him for weeks now that I'm doin' fine. He keeps tellin' me he's worried about this or that, but I feel fine. Maybe the doctor's gone crazy, spending too much time in the looney bin hisself. You know what I mean?" Nancy cackled like a sedated witch.

Sarah let out a little laugh and shook her head. She knew it was best to play along.

Nancy continued. "So, how's things with this Michael guy?"

"Things are..." Sarah paused. She wasn't sure she wanted to go down this road with Nancy.

"He gonna put a ring on it?" Nancy's question interrupted Sarah's search for a deflection.

"We're not there yet." Sarah hesitated. "He's great, but there are a few kinks to work out before any commitment like that. I mean, I'd love to, but..."

"Everything's got kinks. Even a crazy lady like me knows that."

"Well..." Sarah stopped. She'd already said more than she'd wanted to but had little choice but to continue. "He's great in so many ways. He encourages me to try new things.

He wants me to finish school, but... sometimes I worry I'm just a stop-over. I mean, the other day, I'm pretty sure he was flirting with the—"

"Bah!" Nancy cut in. "So he flirts; men do that. At least you know he's got some blood in his veins."

"I guess, but I wish he wouldn't. Maybe he doesn't. I don't even know for sure. Maybe I'm paranoid and should be in here with you. But other than that, it's great we—"

"So you talkin' to him about a ring? Or are you gonna let this one walk too?"

"Mom, no! After I finish school and get a real job, we'll see..."

Sarah felt flustered; she'd said too much and regretted it. Before she could continue, a nurse entered and announced it was time for treatments; Sarah had to leave. It was just as well. Sarah wished she'd just kept her mouth shut.

The doctor's concerns weighed on her mind as she headed home. She hoped they could fix Nancy's pain, real or imagined, and that it wouldn't lead to bigger problems.

CHAPTER 12

"Sarah? She's in back," Loretta said to Bea. "I'll call her up."

Loretta peeked behind the curtain that separated the sales floor from the back room and asked Sarah to come to the counter.

"I'll be right there," Sarah said. "I just have to finish these last screws on this display." Screwdriver in hand, Sarah turned back to her work but wondered what Bea wanted with her and kept a keen ear on them.

"Loretta, while we're waiting, can you wrap up a few pounds of your Earl Grey for me?" Bea asked. "I'm on my way to the airport to meet Tina—you know my granddaughter, Tina—the private flight attendant. We're going to West Palm Beach with Mr. Longheim, aboard his plane, for sun and shopping." Bea emphasized the last word with a high-pitched ring. "I'm in a bit of a hurry and will need to push on."

"Funny, we were just talking about that," Loretta boomed. "I just got back from Florida myself. I took the grandbabies to Orlando. It was *hot*, not to mention pricey, but the kiddos enjoyed themselves. Really, that's all that matters."

Sarah turned the last screw into place and chuckled at Loretta going on about Florida. While she'd never been there, she had enjoyed listening to Loretta and Bernie trade stories about their adventures in the Sunshine State.

"But if you're off to down there," Loretta continued, "what are you doing here?"

"I'm here because I absolutely adore your Earl Grey, and I absolutely must give some to Mr. Longheim. A man as generous as Mr. Longheim must have a gift, even just a token one. Someone with as exquisite tastes as Mr. Longheim must have this tea—his friends too—and I will be the one to take it to them."

"Thanks, Bea, we appreciate your evangelism. We'll gladly sell our products to anyone interested, plus, we ship," said Loretta, never able to resist being a salesperson.

As Sarah scrubbed the dirt from her hands and nails, she cursed herself for having procrastinated on the displays. She'd rather have spent the last forty-five minutes back at Bernie's table with Richard and his new girlfriend Phyllis, who just moved up from Georgia, instead of wrestling with flat-pack pressboard and ill-fitting hardware.

"Where is that girl?" Bea's words were curt. "I'm really short on time, and I have some news concerning Sarah's latest beau that she may want to have, though probably not want to hear."

At her name, Sarah's ears perked up, and knowing that it was about Michael set her nerves on edge as she headed to the counter.

Loretta wrapped Bea's packages, one in pink, one in blue, and rang her up. Bea stayed quiet as Loretta finished but checked her watch twice. Sarah appeared from behind the curtain and was immediately struck by Beatrice's immense state of over-dress. She wore a chartreuse Burberry dress with matching epaulettes and brass studs. Her hat, flamboyant as ever, was custom made to match the dress and featured bright peacock feathers and brass highlights. She looked like a Disney grandmother dressed in high fashion—Cruella de Vil wears Prada.

"Hi, Bea," Sarah said hesitantly as she wiped the dust from her apron and began to roll down her blouse sleeves.

"Little deary, I'm afraid I have some news for you of a rather tender sort. Do you know my granddaughter, Nikki? She's about your age and always about town—a regular at all the fashionable spots. She shops here sometimes." Bea tapped her gloved finger on the counter.

Sarah shook her head no and wondered why Bea thought she and Nikki ran in the same circles. Spoiled trust-fund brats don't usually run with the poor, plain girls. Sarah wished she would just get to the point.

"Well, anyway, she knows who you are, deary. She told me that two nights ago, she was dining at *L'Espérance* with her friend and saw your man, erm, what is his name..."

"Michael," Sarah said, annoyed. She did not like where this was going and wondered why Bea chose to bring this to her attention in front of everyone, especially if it concerned Michael.

"Yes, Michael. Well, he was dining there with a girl and that girl, I hate to say it, wasn't you." The words sang from her lips but were pointed and sharp. "Nikki didn't know her but said she had a bit of an art look—thick-rimmed glasses, reddish hair, young. Does that sound like anyone you know?"

The description was familiar. Though she'd only seen her for a few seconds, her thoughts immediately went to the woman from the information stand at the museum—with the copper jewelry.

"Are you sure it was him?" The words quivered out. "I don't know the girl. I mean, I don't think I do."

"Nikki seemed pretty certain. She had a good view. It sounds like she and Michael may have been friends once, a long time ago. Anyway, deary, I'm frightfully sorry to be the one to break it to you, but someone had to do it." Bea collected her change from Loretta and methodically put each piece of currency into its place. As she tucked the wrapped boxes into her bag, she said, "Now, however, I have to go. I have a plane to catch. I mustn't keep Mr. Longheim waiting."

Bea turned and headed for the door.

"Wait! Was that all she said? What were they doing, just eating? Was there anything else?" Sarah pleaded.

"I'm sorry, deary, that is all I know. I wish I had more for you. Now, I really must be going. Good day, everyone." Bea shook her head and walked out the front door.

The door chimed as Bea left and the store settled into silence. Sarah stood frozen, immobile, as if she had stepped into a snowbank up to her waist. She did not know what to do with the information she'd just received.

Was it true? Was there another reason, or was she just being played for a sucker? She tried to keep up her wits, and, being of scientific mind, she slipped into analysis mode.

What do I know to be true? I was not with Michael two days ago. I did not hear from him two days ago. L'Espérance is his favorite restaurant—he goes there a lot, even without me.

The facts did not seem to be lining up in her favor, but she pressed on with her analysis.

What information suggests it wasn't him, or at least not under the circumstances Beatrice insinuated? We can't completely confirm it was him. *The only real information comes from the word of a bimbo socialite whose business is stirring up trouble and figuring out ways to profit from it. That said, Bea, despite her faults, is not likely to drop a bombshell on a girl's life on a whim. After all, Bea likes me and has helped me before.*

A few years earlier, when one of Nancy's crises forced her to move suddenly, Sarah did not have the money to cover last month's rent at the old place and the first month's rent plus the security deposit at the new place. Bea, who knew the owner of the new apartment, convinced the landlady to accept the security deposit two months later. Sarah only found out that Bea interceded more than a year after the fact. Sarah assumed the landlady was being kind.

There could be a perfectly innocent reason for all of this, Sarah thought to herself and shifted to rationalization. She ran through a litany of possible scenarios that didn't amount to Michael being a total asshole: Maybe it was just someone who looked like him; perhaps she was a platonic old friend; possibly he had a cousin in from out of town and he wanted to show her a great restaurant. She wanted to believe any of those explanations; she wanted to give him the benefit of the doubt and not feel like she had been fooled again.

"Sarah, we couldn't help but overhear," Richard said in his quiet, rough tone, interrupting her thoughts. "Was Bea talking about Michael Kensington?"

"Um, yes, my boyfriend. Why?"

"Well, I'm not sure, but we might have some information that could make you feel better," Richard replied, his gravelly voice turning soft.

"His uncle is Geoffrey Kensington, right? The one who had a terrible fall last winter?" Phyllis chimed in inquiringly.

"Yes, that's the one," said Sarah with caution.

"I think we know him," Phyllis said. "We live in the senior home next to the rehab center. It's all part of the same ol' complex and share the same dining hall. We've actually dined with him—well, both Geoff and Michael, really—several times. We've sort of become friends. With all of his surgeries, he's always in and out of there. We like him; he's a sweet man."

"That's great, but how does that relate to what Bea said?"

"Here's the thing, young one," said Phyllis. Her soft Georgian accent kept her from sounding condescending. "We had dinner with Geoff two days ago, and he said that Michael had been by to see him that day and all he could say was, 'Sarah this and Sarah that.'"

Sarah raised her eyebrows and listened closer.

"So, the boy is talking about you left and right. I know that doesn't exactly clear your mind, but it may give you some comfort, sweetie." Phyllis paused a moment; her eyes rolled as she searched for a memory. "You know, there was another thing." Her finger shook in the air. "It was a li'l uncouth but could still be worth mentioning. See, we were dining with Geoffrey and Michael, and in a moment of joviality he mentioned to Richard that he 'may have to try his hand at monogamy for that one.' He was referencing you, young one. Feels like that could be taken a multitude of ways, I suppose." She shrugged. "But it might help."

"I guess it does, a little; maybe. I hate feeling like I'm being used," Sarah said and sat down in the chair behind the counter. She closed her eyes, dropped her head, and took several deep breaths.

Phyllis and Richard took the hint and withdrew to the table with Bernie.

Sarah sat for many minutes without knowing what to do. She thought about Michael and their future. It wasn't so long ago that she had seen their world collapsing in his eyes, but then he said he loved her and everything changed. Or, she'd thought it had.

The quiet air was cut by the staccato ring of the Kettle's phone. Sarah sucked her breath and pinched her tongue between her teeth as she heard Loretta answer in her office.

"Thanks for calling the Family Kettle. How may I help you?" Loretta asked in her good-natured, cheerful tone. "I'm sorry, who? I can't understand you. Sarah? Yes, please hold."

Sarah's ears perked up, and her stomach tightened. A shot of nauseous adrenaline surged through her system as she wondered what lurked on the other end. From behind her, Loretta summoned her to the phone, which she brought to her ear in near slow-motion.

"Hello? This is Sarah." She forced herself into salesperson mode.

"He's gone, Sarah! He's gone!" Michael was barely recognizable under his sobs.

"Who is gone? What's going on?"

"Uncle... Geoffrey..." Michael wept, "...is *gone*. He had surgery on his leg but spiked a fever overnight; he died this morning..." Michael said as he managed to pull his words together enough to form a few sentences. He let out a whimper followed by a torrent of tears.

"Sarah, I don't know what to do. I'm lost, completely lost. I need you. Please, help me."

"I will. I'm on my way."

Sarah hung up the phone and stood in sullen shock. How could he be gone, that sweet, gentle man? How is it that only a few minutes ago she wanted to tear Michael apart and

MATTHEW KOPF · 129

now she felt nothing but overflowing compassion? He was a wounded animal that needed her help. She would use her love to give him solace and put aside her worries; she needed to be there for him.

———

Sarah stared at Michael in the pissing, grey half-rain as he stood motionless and wept over Uncle Geoffrey's grave. The night had dropped water in leaded sheets, and the damp air clung to everything like bubbles on glass. She watched as the droplets wicked off the drawn hood of his overcoat and onto his pained face. It was evident he didn't notice the sting of the cold.

The humanist preacher and the small, assembled crowd had vanished, evaporated like rain. Sarah stood near Michael but at a distance. He'd asked for space; all she could do was stand and watch. The previous night, Michael had told her about his fears of abandonment and hopelessness in the face of his uncle's passing. He had said it was as if his only familial connection to the world had severed, and he was now just a tribe-less body floating in space.

In the oppressive air, Sarah's heart broke with pity and overran with sympathy as she watched the silent suffering. Michael looked like a man lost at sea, both disorientated and determined, as he dropped a bouquet of white roses and forget-me-nots, his uncle's favorites, onto the lowering casket and ran a palmful of dirt through his fingers onto the polished wooden box. His eyes darted around the scene, as if just awakened from a dream. His lips moved in small spasms as if he were bartering with himself—or the universe—about taking his next steps into a world without Uncle Geoffrey. Sarah could see his mind struggled to calculate it all. He wrung his hands in apparent desperation. It was too much, too final for his unprepared mind—the box, the earth, the end.

Sarah's body was a prolonged ache as she watched Michael grapple with the twist the Fates had dealt Uncle Geoffrey. She wanted nothing more than to race to his side and comfort him. To hold him and soothe his desperate pain.

Her thoughts turned to the first time she'd met Uncle Geoffrey. It was about a month after they'd started dating, and everyone was nervous. Geoffrey, because it was his first time out since the accident; Michael and Sarah, because Uncle Geoffrey was the most important person in Michael's life. Michael had arranged for them to dine at Jacob J's Steak House, which was the best in town. Sarah remembered how Michael's hand was clammy, almost sticky, as she held it when they walked from the car. He was so nervous that he'd dropped the car keys four times on the walk from the parking lot. The memory brought a small smile and some levity.

The rest of that evening went off without a hitch. Geoffrey was sweet and gracious; Michael was charming and deferential; and Sarah was kind and jubilant. That night, Uncle Geoffrey asked her so many questions—he was fascinated by Sarah's interest in chemistry. He was both a keen observer and curious but never nosey. As they ate, Geoffrey asked about how salt worked with their steaks and the chemistry behind the rendering of fat. Michael barely got a word in but seemed to enjoy watching the back and forth.

After that evening, Sarah would see Geoffrey at occasional intervals. He was always sweet and considerate, even when in pain and medicated. Sarah marveled at the contrast between Uncle Geoffrey and her mother. Both had suffered cruel twists of fate, but Geoffrey faced his with steel-eyed determination and Nancy with victimization. In a way, she'd been jealous of Michael's relationship with his uncle in that they were on the same team fighting illness together, whereas Sarah had to fight Nancy and her illnesses on a two-front war of attrition. As she watched Michael crumble before the death of Uncle Geoffrey, she doubted her own reaction would be so severe when the time came for Nancy.

The previous night, on the grey-striped sofa, in the wood-lined living room, Sarah had listened to Michael pour out his soul about his uncle. It seemed cathartic at the time but now appeared inadequate. Uncle Geoffrey had been the one constant throughout the hardships and sorrows of Michael's life. Uncle Geoffrey had been a guide as well as a beacon of hope, throughout the loneliness and loss of his parents to abandonment and death. He was the one person Michael could always count on, no matter how wayward he had been. An uncle in relation but both a mother and father in practice, and now he was gone.

Sarah cried as Michael stood, almost bolted to the earth. The site workers began to fill the grave and moved with professional politeness around the hardened clay statue of Michael Kensington. Then, he started to move. A little at first, as if to break the seal between his foot and the ground. He pulled up one leg and then another before straightening his back, as if at attention. Sarah saw a change in his face, a recognition, that the light that had guided his life since childhood had been extinguished, shattered like a glass bulb cast to the ground, its gaseous elements drifted away like a soul making its escape.

CHAPTER 13

Michael's life corkscrewed to the edge and would have jumped the rails to oblivion if not for Sarah. She became his assistant, aide, and constant companion, able to wield decisiveness like a sword and make decisions where he could not. Though she kept her apartment, most of her time was spent in Geoffrey's old townhouse. She'd begun to view it as a second home, almost as *their* home. In order to handle the lawyers and accountants and to keep Michael fed and out in the sun now and again, she dropped to one class, which deferred her dream of a real career a while longer. A fair price, she reckoned, if it meant being with him. She hoped to ultimately end up with both—her career and Michael.

After Geoffrey's death, Sarah listened to Michael come to grips with his uncle's passing. He talked about how the sudden transition from life to death had left him feeling hollowed and unmoored. How he always figured death would be something they would have seen coming, as if he and Uncle Geoffrey would have stared down the reaper as he rode toward them, sickle gleaming in the air. Sarah felt a mixture of pleasure and disappointment when Michael talked about how grateful he was to her but also how alone he felt. He moaned about how the ties that bound him to anyone felt tenuous and circumspect—none of them family, just people. People who could come in and out of his life at assorted intervals and whose relationships could end with the utterance of a few words. When he spoke like that, Sarah felt cold.

As the weeks passed, glimpses of the old Michael reemerged. An occasional smile or a "lovely" was a reminder that all was not lost and that grief had a terminus. But each step closer to normalcy brought an unanswered question nearer to Sarah's tongue. It had floated in her mind since the last time she saw Beatrice at the Kettle.

On a lazy Sunday afternoon, after a gentle weekend of sameness and quiet, Sarah could take it no longer and forced herself to ask him.

"Hey, Michael, I need to ask you something," Sarah said and set her book aside. She looked down at him from the couch as he sat cross-legged over a pile of paperwork on the floor.

"Yes?" he said and slowly looked up from his stack of Uncle Geoffrey's papers.

"There's something I've been meaning to ask you for months, and, now that you're feeling a bit better, I don't think I can wait any longer." Her palms felt sweaty, and she rubbed them on her thighs.

"I'm not sure I like the sound of that. Should I be worried?" His despondent countenance sagged a little lower as he moved up to the couch next to her.

"I'm not sure how to say this, so I'm just going to come out with it. See, just before Uncle Geoffrey died, I'd heard a rumor that you were out with another girl. Were you seeing someone behind my back?"

"A rumor?" Michael groaned and threw Sarah a look that made her feel six inches tall. "Where does this come from? We're sitting here going about our day and suddenly a rumor from... where? What? Were you on the internet and a window popped up? Maybe you need to have your system checked." He shook his head dismissively.

Sarah wiped her palms again. Michael's defensiveness was not a surprise, but it was disappointing. She knew she had to persist.

"No, Nikki said she saw you and someone who sounded like the information girl from the art museum at *L'Espérance*. Remember, the Miró exhibit? A few weeks before your uncle died."

"Who? I have no idea what you're talking about. I go—well, used to go—to *L'Espérance* all the time. It's my favorite place. You know this. But who's Nikki? Who's the girl from the museum?"

Michael twisted on the sofa.

"Look, I know it's been a few months, but you can't tell me you don't remember. The one with the freckles, with the copper jewelry on her dress!"

"Freckles? Are you feeling okay?" His voice was irritated and full of mock concern. His grief had left him raw and with even less tact than usual. "You might as well be asking me about Bill at the hardware store."

"Who's Bill?"

"Precisely my point. I made him up." Michael's voice was sharp.

"You're being ridiculous. Nikki is a real person, and she saw you." Sarah was exasperated.

"Look, I don't know Nikki or freckle girl or whoever."

"Nikki is Beatrice's granddaughter. Apparently, you guys were friends once."

"That clears it up," he said sarcastically. "I've known a lot of Nikkis over the years but certainly not any Beatrice."

"I bet you have. So, were you out with another girl or not? I need to know. Our future depends on it."

"You're being dramatic," Michael said and half rolled his eyes. "I don't know who, or what, you're talking about. So, unless you have some specifics to jog my memory, it is probably best that we drop it before someone says something they'll regret."

With that, Michael slid off the couch and went back to his paperwork, his back to her. Though unsatisfied, Sarah let it drop and went to the kitchen to make tea.

As the days turned to weeks, Michael's answer continued to under nourish Sarah's desire for the truth, but, like any starved being, she made do with what she had. She began to wonder if she had built up the whole thing too much. Overthought it. *Maybe I'm just being too sensitive.* Over time, she convinced herself that if Michael didn't remember then it couldn't have meant much anyway. Assuming it happened at all. She tried to let it go.

The long shaker-style table was piled with stacks of letters and paperwork on one end—Michael's project to dig through Uncle Geoffrey's correspondence as a way to closure and deeper discovery of his departed uncle. The other side had been cleared enough for two place settings as Sarah and Michael sat down to a meal of pork tenderloin in a mushroom sauce with sides of buttered green beans and jalapeño corn bread. The sauce was the latest in a long line of Sarah's experiments with mushrooms and similar flavors.

They ate quietly until Sarah's gentle voice broke the silence. "You're looking a bit morose; everything alright? I thought you were having a good day."

"I was, I think. I'm not really sure I know what all right is anymore. Lately, I've been plagued with a reoccurring thought."

"Oh? Something I can help with?"

"Unfortunately, no. See, since Uncle Geoffrey died, I can't shake a nagging feeling of aimlessness. I feel like I just wander around without purpose, like some kind of automaton."

"That's not unusual given the loss you've suffered," Sarah responded. "I'd be surprised at anything else."

Michael stretched his arms a little and put down his fork. "I know, but I feel so untethered, so alone in the world. I mean, I know I've got you, but..." Michael paused and shook his head vigorously. "I don't know, it's not coming out right.

"Take your time. I'm here."

Michael rubbed the palm of one hand with his thumb as he collected his thoughts. The creases in his hand seemed to mirror those on his brow.

"He was my family, and now I have none. On top of that, I just don't know what to do with myself. Sorry, this is all coming out in such a mess."

"No, no, I know what you're saying. I think you're looking for a purpose. When your uncle was still alive, you had to help him; it was a driving factor in your life. Now that he's gone, so is it. It makes perfect sense."

"I guess..."

The look on his face showed that Michael wasn't sure if that was what he meant.

"The question is, what are you going to do about it?" Sarah asked.

"I'm not sure yet, but I've been going through Uncle's stuff—"

"You don't say?" Sarah cut him off with a chuckle as she motioned toward the chimney stacks of paperwork that dominated their dinner table.

Michael let out a little laugh and continued. "Well, I've found a bunch of letters, birthday cards, love notes, and what not. Uncle Geoff was quite a ladies' man and a poet in his younger years. It's kind of bizarre to read, but I guess everyone old was young once. Anyway, what I'm trying to say, so inarticulately, is that I've been thinking about taking a short trip."

"Eh? Where, exactly?" Sarah asked with a raised eyebrow.

"You're concerned; you needn't be. See, in all of this correspondence, I've found about a dozen or so letters involving someone named Mildred."

"A lover? Way to go, Uncle Geoff." Sarah smiled.

"Not quite—a cousin."

"Eww." Sarah's face twisted in disgust.

"Sarah! Not like that." They laughed and grinned. A few moments later, they regained their composure and Michael continued. "Uncle and Mildred had a couple of years of letter writing, but the correspondence ended abruptly almost thirty years ago. I've searched and searched, but I can't seem to find any more letters. All the return addresses are from a small village in Wisconsin. I'm thinking of heading out there to see if I can find her or someone related to her." The words sped out of his mouth and his arms moved in wide movements as he spoke. Sarah was pleased to see him excited about something. "Worst-case scenario is that I find nothing and have a nice, relaxing trip to the country. Best case scenario, I've located a new relative, someone I didn't know I had, and then I won't be..." He paused. His enthusiasm stumbled, and melancholy washed over his face. "So... alone."

Sarah winced at his words as she watched Michael shrug and rub the back of his neck. His motions added an air of "lost puppy" to his sadness.

"You're not alone, Michael. You have me. Plus, how would this help you find a purpose?"

"Ugh. I don't really know, it probably won't. There's more going on here than just finding this 'purpose' of yours," Michael snapped. "I think this is something I need to do. If it leads nowhere, I'm no worse off. Plus, I think a nice change of scenery and some fresh air would do me good. It'll be nice to get out of town for a while."

"I could go with you; it could be a holiday," Sarah said with cheerful comity. She pictured them picnicking on some grassy hill in the middle of nowhere.

"No, I want to do this alone. You've been so good to me, and I am so grateful, but I need to be alone." Sarah's shoulders dropped and her head sagged. "I want some time to think and explore and, hopefully, find something. It'll only be a week or so."

Michael's soft, puppy dog creases had turned sharp but hollow.

The conversation halted into silence, and they stared at each other over their pork. Sarah thought a minute and then spoke.

"If you think you need this, then you should do it. Go out there and explore, turn over a few rocks, get lost in the woods, and see if you can find this cousin... Mildred." She laughed a little. She didn't like it but knew she had no choice but to relent to his scheme. "It all sounds ridiculous, you know?"

"Yeah, I know. Honestly, I assume she's dead—thirty years is a long time—but maybe I'll find *something* over there. I've been thinking about going next week, Wednesday probably."

"Okay," Sarah said with a nod and tried to look agreeable. "If this is what you need, I support you." It was clear Michael wanted an adventure and needed the distraction, so she didn't want to quash it.

She imagined him planning the trip: curled on the floor of his bedroom with a map and a stack of letters trying to find some goofy spot in The-Middle-of-Nowhere, Wisconsin. He probably felt like an archeologist on the hunt for long lost treasure—like Indiana Jones or Lara Croft. She chuckled at the thought.

In truth, she didn't want him out of her sight for too long but knew she had no choice but to capitulate.

CHAPTER 14

Sarah dipped her feet into the cold, fresh stream and relaxed as she stretched out on the sun-drenched field. The lush monochrome-green forest swirled around her, and the endless white clouds paraded past as she pretended to see objects in the formless masses. A ship, a plane, a dog, or a pair of lovers; all pareidolia but all good fun.

Whitfield Park sat on the far west side, too far from Sarah for convenience but was a lovely refuge on the outskirts of the city. Michael was on his way back from Wisconsin, and Sarah was there to meet him.

She was excited to see Michael and couldn't wait to hear about his trip. They'd spoken a few times during the week but only briefly, to confirm he was safe. Her week had been dull and lonely; voices of concern crept into her mind about Michael's lackluster response regarding the rumors from Bea. Though she had successfully quashed them, she craved a return to the excitement and distraction of life with Michael. For now, she enjoyed the park and waited.

Sarah soaked in her surroundings, blades of grass poked between the fibers of her shirt and surprised her by being both soft and sharp. She was peaceful and contented. The whirling pops of compacting gravel under tires directed her attention to the distant parking lot. She twisted her body just in time to see Michael park his red rental sedan. In haste, she replaced her socks and shoes and hurried to meet him.

After a hug and light kiss, Sarah said, "This place is gorgeous and so empty, I feel like I have the world to myself. Now that you're here, it feels complete." Her eagerness was obvious. "We should explore."

"Good idea. Shall we go for a hike? I've been in that car for hours and could use some exercise."

Sarah studied the signboard with a map of the trails.

"Let's take this one," Sarah said and pointed to a flowing line on the map. "It's marked 'easy.' Let's enjoy ourselves and not get lost or die of exhaustion," she chuckled.

"Yeah, I can see the headlines now: 'City dwellers lost in woods for days—survived on bark and urine,'" Michael said with a laugh.

They found the trailhead and started down the gentle, winding, well-maintained path. It was easy to follow, as the edges were marked out with long wood slats or, in places, a series of small stones.

Sarah walked just behind Michael and gazed at the treetops, awed by their enormous size and the vastness of the forest. With Michael back, she felt a sense of calm and relief. After a short while, she quickened her step, caught Michael, and took his hand.

"So, how was Wisconsin?" Her smiled beamed. "Did you find Mildred?"

"It was great. Very pleasant," responded Michael enthusiastically. "Once you get out of the cities, it's just miles and miles of hills and greenery and farms. Everywhere I stopped, people were friendly; everyone wanted me to try their pie or cheese or baked good or whatever. I, being a man of food, tried everything I came across; it was all delicious. I bet I gained five pounds."

Sarah stopped and looked him over. He'd developed a little pouch in his normally flat mid-section. *He looks like a snake with a fresh kill in his belly.*

"There was one dessert I found particularly delightful. It's called frozen custard; like ice cream but made with eggs so it's richer and more luxuriant. It's served a little warmer than ice cream, so the flavors develop more fully."

"That's all great, but the tales of feasts and gorging can wait. Did you find Mildred or anyone? After all, you went there for people, not food." Sarah chortled.

"Well, yes... no. Yes and no," Michael said ambiguously.

"And...?" urged Sarah.

"Okay, okay. So, I used the address from the last letter Mildred sent to Uncle Geoff as a starting point, and it took me to the far southwest of the state, almost on the Mississippi River."

As he spoke, he waved his arms as if he were drawing a map in the air. He added an extra squiggle with his finger when he mentioned the great Mississippi.

"The town is tiny," Michael continued. "The population is something like five hundred people—so I found the house easily. It was a small cottage, not more than the size of a small city apartment, probably at least a hundred years old. I knocked on the door and spoke with the owner. He said he had known Mildred but that she died years ago."

"Oh, that's a shame." Sarah frowned a little and put her arm around him. "I guess you sort of expected that, but still. Did he give you any leads on anyone else?" The light filtered through the tall trees and made the canopy glow warm above their heads.

"He wasn't any help. To his knowledge, she had no family or relatives but occasionally spoke about someone named Geoff. He suggested that I check with the post office and the reference librarian at the town library. Apparently, she has worked there for decades and knows everything about the area." He paused and gazed up before he continued. "I asked around at the post office, but nobody knew anything. Which wasn't surprising, because everyone looked about thirty."

"What about the lady in the library? Any luck?" Sarah asked and squeezed his hand with a little excitement.

"No, but she alone was worth the trip. She must have been about ninety years old and four feet tall but sharp as a razor and loved to talk." Michael used his hand to illustrate her height and put a strong emphasis on the word "loved." "She was literally a walking encyclopedia of the town. It was actually pretty funny; see, she'd pace while she talked, but used a cane, so it looked like she was doing a jig kind of thing. Like Yoda but with a full head of hair."

"Wow, that sounds like a trip." Sarah hopped across a small mud puddle in the middle of the trail. All of the fresh air and talking had her feeling free and unrepressed.

"I listened to her talk for forty-five minutes about the founding of the town, their flood problems, everything. Evidently, they're trying to relocate *the entire town* a few miles away from the river."

The wind swayed the green giants and sent a quick chill up Sarah's back. She shook it off and returned her attention to Michael.

"She went on and on. When she finally got around to Mildred, she was of some help. Turned out that she knew a lot about her; she had no kids or family but had a best friend she palled around with who lived a few doors down. Unfortunately, the friend died a few years before Mildred."

"So, it's a dead-end then?" Sarah asked and kissed the back of his hand.

"Yes, as far as that is concerned, but..." He trailed off, sounding uneasy.

Sarah glanced at him; the look on his face caused a troubled feeling to rise in her stomach. Something didn't seem quite right. She dropped his hand and turned to face him.

"Is there something else, Michael?" Sarah asked, concerned. "Sounds like you didn't find anything, so why do you have that look on your face?"

He was pale, much sweatier than he should have been on such an easy trail.

"Are you being haunted by great Mildred's ghost?" She chuckled and tried to ease the tension in her gut. Her earlier feelings of freedom diminished fast.

"No, but there is somewhat more to it," Michael said, his face serious. He paused, looked up at the sky, and took a deep breath before he continued.

"After finding nothing, I was thoroughly disappointed and decided to avail myself of the local scenery—which was splendid, by the way. I found a nearby state park and rented a small cabin for a couple of days. I don't get out to that kind of place very often, so I wanted to take advantage of it. I wanted to rest and reflect."

"It sounds like a good time. I wish you would have taken me along," Sarah added with a small smile. The tightness in her stomach persisted. She tried to imagine the park and his cabin but only saw worry.

"I know, my lovely, but I needed the time alone. While I was out there, I did some thinking about the arc of my life. About my school days, Spain, Uncle Geoff, and you. And I've come to some conclusions."

Sarah braced herself. The wind stayed down but, again, a chill skittered up her back. Michael's words felt like somewhere she didn't want to go. And, as with the ringing phone, she held her breath for a moment as he continued.

"While I was out there, I realized that I am alone in this world. Yes, my mother still exists, probably, but she's dead to me. Throughout my life, everywhere has felt flat and lifeless. Since Uncle Geoff passed, these feelings have only intensified and deepened. I always feel like I'm a three-dimensional person in a two-dimensional world."

Michael looked at Sarah, her face contorted with worry. He frowned a little and continued.

"As I walked through all of those woods, I asked myself when the last time was that I felt real—alive. Again and again, my mind turned to Spain. Always Spain. From the dusty fields to the smiling, charming people. Spain was the one bright spot. So…" He paused again and took a breath. "I've decided that now that Uncle is gone and doesn't need me anymore, I have to return and continue teaching. I don't really know, but that could be my purpose." Michael looked at her with soft, apologetic eyes. He held her gaze for a few moments but then shifted to the forest floor.

Tears streamed down Sarah's face. "I think you are confused; you are not alone. You have me! I'm here for you, just as I have been. As I was when Uncle Geoffrey died and as I will be in the future; in our future, together…"

The forest spun around her as Sarah processed what was happening. Time seemed to speed up, catch itself, and brake in the span of moments.

"I know, I'm sorry. This is something I have to do." Michael reached for her hand and held it gently for a split-second before she pulled away. Her whole arm moved as if his touch were an electric shock.

Sarah took a few steps and stopped. Sullen, tearful, she stood on the edge of panic as she scanned the treetops and tried to breathe.

She paced, and her mind ran. *Is he telling the whole truth? Is it just Spain, or is there something more? Is Mother too much? Another woman?*

When she looked back at Michael, his normally bright eyes were dulled and sunken. A tear or two ran down his cheek as he hung his head.

"Is that really all?" Sarah was quiet at first. "It there something else? Is this really about that information hostess?"

"Information who?" Michael looked confused for a moment. "That again? No."

"Or does my mother have anything to do with this? I know she's a handful, but she's my mom."

"Your mother?" Michael's face exploded with surprise. He diverted his eyes. Sarah watched as they shifted side to side, as if searching for an answer. He hesitated. "I don't know how to make you understand." Michael was almost pleading. "I love you, and we will always be friends, but this is something I must do."

"But why must you do it without me?" Anger seeped into her. "I'll go with you. Then we'd be away from this place, my mother, all of it."

"I'm sorry," Michael said, calmly.

Sarah felt her heart tear in her chest and, with it, a torrent of anger and fear.

"After all I've done to make sure you had what you needed when you needed it? The classes I've dropped, the shifts I've traded, all for you—for us—a life together." Sarah was nearly shouting. "What has all of this been? Am I nothing to you? Just something to pass the time?" Her questions echoed off the nearby hills.

"Sarah, no, it's not like that." He nodded. "You mean a lot to me, and you've given me more than I can ever reciprocate. There is a permanent place in my heart for you, but I need to feel whole, fully realized."

Michael walked closer and stopped a few feet away. His shoulders were stooped as if he carried a large pack. "I just can't do that here. Maybe it's this town, maybe it's the lifestyle, I don't know, but it drains me of everything. Sure, it has some nice points—you, for instance—but this place feels like a stone on my soul. I'm sorry."

Michael was tender and imploring. It seemed clear he didn't want to hurt her. She could tell he tried to be direct, make a clean cut rather than a jagged snag, but it didn't help; all exits led through her heart.

Michael stepped forward and reached for a gentle hug, his eyes compassionate.

Sarah brushed off his advance and returned his look with a hardened steel gaze. Pointed and narrow, her eyes were fixed on him as the tears streaked down her face; wisps of hair stuck to the wet spots. She wanted to strike him. She wanted to make him feel pain like the pain *he* was putting her through. But she knew that would solve nothing: it would not keep him with her; it would not make him love her more than his precious Spain; it would not make her happy.

Instead, she resisted her base urges and spared herself the indignity of a resort to violence. Instead, she turned around and walked away. Briskly, decisively, down the wooded path toward the parking lot and the bus stop.

"Sarah! Sarah, wait... Wait!" Michael yelled, as he caught up with her and grabbed her by the arm.

Sarah stopped, turned around, and pulled her arm from his grasp. "What do you want?" Her words were pinched and angry. "You've said what you needed to say. Now leave me alone." The sharpness of her eyes was chiseled to a point, like a dagger ready to cut right through him.

"I never wanted to hurt you." Michael's voice was thin and brittle, as if he were afraid to speak above a whisper, for if he did, he would shatter to pieces. "I never meant for it to be like this. We've been through so much together. Can't we... can't we... at least be friends?"

Sarah crouched and hid her face in her hands as she sobbed. In her mind, she could see her future fading. School, a career, freedom... It all seemed so far away, so unobtainable. The future with Michael, the one she'd visualized so many times, seemed farthest of all. It was fading to black like the end of a film. After a few more moments, she stood up and turned to him.

"You've broken my heart, Michael. You've torn it from my chest and ground it into the dirt. I believe you when you say you didn't want to hurt me, but you did. You *did* hurt me!" The anguish was evident on her face, and her tone wavered.

Before her composure could break again, Sarah turned her back to Michael and walked away in a hurry. It was all too much; she had to get away. The trees waved and turned around her as she began to jog and then burst into a run.

Behind her, Michael entreated her to stop and come back. She had heard enough.

Sarah arrived at the small, metal-lined bus shelter adjacent to the parking lot and huddled in the corner, her arms around her knees. So far from the city, buses came every hour, at best. She tried to settle herself for the wait.

Michael followed but came no closer than the edge of the parking lot. It seemed that he was trying to respect her space. Still, he called to her.

"At least let me drive you home; it'll be ages before you get home on the damned bus."

Sarah ignored him and sobbed into her knees. After a few more tries, frustrated and at a loss, Michael got into the red rent-a-car and drove off.

CHAPTER 15

Some days you're the dog, others the hydrant.
On mornings like these, Sarah had to admit sometimes her father was right. The last few weeks had been a dizzy haze of semi-autonomous movement. Her body floated from place to place while her mind was carried along like a fashion accessory. Her thoughts were trapped in a feedback loop, fixated on unwrapping the riddle of her failed relationship and analyzing it, beat by beat, probing each decision and extrapolating the outcome if she had made different choices. Scientific in its thoroughness, neurotic in its effect.

The wheels of Sarah's life started to drift and careened between what-ifs, bitter anger, and stormy resentment. Thoughts of all of the love and time she'd put into Michael— the dropped classes and switched shifts and undivided attention to his needs. It wasn't long until she became tangled with the side barricades in an indelicate merger that brought the sharp, jagged rocks of oblivion into view. She was cruising down the cloistered second path she had seen in Michael's eyes, that night at Uncle Geoffrey's, and it was far darker and emptier than she'd originally perceived.

Sarah's moods pivoted by the second. One moment, she was a supernova of anger and bitterness; the next, she was a wet blanket so soaked and weighed down with self-pity and loathing that she could not move. There were days where even she couldn't stand herself.

The stress, the drink, the erratic sleep had left her body racked with the ache of loss. With every move, her muscles strained and stung as they stretched over the empty cavity that used to house her heart. Her life was unraveling in slow motion, one heartstring at a time.

Usually the hydrant.

On a late Saturday morning, Sarah eased her way across the sea of empty wine bottles and plates of partially eaten microwave food to the couch. In search of perspective and solace, she curled up with her copy of *Cosmos* and a nearby blanket in hope that Carl Sagan could reassure her that life had meaning and beauty. She needed Dr. Sagan's eloquence to transport her, soothe her, and grant her a reprieve from her heartbreak.

It had been weeks since Michael left her, and Sarah was low. She knew she had a work schedule to keep and a new semester on the horizon, but all of that seemed like too much. Right now, all she wanted was to get lost in her book. She glanced at the pages but struggled to read even a single one and simply flipped them back and forth in her hand, as if knowing where the next chapter began would help her focus. As she reread the same paragraph for the seventeenth time, there was a knock on her door. Startled, but somewhat relieved, she made her way over and checked the eyepiece. It was Nancy.

"Mom! You're out? You didn't escape, did you?" asked Sarah with a sarcastic huff.

"No, I didn't escape nothin'," Nancy scoffed.

"Your lawyer said you might be getting out soon, but I still had to check." Sarah leaned on the doorway and squinted in the sunlight. "I'm surprised you're here; you never just swing by."

"What? I can't just stop at your place? I've been locked up in that looney bin for months. You gonna let me in?"

Sarah stepped back as Nancy waddled into the small apartment and headed for the couch. The cheap sofa groaned under the strain of Nancy's bulk.

"From the looks of the place, you're not doin' too good, no?"

"It's been rough. Michael and I broke up." She sighed, still standing.

"That's too bad. He was a good one. A keeper." Nancy padded her knee for emphasis.

"I'm not so sure about that. He may have been cheating on me. I couldn't confirm it, but—"

"Bah, men cheat. Not your father, but everyone else. You got lucky. He was straight with you. Before I met your dad, I was with some guys. Like this one—"

"Mom, eww. I don't care." Sarah paced back and forth, shaking her arms in disgust. "I don't want to hear about your lovers, or whatever."

"I'm tryin' to help. You got off easy. He didn' hit you or nothin'. Took you to nice restaurants. I used to get beat. I was stranded on a highway—"

MATTHEW KOPF · 153

"Please, stop." Sarah held out her hands until Nancy stopped and then slouched into a side chair with her feet on the coffee table. "I just can't stop thinking about all the things I could have done differently. Well, that, and what a jerk he is."

"He was handsome and took you good places. You even helped him out with his uncle's stuff. So, how'd you mess it up?" Nancy's tone was accusatorial.

Sarah looked up at her mother startled, as if a pillow had been thrown at her. "What do you mean, me? He ran away to his precious Spain to be 'free' or whatever. You certainly never helped the situation with your orange-eyed men and phone calls. At least when you were at Ruther's, you were out of the way." Her words were venomous.

"Sorry your mother was such an inconvenience. I was suffering, you know; those doctors don't know nothin'."

"Things were never the same after your breakdown at the pharmacy. I've often wondered if Michael held that against me. He never said, but—"

"Sure, blame your mother." Nancy threw her hands in the air; her arms flapped.

"Well, you scared away Christopher! Why not Michael too?"

"Did I?" Nancy snapped back. "Or don't you know how to keep a man? You always blamin' me for that."

Sarah stood up, incensed. *How can she put this on me? Michael leaving wasn't my fault! Was it?*

"I can't keep a man because I have a crazy woman for a mother. One who always has to be the victim and no one else can suffer but her."

Nancy stood up, her nose in the air like a snout. "You little bitch! I'm gettin' outta here. I'm goin' home! Sorry I came to help."

Nancy plodded her way to the door and let herself out. The door slammed behind her and left Sarah standing next to the TV, shocked at what had just transpired. *Fuck it, it's five o'clock somewhere.* She poured a glass of merlot and topped it with a non-so-subtle fortification of brandy. Sagan had been forgotten, and she had moved on to Mondavi.

At three in the morning she awoke on the couch in a haze. In a bleary jaunt to her bed, she checked her phone and saw she had a voicemail. Though tired and drunk, a heavy feeling sunk in her stomach like a lead ball. Sarah stumbled on the bed and listened to the message from Loretta.

"Sarah? Honey, this is Loretta. I know you're going through a tough time right now; I want to help. That said, you missed your shift tonight. I covered it, but in the future, please call. I expect I'll see you tomorrow, right? Let's talk about it then. Take care of yourself."

Steam drifted up from a pot of English Breakfast like thermal currents off a mountaintop and filled the room with the toasted aroma of steeped Chinese leaves. The vessel itself was a well-worn and well-loved ceramic pot painted in a delicate blue vine and pink flower pattern. The lacquered finish had crazed years ago; each little surface crack added a line of character. It was like a gracefully aged woman whose beauty remained well past her youth; each line a sign of defiance and will rather than a random blemish of time and habit. Sarah stared at the steam, lost in thought.

The previous night had not gone easy, but Sarah had managed to get out of bed and made it to the Kettle on time. Her walk to work had raised her spirits somewhat, but a hangover still banged away in her skull. Her thoughts turned to her mother; a few morning texts showed she was still pissy but safe and at home. Inevitably, her mind drifted to Michael as anger and frustration lashed in a constant ostinato of what-ifs and how-could-theys. Sarah didn't notice Loretta as she approached.

"Did you know that was my great-great-great-grandmother's?" Loretta said as she leaned against the counter and pointed to the little pot. Her voice pierced Sarah's drifted attention.

"It's beautiful. I was admiring it, and then just sort of got lost in my head; I can't seem to concentrate on anything these days." Sarah pivoted to Loretta, the kettle between then on the counter. "It reminds me of my life, full of cracks and fading but still holding together, even if it is a little tenuous." Sarah tucked a hand towel into her apron.

"Yep, but you're holding on. Look, I know it seems bad and, right now, you hurt, but things will get better."

Sarah sighed. "Thanks, I needed to hear that. I keep telling myself to think about the good things—food, books, music—but I never seem to get very far. My head just railroads everything." Sarah paused and considered the kettle in front of them. "It is a gorgeous thing, isn't it? You know, that's a lot of 'greats.' That must mean this is... really old."

"It has been in my family for five generations." Loretta beamed and rubbed the vessel with her towel. "My mom had it before me, and my grandchildren will have it when I'm gone, if it lasts that long. See, according to the family stories, it was a gift to my great-great-great-grandmother from her master." Sarah's eyes widened as she listened. "She used to keep the house and was highly valued by the family; so, on occasion, they'd give her hand-me-downs as gifts."

Loretta grabbed a nearby stool and sat down before continuing.

"It was two generations old when she received it. To her, it was a symbol of sophistication and class. More than that, it was made in France, a symbol of freedom. Stories had circulated about slaves traveling there with their owners and then escaping into France's welcoming arms. Those tales inspired her own escape. Our whole family loves that teapot but has a complicated relationship with it."

"Oh, my goodness," Sarah exclaimed as she found a tall chair of her own. It took her a moment to process what she'd heard. "I didn't realize... I just thought it was a pretty old pot. Had I known, I wouldn't have..." Again, she paused.

Sarah imagined all of the hands that had handled the little kettle over the years. All of the souls soothed and thirsts slaked. Then, she thought of the evil and cruelty perpetrated and endured by those who had owned it. What suffering it represented! What injustice!

"That kind of changes things, doesn't it?" Sarah looked to Loretta with inquiring eyes. "Given all of that history, why do you keep it? I would think that something related to such depravity wouldn't be something you'd want around."

"Well, like I said, it's complicated. I think everyone down the line has kept it for different reasons." The timer next to the kettle chirped, and Sarah poured them both a cup from the old pot. "I keep it because it is a reminder that my ancestors were in bondage and of the struggles they must have faced. I don't understand how they endured the immeasurable cruelty, but they did. Every time things get tough and I think I'm out, I think about what they went through and survived. It gives me strength."

Pride glowed on Loretta's face. Sarah saw a strength in her that was both familiar and unknown. As if beneath the strength of the regular Loretta she knew and loved lurked a far deeper reservoir of fortitude and courage than Sarah had ever realized.

"That's incredible," Sarah said in awe. She brought her cup to her lips.

"Also, it was my great-great-great-grandmother's prized possession and one of the only things that survived her escape to freedom. It has been a symbol of endurance to my family for over a hundred years. It is a physical connection to my past and my family."

"And, despite all that, we still use it, here?"

Loretta took a sip of tea and then continued. "That's why this place is called the Family Kettle. It's an object that brings the family together."

"All these years, I just thought it was an old pot. Now, I'm almost afraid to touch it."

"Don't be. If you treat it with care and kindness and something happens to it, then that is that. It is simply the impermanence of all things."

"It'll receive only the upmost care from these hands." Sarah waved her palms in the air. "You know, that's very Zen of you."

"Hey, girl, I've spent some time with that Eastern stuff. I'll tell you one thing is for sure, they are right on that point. We all love that ol' pot, but someday it will break beyond repair. That's just the nature of life. So I try not to worry and enjoy it while I can. I try to be grateful for what I have when I have it." Loretta stood up and tucked her stool under the counter.

Sarah was surprised; she hadn't known Loretta to be so centered. Solid and moderate, sure, but she was seeing a new side to her.

"Wow, I don't think I could ever be that laissez-faire about something so important to my family. If we had anything that important." Sarah slid her tall chair back where she'd found it.

They stood at the high counter and sipped their tea.

"How do you stay so cool? So... in control? Do you ever just feel crushed by circumstances?"

"I've had a lot of success and a lot of disappointments in my life." Loretta pointed to the room around her. "I've learned our lives and fortunes ebb and flow. So much is just luck or things that just happen to us, no matter how much we prepare and plan." With a flick of her wrist, Loretta flipped her towel over her shoulder and started a stainless-steel pot to boil. "But still, we prepare, plan, study, and work hard anyway, so we can face life's challenges with all we can muster. Then, sometimes, when it's all too much, you just have to let it go."

Sarah watched Loretta's eyes, big and round, as they shone upon her, like flashlights of compassion and comfort.

"But how do I do that? When do I know it's too much?" A little frown sprouted on Sarah's face.

Loretta leaned over and placed a hand on Sarah's shoulder. "Letting go means taking a step back, not running away or disappearing. You know how to do it; you do it all the time. Look, you've been through a lot in your life. I've watched you handle things bigger than most people ever have to deal with. From crazy customers to school problems to all of your mom's incidents to your father's death. You've handled it all. And you'll handle this." Loretta sighed. "My dad used to always say, 'it's not about getting knocked down, it's about getting up again.' And you, whether you realize it or not, are a champ at getting back up. Who made the arrangements for your dad, for Uncle Geoffrey? Who comes to the rescue whenever your mother gets into trouble? You! Heartbreaks suck, no doubt about it, but if you can get through all that, you can get through this crucible too."

"I hope you're right. I'm struggling. I felt like I was so close to being happy." Sarah's head sunk low on her shoulders. "It seemed like the pieces were aligned. I had Michael, school was clicking along, Mom was out of the way. I was so close I could almost smell it."

Loretta took off her glasses and looked at Sarah with kind but focused eyes. "People always think that happiness is a constant state to be achieved, but it isn't. It comes in small chunks surrounded by struggle and trial. You have to make each little piece of happiness last until the next one arrives."

"I don't know," Sarah said, unconvinced. "It seems like it should be some kind of state of being. A feature, not a bug."

"Maybe it should be." Loretta let out a quiet whistle. "But in my experience, it isn't. Just hang in there and let me know if you need anything. I'll be here for you." A broad smile bolted across Loretta's face as Sarah looked up at her with an appreciative smile.

As Sarah left the Kettle, Loretta's words percolated in her mind. She had never looked at happiness nor herself in that way and felt both confused and improved by their talk. On the way home, she stopped at a small grocery store and bought fresh food for the first time in weeks.

At home, she poured herself a glass of wine and laid the chicken breasts, mushrooms, carrots, and celery out on the counter. As the hints of black pepper and coriander from the wine hit her palate, an idea started to form. She gathered items from around the kitchen—butter, flour, spices, stock, some garlic—and got started.

Vegetables washed and chopped, Sarah turned to the chicken. With olive oil heating in the pan, she dried and seasoned the meat, then slid them into the cast iron skillet. In another pan, she sautéed the vegetables. The chicken breasts sizzled and popped. A thick, brown crust had formed, and Sarah marveled at the transformation. The reactions of the sugars and amino acids to heat was something she'd studied, but somehow, it still held her attention and felt like magic.

The old aluminum sauté pan clacked against the stovetop as she shook the vegetables. When they were sufficiently browned, she plated them before setting aside the chicken to rest. A splash of wine to deglaze the pan and then some stock and spices as she left it to reduce.

A few minutes later, Sarah added her chicken to her plate and ladled over the sauce. Sprinkles of parsley made the finishing touch. For a brief moment, she stood back and admired her work: a gourmet-level meal inspired by a sip of wine. A sense of accomplishment and satisfaction rolled over her as she sat down to eat.

As she ate, Sarah thought about her conversation with Loretta. She made a mental list of all of the hardships and setbacks she'd had over the years and how she had gotten through them all. The fresh, home-cooked meal tasted far better than the boxed food she'd been subjecting herself to. The sauce, the spices, and the wine all worked together. She wondered if Loretta was right.

Sarah cleared the dishes and sat down in a nearby chair. After a moment's rest, her excitement drained, and darkness crept in. Like so many nights before, Michael and the breakup seeped into her mind as her brain resumed its ceaseless churn through the usual questions. As angry as she was, she still missed him. The warm strength of his embrace, the way he called her "lovely." Loneliness strolled in and sat on her chest, using anger as a bench.

Sarah felt herself sink; her lightness reversed as if a demonic jailer were pulling her back into her pit. The relentless circular questioning pummeled and clawed her psyche. The chains were on again.

CHAPTER 16

Third term: the tiny semester crammed between the end of spring and the beginning of fall terms. For Sarah, it was a slow-speed crawl through a dark tunnel on her knees. With only two classes, it shouldn't have been much, but as she still reeled from the breakup with Michael and the continued strain of her relationship with Nancy, it was a struggle.

The week before the end of the meager semester, Sarah was pulling C's. Loneliness and despondency tripped her up at every turn, and she knew it. It had all been a rote exercise. Go to school, go to work, study, repeat. There was no joy or accomplishment, just hoops to jump through.

One night, while studying—the constant ostinato of blame and doubt churned and clouded her thoughts—she let her mind go and left it free to wander.

First came the dark. The waves of blame crashed on her shores: *Why didn't you tell him about your mother sooner? Would it have mattered? Why can't you keep a man?*

As her doubt and loathing heaved and turned, she started to look, really look, through the books in front of her: *Advanced Food Science*, her notebooks, and folders full of papers. She thumbed through her journal—page after page of ideas and recipes and formulas tumbled forth in scribbled blips. Then, it started to break; the darkness lightened with each turn of the page.

Sarah remembered something she had hidden away, almost from herself. She dragged her chair into the bedroom. The closet door slid open with ease, and she set the wooden seat in the gap. With a quick hop, she stood upon it and reached for the back shelf. There, buried under piles of old clothes and long-dormant board games, was what she was looking for: the red shoe box, the archive she'd almost forgotten.

In a flash of excitement, she hurried to the bed, opened the box, and spread its contents across the comforter. The first thing she looked at was a chemistry test from senior year in high school. Scrawled on the top in bright red ink *A. Great job! Keep it up!* The next, a report she'd written from Chemistry 154: "Preservatives in Food: A Survey." Sarah flipped to the back: *98 percent. Excellent work. You have a knack for this, but watch your spelling!* There was a whole pile of similar papers from throughout her long school career. She wondered how she'd let this treasure trove slip from her memory.

Sarah looked at a few others: *97 percent. You have this down;* or *100 percent. Nailed it!* Pride swelled within her, and her confidence rose. *I am good at this.* A smile stretched across her face as her thoughts shifted to Loretta. *She placed confidence in me when I made my blends, and those were a hit.* Their last conversation drifted into her mind, and Sarah thought about all the times her mother or father had thrown her life into the dirt, she got back up. When Dad died, she got back up. When Christopher left, she got back up!

Then it clicked.

She didn't need Michael; she had talent. The food, the flavors, her palate—that was her ticket out of her hole. If she achieved, happiness would follow either in small pieces or continuous loops; it was in her hands.

With this realization, Sarah was reborn. She could not allow herself to become a calcified rock of anger and bitterness. No, she had to pursue her goals, and to get there she needed to finish school. From this point on, she would hoist herself upon the world and make it reckon with her. She would be action.

A quick calculation revealed that if she went full-out—eighteen credits a semester, maybe another third term—she could graduate in a year, then possibly grad school and on to her dreams. The fall semester was weeks away, and she would be there. Present, ready, and undeterred. She would no longer be the girl of heartbreak and loneliness but an independent woman—a rocket that ignites itself.

Fall semester began and determination boiled inside Sarah like a kettle set to high. From the moment she set foot off of the bus, she resonated with the dynamic rhythm of campus. Everything seemed to pulse and fill her with energy, exciting her molecules.

Today was Chemistry 452, housed in an old building in the far corner of campus. The long, narrow hall was an up-to-date facility despite being clad in the aged, stained oak of its original vintage.

Sarah's new understanding about her role in her own future had caused a reevaluation of her perspective on school. Previously, it was a box to be checked or a hoop to be jumped through: one more shift before the Kettle or home. Now, she understood what the university classroom actually was: an arena. A place to challenge oneself against the class, the professor, and in some respects, the rest of the civilized world. The classroom was somewhere to strive mightily and propel herself forward, to learn to be successful on her own merit. Education was a path to her independence, and independence was her path to self-realized happiness.

Sarah was ready. In preparation for battle, she'd read through the material—twice. For class, she chose a seat eye-level with the professor and arrived early to size up the competition. The rest of the class filtered in around her, and the temperature began to rise. The classroom's scent of old wood was gradually replaced by whiffs of colognes and perfumes. Looks of seriousness and determination predominated; it was clear the others were also ready for action.

The seats filled, and the classroom hummed. Rumors circulated about the professor's unusual style and strict habits. It was said that she didn't lecture but questioned students like a prosecutor and humiliated wrong answers.

The wall clock struck eight, and Professor Hart entered the room through a side door and walked to the podium. In seconds, the room fell silent. The professor, a slight woman in her early fifties, looked like a learned academic but with far more style. Sarah had expected someone dour and was taken aback by the professor's tan tweed Lauren jacket with elbow patches and tall chocolate-colored riding boots. Her wiry, frizzy, blond hair was pulled back in a loose bunch by a small cream ribbon. She unpacked her brown leather satchel and placed her notes in front of her. With a few rapid clicks, her presentation was on the digital whiteboard, and class began.

"Because you all can read, I will dispense with the review of the syllabus and get right to it," Professor Hart said in a terse, business-like voice. "There will be days when I lecture and days when I question. I use the Socratic method, so you all might as well get used to it. I will ask questions and you will stand and answer. If no one volunteers to answer, I will call on someone. If you have already spoken, you will not be required to speak again until all others have spoken."

A pause. The class whispered to itself; anxiety rippled palpably through rows of desks like wind through a field of wheat.

"A word of advice," Professor Hart continued. "Come to class prepared, be prepared to speak, and know that I intend to get to everyone. Now, let's get started. Who can explain to me the geometric properties of a chiral molecule?"

The room was silent. The students gazed at one another like sheep facing the abattoir. The shock subsided, and the students toughened and began to take measure of each other in attempt to figure out who would be forced to speak and who might be bold enough to put forth an answer. A few seconds later, Sarah stood up.

"Professor, a chiral molecule is an ion that is non-superposable upon its own mirror image." The words came fast and flowing, like a river of knowledge and facts; so quickly Sarah could barely process what she was saying, but she knew it was right. With each word that passed her lips, she seemed to grow larger, more confident. "Further, the angles of the molecules affect how the molecule interacts with other molecules, and outcomes can vary significantly based on those angles."

Prepared indeed.

MATTHEW KOPF · 167

"Good answer." Sarah smiled but stayed sharp as the professor continued. "Someone's done the reading. Can you give me an example?"

"Well, there are many. The chemical carvone in spearmint and caraway seeds, for example, but really a wide variety of amino acids and sugars—"

"That will do, thank you. Ms...?"

"Hall, ma'am. Sarah Hall."

"Hmm, yes. Take a seat, Ms. Hall."

The class seemed impressed. Most of her classmates were reluctant to speak until called upon. They very likely knew the answers but remained mum in front of a professor known for her verbal eviscerations.

As the class wore on, more students spoke. Correct answers were praised; incorrect ones were treated to a verbal lashing. Anyone with a wrong answer was unlikely to be caught unprepared in the future.

For the rest of class, Sarah sat in quiet satisfaction. She could have answered any of the questions posed. She was proud of herself for being the first to speak and even more so for being competitive amongst her peers.

The semester progressed, and Sarah's vivacity and urgency paid off. From class to class, she moved from stride to stride; with each effort, her self-confidence bolstered. At home, graduate school applications dripped out of her computer. Slowly at first, but the pace picked up as she found her groove. Her enthusiasm began to make tangible the idea of happiness through her own work and the possibility of being alone without being lonely.

CHAPTER 17

The bright days of early autumn had given way to the grey, dull days of late fall. The trees, completely relieved of their leaves, stood naked in front of the world; the spindly spires of their upturned branches stabbed at the sky like a dead spider's useless legs. Light patches of snow dotted the sidewalk as Sarah plodded up the faded path that led to Nancy's house. She was struck with a pungent mixture of twisted nostalgia, mild disgust, and a pinch of anticipation. This potent and disparate cocktail hit her every time. Every little detail reminded her of some thought or feeling she had as a child, or some reflection of that world onto her adult life.

Even now, she cringed with embarrassment as she walked up the path, just as she did coming home from school when she was a child. The dusting of snow was unable to cover the overgrown lawn that stung with neglect. Nor could it hide the derelict front screen door that had fallen off its hinges and been haphazardly placed next to the porch.

The moment she entered the house, she was twelve years old again and just off the bus from school except for the eerie silence of a blank TV and Henry's empty La-Z-Boy.

Nancy was at the kitchen table with a cup of coffee and a large snap-case of pills, her immense frame wrapped in a pale blue blanket as she stared blankly into the newspaper advertisements. Nancy coughed as Sarah patted her shoulder and sat down across from her at the aged table.

The rest of the kitchen fared no better. The cracked, dingy, and yellowed linoleum floor was coated in a thick layer of grease and cigarette smoke, littered with roach traps. The kitchen counter had faded to a grey-brown from decades of use—continually covered in a tangled mass of mail and old food wrappers.

"You don't look so good, Mom. You okay?" Sarah asked with concern.

"I still have a cold. It's been like this for a cupl'a weeks now. I just can't..." Nancy hacked, coughed, and spit before continuing. "I just can't seem to kick it. But I'll be fine."

"Take care of yourself. Be sure to drink plenty of fluids and get rest," Sarah said in a gentle tone.

"Oh, I know. I've been drinkin' plenty of these." Nancy patted a large bottle of Diet Coke and an oversized mug of coffee with her hand as if they were small dogs.

"Diet Coke? Coffee? Mom, you need to drink water," Sarah admonished.

"What? I'm tryin' to..." Nancy was interrupted by another coughing fit. This one left her face a slight tinge of purplish-blue. "I'm tryin' to lose weight," Nancy finished.

"Mom, water has no calories. Drink that."

"Hey, I'm gettin' plenty'a rest. I sleep, like, ten hours a night. And I take naps. Plus, this is the last of the coffee; machine broke this morning. Think you could take a look at it?"

"Yeah, if I can find room on that counter, geesh. Anyway, have you been taking all of your other meds?"

"I have, but I'm not sure they're workin'. I felt good when I got home from the bin, but lately, I can hardly get out of bed in the mornin'." Nancy reached for a fistful of tissues as another wave of coughing came on. "But enough about me. How are you doin'?"

"It's been a tough week. Finals are coming up, and it never seems like I have enough time. I'm taking six classes, two of them have labs, one has a final project. I've got a few more graduate school apps to go out, but I'm already getting rejections, and I'm doing the best I can to help Loretta keep the Kettle running. It's getting to be a lot."

As soon as the words passed her lips, her father's voice haunted her: *Welcome to the real world.*

"On the upside, I'm getting the best grades I've ever gotten," she said in a hurry as if responding to her father.

"That's great. You've got, what, another semester or somethin'? What's you goin' to do when you graduate?" Nancy strained her voice as she spoke and provoked another coughing fit.

Sarah watched as her mother's body twisted and hacked. The blue blanket fell from her shoulders and scraped the floor.

"Not sure yet," Sarah responded after Nancy's coughing settled. "Probably look for a job? A real career, you know? Depends on if I get accepted or not. I've always had it in the back of my mind to go to graduate school but was a little intimidated. Though now, I think I could do it if I get the chance."

"That could be good. Do you need grad school? Maybe it's too tough," Nancy equivocated but still tried to be supportive.

"I think it will further my chances of getting a good job. I mean, a real good job. I've been applying to schools. Several around here and a few... farther away."

"Oh? Just how far away are we talking? Spain?" Nancy cackled.

"Ugh, no! But it feels like I've applied everywhere, and it takes forever. I've applied to a place in Northberg and another in Johnson, but the ones I'm really excited about are the State University, a program at California University in San Francisco, and one at London College in London."

"California! England! How are you going to get all the way out there? What's gonna happen to me? You gonna leave me here all alone?" Nancy asked incredulously.

"Mom! I'll still call, and I'd visit now and then. I mean, really, I'd be happy with any of them, but those three have really fired my imagination. I'd get to see new places and learn new things. A degree from either would practically guarantee me a job with a good company."

"I know you like all of that food and science stuff, but you can't just up and leave your mother, especially now that I'm all alone." Nancy turned her head and slowly glanced at Henry's vacant chair.

Sarah's heart sank. "I have to do what's right for me. I've been working at this for so long, I—"

Sarah was interrupted by a long, loud, coughing fit followed by several long gasps for breath. Nancy's face was almost purple.

"Good god, Mom. Have you seen a doctor about this? Maybe it isn't just a cold!"

"It's all right, it's all right," Nancy wheezed as she slowly caught her breath. "I think I just need a hot shower to clear this out. You mind takin' a look at that coffee machine?"

"Yeah, okay. While you're in the shower, probably all of the damned bugs."

"Okay, thanks. I'm goin' now."

Nancy wearily rose from her chair and teetered off to the bathroom. The floor creaked under the strain. Sarah heard the light scratch of Nancy's hand on the hallway wall as she ran along it for support.

Sarah turned to the counter and groaned. Every square inch of surface area was crowded with debris. On the stove, a greasy, cracked Teflon pan sat on the burner with bits of overcooked eggs singed to the sides. The rest of the stovetop was the only unfilled space. Uninspired, she sat back down and turned to her phone. After some time, she finally turned her attention to the gummy black coffee machine and wrested it from its nest, placing it on the stove. As she turned it around, a loud crash emanated from the other side of the house: the bathroom.

"Mom!" Sarah yelled and ran down the hallway.

Sarah pushed open the bathroom door and was greeted by a blast of warm, sticky air. The walls and mirrors dripped with condensation, slippery to the touch. A loud crackling noise drew Sarah's attention to the bathtub where the shower curtain had been partially pulled off the rod and water pelted against the plastic. Nancy's arm draped over the side of the tub, and her naked body was half covered in the torn shower curtain. Blood streaked down the plastic-lined wall and sides as it rushed down the drain. Sarah hurried to turn off the shower and attend to her unconscious mother.

Sarah had taken a first aid class at school and knew what to do. She dialed 911 on speaker and laid the phone on the counter. Careful not to slip, Sarah reached into the tub and rolled Nancy onto her back with a towel under her head.

Nancy's mammoth legs had to be propped against the side of the bathtub and the wall to elevate them above her heart. From the side closet, Sarah grabbed a stack of towels and applied pressure to the wound on Nancy's forehead with one hand while she attempted to dry her mother with the other. The remainder of the towels were tucked along Nancy's side and draped over her body to keep her as warm as possible.

As she worked, she heard the distant wail of an ambulance siren. They were close.

Sarah whispered to her unconscious mother, "Hang in there, Mom. We'll get you through this. I can hear the paramedics now."

Nancy's eyes began to flutter under their lids as they slowly opened to a squint.

"Can you hear me? I've called 911, and the EMTs should be here soon," Sarah shouted.

Sarah heard the murmur of voices and a series of heavy knocks on the front door. In a smashing blur of blue and grey, the house was flooded with firefighters and emergency responders. Sarah stood back and watched, shocked at just how many responders had come. EMTs, police, and firefighters filled the bathroom, bedroom, and hallway; they crowded almost every room of the small house.

The EMTs maneuvered a stretcher into the cramped bathroom and prepared the ambulance for the trip to the hospital. A shout from the room alerted her that Nancy was awake and that they had begun the GCS assessment to test her level of consciousness. Moments later, Nancy was wheeled through the house in a commotion. It was almost as if someone had just reversed the playback of their entry. The moment the back doors of the ambulance closed, it sped away in a blaze of red and white lights and the blare of sirens, without an instant of hesitation.

A cop offered Sarah a ride to the hospital. As she grabbed her bag, she caught a glimpse of herself in the mirror. Her face was grey and rimmed in deep lines of worry.

CHAPTER 18

Sarah burst through the Kettle's door with an enthusiasm that nearly knocked the bell from its mount. With a gleaming smile, she sauntered behind the counter and took her apron from the smooth wooden peg. After weeks of tending to Nancy, both in the hospital and out, and studying between the cracks of her schedule, Sarah finally had something to be happy about.

"Congratulate me, Loretta. I did it," Sarah said as she tied up her brown curls and lifted them over the back of the apron.

"Okay, I'll bite. Congratulations! For what, exactly?"

Loretta smiled in good humor. The lunch rush had just died down, and she hustled to tidy up the mess.

"Today was the last exam of the semester. I got through it and did great! I'm still waiting for today's grade, obviously, but everything else is in, and I got straight A's—my best semester *ever*!" Sarah threw her hands in the air in excitement.

"Line it up and knock it down. Well done! I'd say break out the champagne but, you know, it's a tea shop. And we've got work to do." Loretta feigned a sideways glance.

"Yeah, yeah." Sarah chuckled. "It feels good to do well. Is this what it felt like back in your big money days?"

"My what?" Loretta tilted her head and looked at her with sarcastic confusion. "In my experience, success certainly feels good. Especially in my 'big money days,' as you called it. Back then, I was surrounded by frat-boy-elitist-coke-heads, and anytime I could show them up, it felt even better."

Loretta grabbed a large steel pot and began to fill it with water.

"Ick. Was it as bad and as gross as it sounds?"

"Sometimes worse, but oftentimes not. I was lucky to have a mentor who believed in me and, as my career progressed, a loyal team who trusted me and my instincts. We all made money and made a lot of foolish people eat crow." Loretta nodded in satisfaction at the memory as she set the pot to boil.

"Wow, what was your biggest triumph?" Sarah measured tea leaves from a nearby canister.

"Oh, Sarah, that's in the past." Loretta waved her off. "Let's talk about the future. How's your grad school search going? You moving on to bigger and better things?"

"Not yet, but not for lack of trying." Sarah's enthusiasm for Loretta's stories were felled by the reality of her own life. "Fourteen applications, twelve rejections, two no replies—still waiting."

"Oh, I'm sorry. On the upside, it only takes one." Loretta's tone oozed optimism and apology. She poured the boiling water into the kettles and set the timer.

"I'm holding tight to hope."

"And you should; something will come. Don't get too down about it. If it all goes south, you can work here as long as you need to. I know it isn't what you want for the long run, but it's something until you get something else going."

"I appreciate that. You've done so much for me over the years. I hope you know how grateful I am."

"Of course, I love having you here. You're like another daughter to me. You're always welcome."

Sarah's posture straightened, and a shallow smile curled over her lips. She was truly grateful for Loretta and hoped to one day be as strong of a woman as her.

"Say, have you ever thought about looking for internships? I read an article a while back in the International section of *The Post* about some European companies doing innovative things. One may have even been food related, but I don't recall. Maybe you can find something like that?"

"That totally sounds like something I'd be interested in." Droplets of excitement sputtered from her lips. "Do you still have it?"

"Not sure. I'll have to look back and see if I can find that article."

"That would be great!"

Their conversation was interrupted by the jingling of the bell on the door. Richard and Phyllis came in, hand-in-hand. They made a cute, but odd, couple—Phyllis's nimble form connected to Richard's creaky, deliberate movements.

"Hey, y'all. What's good?" Phyllis asked in almost a yell. Her irrepressible zest lifted the room.

The group stood around the café counter and learned about Sarah's good news. Soon the gab turned to Richard's new hip and Phyllis's yoga class. After a while, the conversation moved to Nancy.

"We heard your mom was in the hospital. How's she feeling?" asked Richard in his soft, deep voice.

"Good, I think. She was released last week. The doctor said she had double pneumonia. That's cleared, and she's taking all of her meds, so she should be fine. But she's still complaining about leg pain, which goes back to her time at Ruther's." Despondency leaked into her voice. "All the doctors say it's nothing, but it's almost all she talks about. I get over there regularly and I try to distract her, cheer her up, but it doesn't seem to work very well. How do I help someone with pain that doesn't exist?"

The conversation drifted to other topics until the late-afternoon rush swept Sarah and Loretta back into the swirl of commerce.

Her head on a soft blue pillow, eyes closed, Sarah laid back on her couch and visualized the future she wanted: a degree on her wall, a lab coat and safety glasses—a nice job, a career. Her mind wandered.

With a few days off of school and work, Sarah put her extra free time into catching up on her reading, cleaning her neglected apartment, and hoping for good news on her remaining applications.

In the formless space between wake and sleep, her guard down, Sarah's thoughts turned to Michael. She wondered what he was doing and how he was getting on. Was Spain everything he'd hoped for? While at ease with the dissolution of their relationship, she still missed him sometimes. Caution flags arose, and she steered her thoughts away as they treaded too close to the waiting trap of regret, self-pity, and self-loathing.

Quick bursts of vibration rattled the coffee table, and Sarah felt her breath catch in her throat. She shook it off and looked for the phone. *Where is it?* She moved school brochures and take out boxes. *I hear it, but I don't see it.* "There it is!" She lifted her special edition of *I, Robot* and grabbed her phone just before voicemail picked up.

"Hi, Mom. How's it going?" Still bleary from her nap, Sarah hid it as best she could.

"It's goin' fine." Nancy's cadence was slow and distant, as if her simple response took significant effort.

"Why do you sound so out of it? You okay?"

"Oh, I'm fine. My leg's still botherin' me, but I've been takin' my meds. Hopefully that'll help." The words dripped out if her mouth like a leaking faucet.

"Mom, you need to be careful with those meds. Do you want me to come by? I'm worried about you."

"Oh, no, no. I'm okay. Don' come." Nancy's speech was sluggish. "What have you been up to?"

"Not too much, just waiting on grad school applications and hoping for the best."

"Oh? Okay. That's great," Nancy said, as if hearing of it for the first time. "Where have you applied?"

"The only ones I haven't heard from are Northberg and London College."

"London? You mean England? That's a long ways away. You're leaving me? How will I survive? Am I gonna die alone?"

"What are you talking about?" Sarah said, surprised. "We've been over this. Either way, it'd only be for a couple of years, then I'd be back. Realistically, you don't need to be worried. I probably won't even get in. Those are some of the best in the world, and everyone else has already rejected me."

"I guess that sounds nice. I hope you get in." Nancy's voice sounded far off, like at the other end of a long chasm. "Maybe I'll survive. Well, it's been nice talkin' to you, but I think I need to get to bed."

"Wait, what? We're done?" Sarah looked at her watch. "It's only seven! Why are you going to bed?"

"I get tired lately. My leg hurts, and I do lots of sleepin'." It took several moments for her to finish the sentence.

"You do sound tired, I guess. I can let you go. Have a good night."

"I'll try."

"I love you, Mom."

The call clicked off before Sarah finished her sentence.

CHAPTER 19

Sarah's eyes glossed over as she stared into her laptop screen and scrolled though endless monotony. Tired, bored, and frustrated, she worked on what had become her new evening routine: the job hunt. Graduate school was nearly a bust and graduation day drew nearer. She needed a job—or at least prospects. Deep inside, an anxiety gnawed at her and her confidence. *Get a helmet.*

Loretta's generous offer to stay at the Kettle was appreciated and gave her some respite, but Sarah was ready to move on. The Kettle meant the world to her, but it wasn't a career; she was just a drone. No career meant no future, and she needed a future. Sarah started to look for things related to food science, something to get her foot in the door.

Her research turned up three companies in town that could lead somewhere. Each dealt with food and, she hoped, food science.

She was wrong.

One made all of their food in California and only offered transportation jobs in Sarah's area. Another bought their food from a supplier and were basically a marketing company.

The third seemed promising, local, and had a catering division, but led to nothing when she learned they only employed family members and a chef. Unless she wanted to work the production line for minimum wage, it was a bust.

Disappointed and disillusioned, Sarah expanded her search and spent her evenings looking for something, anything, she might be qualified for, something remotely related to her field. Bubkis. Everything was either low-wage service jobs or engineering positions. Though she had a background in chemistry, a chemical engineer she was not.

Every night, she would search and send off résumés and cover letters never to be heard from again. Any attempts at follow-up were usually stymied by a lack of a usable phone number or email address. Sarah spent hours upon hours sending documents and wishing for some kind of response—even a rejection—but almost nothing arrived. It was as if everything she sent was simply sucked in an HR black hole.

Disenchantment set in, but she continued, nevertheless. Night after night, Sarah persisted in the futility dance between herself and the inhuman human resources departments and their faceless computer systems in hopes of getting somewhere, anywhere.

It's tough out there.

Weeks of frustration had been sacrificed to the false gods of human resources, but today was a new, different day—graduation day.

The bright morning sun filtered through the blue curtains of the Family Kettle and lent a cheerful air to the busy morning but did little to ease Sarah's stress and worry. Tired and overwrought, Sarah slumped across from Bernie and sighed the sigh of the relentlessly overburdened.

"You look a bit exhausted, sweetheart. Take a load off," Bernie said as he looked up from his *Freedom Gazette* and Irish Breakfast. His voice was grandfatherly and pleasant.

"You're working on the big day?"

"Only the morning. We're about to shut it down."

"Oh?" He checked his watch, shook it, and checked again. "It's only ten o'clock."

"Loretta's closing up early so she can help me get ready and attend the ceremony." Sarah perked up as she mentioned it.

"I'm so excited for you." His words were full of pride and joy. "You've worked so hard to get here. Enjoy it, sweetheart."

Sarah smiled, and a wind of excitement built in her. "I can't wait to walk across that stage and shake the dean's hand. If there's one thing I know, I've earned this."

"Indeed, you have. Is your mom going too?"

"Well..." Sarah exhaled sharply. "No. She's still complaining about her leg and says she can't leave the house."

"I'm sorry to hear that." He frowned slightly and took a sip of tea. "How about everything else? Anything definitive yet for your future plans?"

"I've pinned my hopes on a couple of food science internships, but they're in Marseille and Sarasota and neither seem too likely. Everything else has fallen through."

"That's disappointing. Wait, food science? I thought you were into chemistry? I've heard the term, but isn't that sort of Frankenfood?" Bernie asked with kindness.

"It's funny, I get that a lot. But not really. See, people never think about their favorite chip or snack cake and how they came to be. How the flavors were deliberately designed to evoke a response; studied and planned—the crispiness of a chip, the exact blend of spices, or the texture of icing or chocolate on a sweet snack—all calculated and specific, nothing by accident. That is the science of food science: consistent results, reliable food."

Sarah's voice was a staccato clip. As she spoke, her excitement accumulated.

"Hmm, you're right. I have to admit I've never really thought about it either. But with all of this interest in food, why not culinary school?"

"That's a different thing. I'm really into the actual chemistry of it all. How different molecules and substances impart different flavors and textures and how the interaction between all of the parts can be controlled with great precision. It's like what a chef does but in much more granular detail."

Usually, at this point in the conversation, people would start to look at her as if she were crazy, but not Bernie. He smiled and basked in her excitement. "That's way too complicated for this old dog, but it certainly sounds fascinating." His eyes shifted back and forth. He appeared to be trying to imagine it all.

The shop talk and excitement had refreshed her worried, weary body. She felt ready for the rest of the day.

Loretta approached the table. "Okay, Bernie. I hate to do this to you, but—"

"Oop, it's time?" he interrupted. "Glad to go if it's for her." He pointed to Sarah with a magnanimous smile. With his ivy cap on his head and cane in his hand, Bernie teetered out the door.

Sarah locked it behind him. In no time, the practiced hands of Loretta and Sarah had the register down, the shelves stocked, and the floor vacuumed. Sarah pushed the Hoover, as Loretta called it, into the closet.

"Sarah, I have something for you. Follow me," Loretta called.

"A surprise? I love surprises." *Well, good ones, anyway.* She followed Loretta into the backroom and sat down on a bench next to her bag.

"Okay, close your eyes." Loretta's broad smile showed her sparkling teeth.

Sarah did and waited.

"Now, open them."

Loretta held a white Anne Klein dress. Sleeveless and cinched slightly at the waist, the dress flowed with simplicity and elegance.

"Oh, my gosh! Loretta! It's beautiful! Thank you!" Sarah put her hands on her head in excitement. In a flash, off came her dusty apron, worn jeans, and simple blouse, replaced with the pleasant dress. Sarah stood back from a small mirror on the wall and tried to see herself as she swished the bottom of the dress back and forth.

"You look positively lovely," said Loretta.

Sarah curtsied in appreciation. For a moment, the word "lovely" triggered thoughts of Michael, which she quickly buried. She fetched the gown the school had sent her from her bag. The manufacturer had folded it into a compact square shape and sealed it into an equally square plastic bag. She removed it and realized it was creased at right angles from its long slumber in its packaging.

"Looks like I'm getting my Bachelor of Science degree in a rain poncho." She laughed as she held it up for Loretta.

The phone rang. Instinctively, Sarah held her breath.

"We're closed. It'll go to voicemail." Loretta waved her arm at the ringing phone as they turned back to the poncho… er, gown.

Loretta helped swing the plastic sheath over Sarah's head, and they attempted to make it look like an approximation of flattering.

Sarah turned back to the mirror and collected her hair and drew it up into an artful bun. She tilted her head back and forth to check her work as Loretta helped tuck in stray strands.

The phone rang again. Startled, Sarah jumped and bit the inside of her cheek. At ring four, Loretta moved to answer it. From the other side of the curtain, Sarah heard Loretta exclaim something that she couldn't make out. Then, she called Sarah to the phone.

With apprehension, Sarah took the receiver.

"I think somethin's wrong wit' Nancy," the voice said.

"Karen? Is that you? What's going on?" The words were tinged with panic. *Why the hell is Karen calling me? Why now? Why here?*

"Yeah, it's me. I just tried to stop by and visit your mom, and she didn' come to da door. Didn' answer da phone neit'er."

"She's been sleeping a lot lately. Maybe she's napping?"

"I banged pretty hard. Tried a coupl'a windows too. Somethin's not right. You need to check on her."

In her mind, Sarah imagined Karen's deep wrinkles shaking as she spoke.

"But it's gradu—" Sarah stopped herself. It didn't matter. She knew what she had to do.

Sarah thanked Karen and hung up the phone as she stood stupefied in her new dress and poncho-like gown.

After a quick discussion with Loretta, they headed to Nancy's on their way to the university. Sarah, unsure whether to worry or relax, inhaled in tension-filled breaths.

CHAPTER 20

Loretta's green SUV had barely pulled to a stop as Sarah jumped from the car and ran to Nancy's front door. Even in her hurry, she still cringed with embarrassment at the state of the lawn. The broken, removed screen door now had a band of rust along the bottom quarter where the snow had covered it. The keys fumbled in her hand as she struggled with the lock. *Why does nothing ever work?* Then, the brass key aligned with the pins, and the lock clicked open.

The house was still and quiet. TV off, Henry's chair empty and ghostly, she proceeded to Nancy's room. *Please be napping. Please be napping.* Sarah took a deep breath and planted two firm knocks on the bedroom door and went in. The room was dark. Blackout curtains were drawn, but, as it was midday, some light seeped into the room around the edges of the heavy fabric. Her eyes adjusted to the light, and she saw a faint outline of Nancy in the covers. As she waded into the room, her legs felt a resistance her eyes could not see; the tug of fabric pulled against her legs as she inched toward where she expected the edge of the bed to be and sat down. With a quick series of scooches, she made it to the nightstand and clicked on the small light.

The harsh glow revealed the mess within. The small bedroom was almost wall-to-wall bed with tiny aisles on each side, capped with small wooden nightstands and ceramic reading lamps. The floor was covered with old clothes and excess pillows—fancy, decorative types from one of Nancy's "getting her life back together" periods. Sarah could now see her mom in full.

Nancy laid on her side with her back to Sarah. Her immense frame was covered in blankets and quilts of various colors. The effect was a hilly landscape, like something out of a Doctor Seuss book. *She looks fine.* Sarah reached out and pushed on Nancy's shoulder.

"Mom, it's me, Sarah," she said loudly in hopes of waking her.

Nancy was silent. Tufts of brown hair jetted out from beneath the heap of blankets.

"You okay?" Sarah shook her.

Nancy did not respond. Sarah tried again but with more force.

"Mom! Mom!" she shouted and shook Nancy vigorously.

Nancy did not move. A deep sense of fear and terror began to rise through Sarah as she pulled away the top layers of blankets. The light was dim, but Sarah could see that something wasn't right. She hurried back to the wall switch near the door and turned on the overhead light. In the illuminated room, Nancy looked ashen and grey. Only then did Sarah realize that Nancy wasn't breathing.

"Holy shit!" she shrieked and fumbled for her phone. In a flurry of button presses, she dialed 911.

Terrified, Sarah's protective instincts kicked in: She was going to save her mother's life. Sarah leapt across the bed and threw the blankets to the floor. There was no space on the ground for Nancy's bulk, so, despite her training, she rolled Nancy onto her back and started chest compressions while she shouted to the operator. Without thinking, she found herself singing "Stayin' Alive" as she thrust her folded palms into Nancy's chest with rapid succession.

The seconds turned to minutes as Sarah pumped hard. "Come on, Mom! Breathe, goddammit!" Nancy's face was blue, yet Sarah persisted. As bad of a mother as she was, she was all Sarah had. Sarah was going to fight to keep her.

Arms on fire, Sarah paused for a moment to rub her muscles and take stock of the situation. Her long, strenuous minutes of pumping had no effect.

A loud commotion came from the front of the house—the ambulance, the police. Loretta burst into the bedroom, emergency services in tow.

"I saw the flashing lights. I knew something was wrong and came running! They followed me in." Loretta's voice was rapid but confident. "What can I do to help?"

As the paramedics rushed in, Sarah knew the situation was out of her hands. She turned to Loretta with a distorted face and hugged her.

"I think this is it," Sarah sobbed.

The EMTs continued the chest compressions and oxygenation with a bag valve mask. No pulse, no respiration. After a few more minutes, they called it. Everything that could reasonably be done had been done. Nancy was gone.

Almost as fast as they'd arrived, the first responders retreated to their mobile enclave of squad cars, fire engines, and ambulances and prepared to move the body. The police officers cordoned off the area and strategized about how to proceed with the investigation while the firefighters and EMTs arranged the stretcher, the body bag, and straps.

With the room clear of personnel, Sarah and Loretta stood and stared at the shell of a body that had been Sarah's mother. Sarah shivered, feeling as naked, cold, and alone as Nancy looked. With covers pulled back, Nancy's full mass was laid out in plain view veiled only by the thin strands of her favorite nightgown. From that vantage point, all of her scars, scrapes, folds, wrinkles, rolls, and purple, hardened veins were on display, and it was clear that the full force of life's punishment had been dealt to that body.

The police officers poked around the house and gathered evidence for their investigation which, Sarah soon learned, the law required. No one suspected foul-play, and the investigation proceeded in a perfunctory fashion. The officers found a bottle of hydrocodone with a loose lid and several pills missing.

The paramedics packed Nancy into a body bag, strapped it to the gurney, and carried it away for post-mortem evaluation. Within an hour or two, the entire legion of emergency services was gone. The house was empty except for Sarah and Loretta, who were numbed into silence.

They stood on the threshold between the filthy kitchen and small living room, staring into nothingness. After some time, Loretta took a small step toward Sarah and embraced her. Sarah collapsed into her warm, comforting arms and wept. The tears flowed, not just for the mother she'd lost but for the hope that died with her. Somewhere, deep inside, Sarah had harbored a dream that Nancy really would get her life together and be the mother Sarah wanted, needed, and deserved. But now, along with the Nancy of reality, that too was dead.

With a groan, Sarah sat down on her couch and dropped her crumpled poncho gown on the floor beside her. She closed her eyes and sighed. The day had started with such hope and promise. She was supposed to graduate. It was supposed to be her day—the culmination of years. Thoughts about her life—her mother, her struggles at school, and even Michael—entered her mind as a smattering of tears drizzled down her face. Before long, the memories and pain, heartbreaks and triumphs, flowed like a faucet with the handles broken off. Awash in a downpour of tears, Sarah sat, helpless. The full waves of her emotions crested and crashed into the shore of her being. Grief and sadness overtook her one moment and were subsumed by guilt the next. The process repeated itself in cascading waves until Sarah collapsed into sleep, worn to nothing by exhaustion.

CHAPTER 21

Sarah sat at her kitchen table and stared at the list in front of her. There were arrangements to be made, phone calls to place, actions to be taken. The funeral home wanted directions; the police needed information she didn't have; and a handful of distant relatives, who she didn't actually know, needed to hear about Nancy's death.

It all had to be done, but Sarah was numb. Because of Henry's death, Sarah knew how to proceed, but this time it was different. She was completely alone. Alone but for a sidecar of guilt. She wondered what would have happened if she had checked in on Nancy that morning? Would a simple phone call have saved Nancy's life? Sometimes she did call Nancy in the mornings but not that day. Would it have made a difference? How could she have known?

At the same time, another kind of guilt assailed her. The guilt of relief. With Nancy gone, Sarah was free and unencumbered by the constant demands of Nancy's ever-present illnesses. Of course, it wasn't really that simple. According to the lawyer, the demands of Nancy's debt, medical bills, and other casualties of her lifestyle would probably tail Sarah for years. The sale of the house would likely cover most of it, but she still had to get it ready and would pay in time and energy.

Loretta had stopped by and brought her enough food for a week, but Sarah still felt alone and sourceless. For a moment, she wondered if this was how Michael had felt. Despite all of the trouble and hardship Nancy had caused her, now that she was gone, Sarah missed her. *You only get one mother. I loved her even when I hated her.*

The heat from the stale, black coffee caused the foam cup in Sarah's hands to soften as she sat in the tiny office of Detective Goodall.

"Good morning, Sarah," said the detective in a kind voice. "Thanks for coming in. I know this is hard to do, but I will try to make this as quick and painless as possible." The detective was a heavyset man of dark complexion with black, close-cropped hair and a short, well-trimmed mustache. He spoke in soft, reassuring sentences, nothing like the TV show detective Sarah was expecting.

"Thanks," Sarah said. "I'm hoping this will give me some closure. Her death is still very much a shock."

Sarah sipped her coffee as the detective fiddled with his computer. It tasted a little like nutty dirt but still calmed her.

"I hope that it does. So, cutting right to it." The detective glanced at his screen and then found a manila file folder. "From the get-go, we were not suspecting foul play, and our investigation offered up no information to change that presumption. Nancy's toxicology came back with large quantities of hydrocodone, lorazepam, and trazodone in her system, but no alcohol was found."

Sarah sighed and twisted her hair around her finger as the detective continued.

"After reviewing the Medical Examiner's report, we have concluded her death was from an overdose of prescribed drugs and accidental in nature. As such, we now consider the investigation closed, unless you have anything to add or any additional questions?" Sarah could tell he was trying to humanize the stiff police-speak of his report with kind tones.

"No, that's what I expected too. It is good to get the confirmation, though."

Sarah thanked the detective for his time and made her way through the parking lot toward the street. The closer she got to home, the heavier her steps became. She was now parentless and alone and felt sorry for herself. It was as if the weight of her loneliness was gradually driving her into the pavement.

In a surprise turn, her thoughts shifted to Henry. Sarah wondered what he would have thought of that detective, of Nancy's death, or of Sarah walking through the city dripping with self-pity. She knew the answer; he would have said, "Toughen up, cupcake," or some other stupid shit and then popped himself a beer. In its way, the thought made her chuckle. Her father was a man unsuited to handle the intensities of real life, and alcohol was his shield and his savior. But he expected everyone else to take life's hits unprotected.

She hated her father yet missed him. While not an entirely bad man, he was a crap dad. Whenever she reached out for help, especially during those firestorm years of adolescence, she was met with hostility or, at best, casual indifference.

Henry never understood what it meant to be a father or that a girl needs her father to be there for her, even when she thinks she doesn't. Someone to protect her and tell her she's pretty and smart when it feels like the whole world is telling her the opposite. He never understood that a dad is supposed to fight by his daughter's side, an ally against the slings and arrows of the world—the haters, the creeps, and the users. Henry just hid behind his little slogans and cans of Old Milwaukee.

Sarah remembered a conversation she'd had with him a few months before he died. He told her that he felt it was his job to toughen her up so she wouldn't grow up to be a coward. *He never realized that I didn't need toughening; the world does that all by itself. I needed a dad to support me and help me build self-confidence and courage. He never did any of that.*

When Sarah finally made it home, she was spent. Too much time thinking about her crap dad and crap mom and how she still missed them despite all they didn't do for her. She opened a bottle of pinot grigio and tried to pick up where she'd left off on Clarke's *Childhood's End*.

CHAPTER 22

Sarah caught her breath as her phone buzzed on the kitchen counter. The display flashed a picture of Loretta with a big smile on her face. It was Sunday night, and the Kettle had been closed for hours. *What could she want?*

In a brief and hurried conversation, Sarah learned there had been a small, but messy, accident at the Kettle. Loretta needed help to clean it all.

As she hustled out the door, Sarah wondered what Loretta had been doing at the Kettle hours after they'd closed the store together. The weather had turned damp and fog had rolled in. With the weekend bus service finished for the night, Sarah went on foot. The dark streets felt ominous in their grey, misty coating, but Sarah had done this walk a thousand times and was on guard but undaunted. In the still of the evening, Commerce Street looked abandoned; the whole commercial section was a ghost town. The vapor danced in the light of the street lamps, making phantoms and human-like shapes with every sweep of the eye. *More pareidolia.*

From the street, the Kettle was dark except for a small light that glowed from the back room. The sign, the window lights, and the store overhead lights were all extinguished. *Did Loretta finish and go home?*

The bolt clicked and the bell chimed as Sarah turned the key and opened the door. To her surprise, the alarm system was silent.

"Loretta? Loretta, are you here?"

No response.

The lights flickered on silently, and Sarah took stock of the store. It looked precisely as she had left it, and there was no sign of Loretta. Sarah locked the door behind her and proceeded toward the backroom in a slow crouch with her keys poised between her fingers like mini daggers.

"Loretta! I'm here! Where the heck are you?"

No response.

As each of her calls died away into silence, Sarah's heart beat faster and faster, like a pendulum clock gone haywire. She prepared herself for the worst and tiptoed behind the café counter and pushed back the dividing curtain to the backroom.

"SURPRISE!" screamed a chorus of voices.

Close to fainting, Sarah put her hands over her face in shock. Loretta, Bernie, Richard, Phyllis, a few friends from school, and even Beatrice were all there with broad smiles and pointy hats. Across the back wall hung a sign that read: *Congratulations, Sarah. We Love You.*

Overwhelmed by the ruse perpetrated in her favor, Sarah stood still and started to cry. The sudden jolt between fear, surprise, and joy knocked her off-balance, but after a few seconds, she composed herself enough to speak.

"You guys! Thank you!" she said, still visually startled. "I was not expecting this! Loretta, did you plan all of this?"

"Of course I did, honey. You've worked so hard and had to deal with so much. We all figured you needed some celebrating."

"It's wonderful. After missing my graduation and, well, you know, everything else, I never even thought of a party. Thank you." Tears streamed again, and she managed to mutter, "I'm sorry. I'm still in shock."

The room was decorated to the hilt, packed with streamers and balloons in the university's colors of black and gold. Celebratory latex and mylar balloons of all colors hung from the ceiling and crowded the floor.

On the far wall were tables of drinks and hors d'oeuvres, more than enough for the assembled guests. Loretta had spared no expense: champagne, craft beer, pinot noir, and catered food.

With Sarah's arrival the drinks began to flow as everyone devoured the rumaki, bruschetta, and mini beef wellingtons. For the first time in a long time, Sarah felt unburdened and let loose.

Loretta poured champagne and said a toast. The chorus of hoorahs subsided, and Bernie was the first person in line to greet Sarah.

"Congratulations, sweetheart. This is for you." He handed her a rectangle wrapped in blue and gold. "Please, open it."

"Bernie! You got me a gift, that's so sweet." With gentle tears, Sarah opened the package. Inside was a leather-bound copy of the *Foundation* trilogy.

"I hope you don't have it. If you liked *I,Robot*, and I know you did, you'll love this."

"I do! Thank you." Sarah hugged him. "I'm so glad you came."

"I wouldn't miss it for the world." Bernie squinted and knocked his cane against the ground for emphasis. "I heard about those internships and jobs. Those folks have no idea what they're missing. You're a great kid, and you'd be a gleaming addition to any of those places. Chin up. It'll work out one way or another; just keep pushing."

"Thanks. I hope you're right."

Beatrice came up and stood beside Bernie. For the occasion, she wore a tight-fitting black cloche hat with a gold ribbon.

"Well, I'm going to allow myself another little drink and mingle with your fine guests," Bernie said with a wry smile and a wink. "I have to get some living in before I have to teeter myself home. Old-timers like me have to get to bed early... but not too early." He nodded toward Beatrice and headed to the makeshift bar.

"Sarah, deary, congratulations. I brought you a gift." Bea handed her a heavy box about the size of two shoeboxes. "But it may be a bit silly, now, if I overheard correctly? Did he say you were unsuccessful in your internship pursuits?" Beatrice asked, her voice like a bossy robin.

"Yeah, you heard correctly," Sarah said with a shrug. "It all came up bubkis."

"That's strange. I expected you would get accepted. I was speaking with my granddaughter-in-law about how intelligent you are. Maybe not when it comes to men, but... nevertheless, you're a sweet, smart woman. Hmm..." She paused for a moment and crinkled her lips in thought. "I am very surprised, indeed. I am sorry, but you must excuse me. I have to make a phone call. There is some urgent business that requires my attention." She walked away from Sarah in a hurry and placed her champagne glass on the shiny, black tablecloth as she hastened to the other room, phone in hand.

"Um, okay," Sarah said, mostly to herself. "Thank you for the gift."

That was strange. I wonder what that was about. Sarah shook her head and opened the hefty package—a hardbound copy of *The Count of Monte Cristo*, in French, as well as a French-English dictionary. There was a note attached: *I know it's one of your favorites. You'll love it even more this time.* Confused but excited, Sarah put the gift with her other presents and moved on to be with other guests.

For a few hours, Sarah's problems were banished, and it was only drinks, foods, and friends. The assembled group was small but meaningful. Each person present was precious to Sarah, and seeing everyone together reminded her that she had good people who cared about her.

The night wore on and the guests veered, in varying degrees, away from sobriety. Timed perfectly, Loretta had one more surprise in store: karaoke. The crowd cheered as Loretta wheeled in a large cart with a huge screen and several microphones followed by lights, more screens, and a disco ball.

The assembled sang and danced well into the night, and the joviality lifted Sarah's spirits. The encouragement of her friends and the effects of the alcohol buoyed her self-confidence and her self-respect. It was not to last, however. The next day, reality bit back.

Sarah awoke in a tangled nest of blankets and stared at the ceiling to settle her pounding head and aching stomach. The curtains glowed in the late morning light and gave the room a warm, sensual feel as she recalled the previous night with a smile.

Determined to push forward, Sarah disentangled herself and swung her legs around the side of the bed. Her calf muscles ached as she stood up—too much dancing. In an instant, her head spun, and her stomach somersaulted. She bolted for the bathroom. Bleary-eyed and rough but undeterred, she downed an aspirin, donned her robe, and made her way to the kitchen.

The coffee machine is a miracle of the modern age. Sarah poured herself a fresh, steaming cup of black liquid from the awaiting pot. She had no recollection of filling the machine the previous night but was glad she had. Taste for taste, she preferred tea, but when a caffeine fix was in order, she turned to coffee. The bitter, steaming liquid made her feel more like herself. The nutty, fragrant aroma calmed her nerves and eased her stomach as she assessed the state of her affairs. The tasks that laid before her were as simple as they were insurmountable: find a future, clean the apartment.

The whole apartment suffered from neglect and was in desperate need of a deep clean. The carpet, for want of a vacuum, looked worn, sprinkled with bits of lint and food particles amongst the nylon fibers. The bookshelves and cabinets were coated in a layer of dust thick enough to be seen across the room. In a fit of fancy, Sarah stepped over to a small bookcase and wrote *dust me* with her fingertip.

The more Sarah surveyed, the more tasks she saw that needed her attention. Dishes filled the sink and emitted a faint odor. The mail had piled up and coagulated into a clot of mailing envelopes, magazines, and chunks of junk mail on her coffee table. Since Nancy's death, anything not related to

Nancy or finishing school was pushed aside. Overwhelmed by the immensity of cleaning required, she staved it off and concentrated on her immediate need for a job.

Encamped on the couch with her laptop, Sarah searched for anything that resembled a career; anything she might qualify for—a workable profession of any type. What she found was less than encouraging: an administrative assistant to a logistics manager; a warehouse supervisor position at a company whose clients included chemical companies like Dow, BASF, and DuPont; and the city needed an independent water quality technician (i.e., city job with no benefits or pension). Despite her dejection, she applied to them all. She hoped that wherever she landed might lead to something better down the road. She resigned herself to a temporary detour but didn't know if she could handle a permanent redirection.

The day was spent on cover letters, résumé editing, and web-application tedium. Sarah resented wasting her day on banal minutia that would likely lead to nothing, but it had to be done.

Day complete, Sarah was drained and in need of distraction. After fetching the latest issue of the *Journal of Food Science* off the top of "mail mountain," she grabbed a glass of wine and sank into the couch with a sigh. Sarah was tired—tired of grief, tired of death, tired of disappointment and despair, tired of being let down, and tired of being tired. With a crash, the reality of her situation slapped her in the face—she had no father, no mother, no prospects for graduate school, and no career. She cried to herself in soft sobs, each accompanied by ever larger gulps of pinot. Despite her best efforts, she couldn't help but feel that her dreams had been derailed.

MATTHEW KOPF · 207

―――――

The next day, Sarah awoke in better spirits. The long night of sleep did her good and gave her energy to face the day. With no stomach for the job hunt, she turned her attention to her under-cleaned, overwrought apartment.

The crunchy guitar strings of Depeche Mode's *I Feel You* clanged through the air as Sarah set to work. Dusting came first because it required only one hand; the other was for her tea. With broad swipes, she relieved the bookshelves, cabinets, and tables of the mighty layers of accumulated dust. The furniture shined in appreciation. Tea finished, Sarah focused on the rug and dragged the vacuum across the floor. The weight and motion left little ridges and patterns on the carpet; a look Sarah had always liked as it gave her a sense of accomplishment.

Sarah pulled the plug from the living room wall and moved on to her bedroom. On the kitchen counter, the shrill chirp of her phone cut through the musical din and set Sarah rushing to answer it. The accent on the other end startled her.

"Good morning. I, um, am looking for a Ms. Sarah Hall," said a female voice with a pointed French accent.

"This is she," responded Sarah meekly.

"Ah, yes, Ms. Hall. I'm calling from Avenir D'or about your internship application…"

"Wait, from Marseille?" asked Sarah, her voice shaking with nervousness.

"Ah, yes, that is where we are located," the voice said, somewhat surprised.

"Okay, great, what can I do for you?"

"Well, see, we have not heard from you so I'm calling to find out if you are still interested. We only have a limited number of spots; there are others on the list."

"What do you mean? You guys rejected me. I have the letter here... somewhere."

"No, no, see, there was a misunderstanding. We sent you another letter. Did you not receive it? We sent it several weeks ago."

Sarah glanced at the overflowing pile of mail on her coffee table in alarm.

"May I put you on hold a moment?" she asked in a polite voice and hoped she didn't look like a fool.

The voice answered in the affirmative, and Sarah placed the phone on the kitchen counter. She hurried to the mountain of mail and sifted through it like a game show contestant running out of time. The stack seemed endless as the seconds ticked. Then, she found it. A roughed-up envelope with a gold and white square—the company's logo—in the corner. It was toward the bottom of the heap and battered. Sarah pulled the ruffled correspondence from the pile and flattened it against her thigh. It was still sealed. "I don't remember seeing this," she said out loud to herself as she tore open the letter and read it at a breakneck pace before rushing back to the phone, abandoning all sense of decorum.

"I accept, I accept," Sarah shouted into the phone. "I don't know what happened. It must have been some kind of mistake!"

"Sounds great, Ms. Hall. I will mark it on your file. We look forward to welcoming you in the autumn. However, we need a formal acceptance email by the deadline three days from now. Your packet should contain more information about your internship and the benefits and perks involved. Congratulations, Ms. Hall."

"I will send the email at once! Thank you, thank you. I can't wait." Sarah hung up the phone and pumped her fist in the air. "Yes! Yes, I did it! I'm going to France!" she shouted to the empty room.

Without delay, Sarah drafted an acceptance email. Excitement swelled within her with each keystroke. Her mind raced with preparations—what to take, what to leave. What about her apartment?

She took a deep breath and reminded herself that she had made it; she was in. One step at a time and everything would work out fine. The job searches, the fretting over graduate school, the search for a future was over. She was going to be interning with one of the biggest food innovators in Europe.

Sarah dialed Loretta and danced around the room like a sprite as the phone rang. When Loretta answered, she burst at the seams and tried to explain the whole situation in one breath. After a pause, she tried again and gave Loretta the news in a more measured fashion. Loretta's voice crescendoed with delight as the pair talked and planned Sarah's next steps. They both bubbled with glee, neither fully grasping what lied ahead.

CHAPTER 23

Sarah wheeled her shiny, new carry-on down the jetway and set foot into the mammoth Boeing 747-400. Anxiety and curiosity filled her as she hunted for her seat, 23B, amongst the seemingly endless rows. Her first time on an airplane, Sarah was nearly overwhelmed, but thankfully a friendly flight attendant came to her aid and showed her to her seat.

She settled into cramped coach and reflected on where she was going and who she was leaving behind—Loretta, Bernie, and the rest of the gang. Her thoughts shifted to her mother. While she still missed her, she was glad to put some distance between herself and the mess the lawyer had to sort out.

With most of her things in storage, Sarah carried only her essentials. Her only concession to luxury was her beloved Miró eight-by-ten that she'd carefully nestled between the sweaters in her checked bag.

Within the hour, the wheels of the sky titan lifted from the tarmac, and Sarah gazed in amazement as her city, the only home she'd ever known, grew smaller and smaller until it all gave way to earth-toned plaid. The plane soared and, with it, Sarah's hopes and dreams about who she would become and what kind of a future would unroll before her.

The grey taxi sped down the sun-drenched A55 away from the Marseille Provence Airport toward the Avenir D'or headquarters. After an overnight layover in London, her mid-morning flight had been brief and uneventful, but the taxi ride hit turbulence. The driver spoke no English and didn't understand Sarah's French, so hand gestures stood in for conversation. After a short game of charades, the taxi got underway. Five minutes into the ride, near Plan des Pennes, the car's air conditioning broke and left Sarah and the driver with no options but to roll down the windows and swelter in an early summer heatwave.

The taxi rolled through the baking sun as Sarah fanned herself and thought about why she was here and what she needed to do. In order to craft this experience into a real job, she needed to perform. For her career, this was do or die; this was her shot. This was her chance to learn from the best, work with the best, and hopefully, get employed with the best. If not, she hoped the experience would still lead somewhere. If she failed, it was back to the lack of opportunities and trying to shoehorn herself into any HR box into which she might fit just to exist, her food science dreams deferred indefinitely.

Brown rocky hills guided her path into town. The small rocks looked like crumbling earthenware pots baking in the Mediterranean sun. As the grey car turned onto city streets, it became clear just how diverse and complex Sarah's new home was. It felt simultaneously gritty and vibrant, teeming with life but with an undercurrent of danger, or, at the very least, uncertainty. They passed through the *nord quartiers* and into a business district in an adjacent, and more prosperous, section of the city.

The car steamed as it caressed the finely curved boulevard that led to the Avenir D'or campus, the sun gleamed off the blue glass facade that Sarah recognized from their website. The main building was a squat four-story warehouse with offices attached to the front. Dressed in the blue hue of tinted glass and offset by black chrome paneling, it made for a stunning statement.

The company was headquartered in a light industrial area sandwiched between the airport and the heart of Marseille. Over the last twenty years, the company had quadrupled in size, and the layout of the campus reflected the rapid, spasmodic growth. The smattering of buildings bore little aesthetic relationship to one another, like random toys placed there by a giant toddler.

At the door, Sarah was met by Theresa Hackingham, the woman who would oversee her internship. She was a tall, thin Brit who looked firm and durable but without a trace of malice. She had lived in France for thirty years and been on staff with Avenir D'or as the VP of Operations and Training for the past eight.

They passed through the double-height doors into the vast atrium. From the inside, the building's components were exposed, and Sarah marveled at the enormous panels mounted to a lattice and truss system of chromed steel. The reflective metal caught the light and bounced it around the large room at dramatic angles, creating artistic shadows. The effect was inspiring, airy, and inviting.

The floors were polished concrete, and the walls were black, blue, and silver, which contrasted with the bright works of the rest of the atrium. In the center sat a large set of black chromed steel desks that housed security and reception. Behind which were a pair of escalators to an open-floored mezzanine level and banks of elevators to the rest of the building.

After Ms. Hackingham helped Sarah check her luggage with security, she pointed out the features of the soaring lobby and took Sarah on a full tour of the facility. She explained that during her internship, Sarah would be introduced to all of the areas of the company but would be embedded in a research and development team. The program also granted her some discretionary time to focus on her areas of interest. The tour concluded, and Ms. Hackingham took Sarah to see her apartment a few minutes away.

"Well, Ms. Hall," Ms. Hackingham said in pointed British diction. "I will leave you to unpack your things and settle in." She looked at Sarah's paltry bags. "Once you've finished with that, five minutes from now, I suggest you avail yourself of the local cuisine. You may find it inspirational."

Ms. Hackingham smiled just a little, then turned and left. Despite Ms. Hackingham's formal exterior, Sarah had a feeling she was going to like her—no nonsense but not without a sense of humor.

The apartment was small, scarcely more than three rooms, but more than adequate. It consisted of a small bedroom; a pleasantly furnished, in a modern style, living room/kitchen; and a modest bathroom. The furniture was cheap but functional. It looked like a model out of an IKEA catalog. The wood floors and a wood-look paper coffee table gave the room a warm, stylish feel. It was rounded out with an olive-green couch and a set of multi-colored glass pendant lamps.

Sarah unpacked her limited possessions and settled into her new abode. She arranged her clothes into the small paperboard dresser and found a home for her toiletries in the bathroom. Then, the hunt began for a good place to hang her treasured Miró print.

Sarah held the small print against the wall in several places before she decided on the wall across from the small green couch, just above the little television. The colors of the painting and the sofa tied the room together, as if it were meant to be.

Sarah stood back and looked at the little Miró. It had a calming, reassuring effect. The bold, confident stripes bolstered her while the beautiful flowers brightened her day. But as much as she loved it, it still reminded her of Michael. Sarah spared a moment to wonder about him and how he was faring in Spain. She wondered what he'd think if he could see her now—blazing her own trail, in Europe nonetheless—ready to take on the food science world. The thought put a smile on her face as she set out to do as Ms. Hackingham suggested, and Michael would have insisted, and explore the culinary adventures of her new city.

CHAPTER 24

The morning sun glowed indigo through the Avenir D'or atrium and gave the room the feel of a four-story aquarium. Sarah beamed with pride as she introduced herself to Gunter at the security desk and checked-in with her newly minted badge for the first time. Gunter smiled and politely told her, in his Alsatian accent, how to use the elevator to get to the third floor. She thanked him with a sweet smile and a courteous wave.

As the elevator rose, Sarah tingled with excitement and shook her arms to ease her nerves. It was her first day; she couldn't wait to meet everybody and get started. While she felt like she'd been preparing for this moment for years, she still wondered if she was really up to the task.

The elevator dinged, and Sarah stepped into the Research and Development Department. Ms. Hackingham met her as the elevator doors slid closed behind her.

"Good morning, Ms. Hall. Glad you could join us. We are going to have our Monday meeting, and I'd like you to sit in, meet the team, and get up to speed."

The two sat down at the stark white conference table. Sarah ran her hands on the smooth surface as she set out her notebook and pen. Sitting made her stomach clench, and as it twisted, Sarah became aware of just how nervous she really was. Her excitement and anxiety seemed to be competing for dominance. Three others joined them at the table and were introduced in turn.

First was Marc Laurent, a senior food scientist and team captain. He was in his early sixties and tall and slender with almost no hair. His scalp was marked with blemishes and age spots. He looked as if someone had dripped ink on his head and he'd been too absentminded to remove it. He wore his typical, as Sarah would learn, well-tailored dark brown slacks with a white shirt and light brown sweater covered with a lab coat.

Next was Josephine Blasier, a food scientist and a handsome woman in her mid-forties with a dark complexion and large brown eyes. Her hair was short and stylish. She spoke with a soft accent that Sarah found charming and had previously only heard in movies.

Last was Jean-Pierre Arnoult, the department's lab technician. He had a mop of sandy blond hair and green-blue eyes, which looked at the world through round, rimless glasses. He looked like a French cross between John Lennon and Bill Gates. He was not tall but very skinny, which gave him the appearance of greater height.

"Okay, team," said Ms. Hackingham. "As you've all figured out by now, this is our new intern, Sarah. Sarah, would you mind taking a minute or two to introduce yourself?"

"Hi, everyone," Sarah said with enthusiasm. "As you can tell from my accent, I am American. I recently graduated with my bachelor's in chemistry and have a passion for the intersection of tastes and science. I will be interning with you for the next year and am really excited to be here. I can't wait to see what I can learn and contribute."

"Welcome aboard. Where did you do your masters?" Marc's voice was wooden and slightly prosecutorial.

"My Masters?" Sarah swallowed hard and began to sweat. A spotlight had been turned on her and caught her by surprise. "Um, I don't have one. I've only just completed my bachelor degree."

"Oh? I thought our interns had advanced degrees?" Marc glanced at Theresa.

"Often times they do," Ms. Hackingham chimed in. "We look for excellent candidates. Degree status is secondary."

"Okay, that should still be all right then as long as you guys have vetted her." Marc turned his gaze from Theresa and back toward Sarah. "While our company has a long tradition of successful internships, you're the first one I've had on my team. Regardless, I'm pleased to have you here. I'm looking forward to getting your fresh eyes on some of our newest products."

Sarah's heart beat hard in her chest but slowed as Marc's tone softened. Still, nervousness was winning out over excitement. She curled her hair around her finger as the meeting moved onto other matters.

With the spotlight off of her, Sarah soaked in every detail of the discussion and jotted notes as they went. They discussed the results of a recent launch of a new frozen pastry—a personal-sized ring-shaped pastry in three flavors: blueberry, strawberry, and apple-cinnamon. Turns out, the initial consumer feedback data suggested that people liked it but wanted more flavor varieties. Then, they discussed the products that had been finalized but were still in the works at the production stage. Josephine brought out a series of large cookies, normally singly wrapped.

"As you all may recognize, these are our new Jumbo-Cook Specials. Oatmeal, chocolate chip, and shortbread." She pointed to each as she spoke. "They've been stuck in pre-production because quality control keeps finding these." Josephine held up a smushed, under-baked cookie next to an over-firm, hard one. "Why?"

The room went quiet, and everyone stared at one another. Sarah felt like she was back in Organic Chemistry but having studied the wrong textbook.

"Sarah," Josephine asked, breaking the silence. "What do you think?"

Sarah's palms felt moist. She could feel the color drain from her face. "Umm, uneven heat in the baking elements?" she guessed.

"Nope, we looked into that. Anyone else?"

The others continued to discuss the cookie problem as Sarah climbed into herself and shuddered. Day one and she'd already not known the answer and proved to be a disappointment education-wise. Her innards churned as she forced her attention back to the meeting. A few minutes later, the discussion turned to projects under development, and the group moved to the lab.

"As you all know, we've been trying to perfect a new cream for our upcoming horn pastries," Josephine said as she walked the group to a worktable laid out several dishes of white creams. "We've started with our standard vanilla cream, but for this product, we want something with a smoother finish. We've tried several iterations, and now we're smoother but blander."

Each team member took a small wooden paddle and tasted each sample, commenting to themselves as they went.

"I like the middle one the best," said Jean-Pierre.

"I prefer the newest version, but it's a little bland," chimed in Marc.

"Personally," added Ms. Hackingham, "I think we should use the standard vanilla."

"Sarah," asked Josephine, "what do you think? You're the newest palate here."

Sarah felt herself redden as attentions shifted back to her. She'd hoped to stay unnoticed for the rest of the meeting. She wanted to shed her nervousness and regain her excitement. Not sure what to say, she just said what she thought.

"I like them all. The standard cream is good, but it is a little grainy. The other two are definite improvements in mouthfeel and texture, but the flavor doesn't seem that strong to me. If I may be so bold, have you thought about using benzaldehyde to add a little almond flavor? Or maybe maltol? Or perhaps a little almond extract if the budget allows?" Sarah asked, unable to hide her excitement.

"We'll have to try that. I've been so focused on texture that I didn't even think about benzaldehyde," said Josephine happily. "Great suggestions, Sarah. Glad to have you onboard."

Sarah smiled. She was glad to have scored some kind of a win. She hoped it was upward from there.

CHAPTER 25

The shade of the building gave Sarah a reprieve from the afternoon sun as she ate her lunch at a picnic table in the courtyard of Building Forty-Seven on the Avenir D'or campus. Before her sat her new favorite meal: ham and brie on a baguette with a pinch of horseradish and a sprinkle of dill from the *boulangerie* near her apartment. The shadowy garden sat in the center of a fourteen-story cylindrical building with thin, narrow windows and a dark, orange-red exterior. It looked like a giant oatmeal box with a hole through the middle.

It was only her second week, but the courtyard had quickly become her go-to spot. She liked how the light hit everything at steep angles and cast deep, oblong shadows. There was a pleasant path that wound around trees and large circular raised plant beds filled with flowers, herbs, and other vegetation to be used in research and development.

Sarah ate alone with her new copy of *The Count of Monte Cristo,* her French-English dictionary, and an open notebook to capture inspiration. A coworker approached her from behind.

"Excuse me, Sarah. May I sit here?" a voice asked in perfect English but with an unmistakable French accent.

Startled, Sarah looked up and saw that the voice belonged to Jean-Pierre.

"Oh, bonjour, Jean-Pierre. Yes, please take a seat," Sarah said and motioned for him to sit across from her.

He was dressed in a European version of business casual—a pair of grey tailored wool trousers and a blue button-up business shirt, sans tie, covered with a dark green, sleeveless pullover sweater.

"How have you enjoyed your first weeks in Marseille?" Jean-Pierre removed his neatly wrapped sandwich from a sheet of cellophane and took a bite. "Have you been able to take in the sights?"

"I've tried but haven't had much time. I got a look at Fort Saint-Jean but only for a few minutes. I've walked around the Old Port area too. I'm fascinated by all of the restaurants here; so much to try. The styles here are so different from back home."

"Yes, there's a great deal of variety. While you're here, you must try the Bouillabaisse. In fact, try it in as many places as you can. They're all different and most excellent." His head bobbed with enthusiasm as he spoke. "Then try the daube. For me though, lately, I've grown especially fond of our mideastern restaurants—particularly the Armenian cuisine."

"That's funny, the other day I spotted a little Armenian place downtown. I think it was called *Saveur Arménienne*. I made a note to myself to try it."

"I know the place. In fact, I know the owner—well, the owner's son, technically. The prospective owner, you would say. I've grown fond of their lentil kufta. They serve them with sliced tomatoes on the side—the freshest tomatoes you've ever eaten, I promise."

"That sounds amazing! I will have to try it."

Sarah took a bite of her sandwich. The cool brie and the spicy horseradish danced in her mouth.

"Would you like me to take you?" Jean-Pierre asked. "I know what it is like to be new in a strange city. I'd be happy to show you around. I'll be your—how do you say—personal tour guide. I've lived here a long time. I know all the spots to see, and what to avoid."

Suddenly, Sarah's guard was up. The prospect of having someone show her the city sounded great, but she was leery of overly friendly male coworkers.

"That sounds nice," Sarah said, her voice turned cold but polite. "But I don't date coworkers. I hope you understand. I can't jeopardize my future with the company on a romantic endeavor."

"Oh, um, Sarah," Jean-Pierre interjected, "I think you may have gotten the wrong idea." His face reddened as he spoke. "I wasn't trying to suggest a romantic evening. You're—er, not my kind of date. But you do seem like my kind of friend."

"Oh, um, thanks. I think." Sarah couldn't tell if he was being earnest.

"Agh, I did it again. Sometimes my English is not so perfect." His face grew as red as the building. "I didn't mean to offend you. You're a very pretty lady, but I don't take ladies on romantic evenings."

"Oh, so you're gay?" Sarah asked with hesitation. The color of her face now matched his.

"Yes," responded Jean-Pierre flatly but with a nod and a smile.

Embarrassed but relieved, Sarah dropped her guard. In an instant, she became her usual, warm self.

"Okay." Sarah's smile brightened like the sun after a cloud drifted away. "In that case, yes. I'd love to see the city with you. It sounds like fun."

"Great! How about Saturday? I'll give you an insider's tour of the town, and we'll go to dinner," Jean-Pierre said with a satisfied smile. "Let's meet at the gates out front. Say, one o'clock?"

"Sounds good to me."

"Okay, see you then." Jean-Pierre smiled and waved as he walked away.

Sarah turned back to her lunch, thrilled and exhilarated to have a new friend in her new town.

In a yellow sundress that sat loosely on her shoulders, Sarah began her short walk to meet Jean-Pierre. Her sun-lorn body was grateful for the opportunity to absorb the bright Mediterranean light. As she walked, the beauty of the old buildings inspired and energized her with their red-tiled roofs and long slender windows with painted shutters. The beautiful patina of age gave the neighborhood a weary but wise look, as if it had experienced more than a few centuries of human life with little more than a shrug.

She approached the gates of Avenir D'or and saw Jean-Pierre against a wall with his arms crossed. He looked relaxed in a blue Panama shirt. Jean-Pierre greeted her with warmth and guided her to a nearby metro station as they headed toward Palais Longchamp.

The lime-colored blur out the side of the metro window slowed into focus as the sleek train glided to a halt at the Cinq Avenues—Longchamp station. Sarah and Jean-Pierre hurried from the car and headed up the tight, concrete stairs. When they reached the top, they were welcomed by the green glory of Longchamp Park.

"Have you visited this park before, on your exploring?" asked Jean-Pierre.

"No. I've seen it on the map and read a little about it."

"Oh, it's great," Jean-Pierre remarked. "There is a fountain, a natural history museum, an art museum, and an observatory. There even used be an old-fashioned zoo here until the old-fashioned zoos became, well, old-fashioned."

As they strolled down the broad boulevard of turf, Sarah caressed a hedge with her palm. It felt smooth and cool. In its way, the park was another world, one of glittering green and wide strolling paths. Sarah admired the deliberate balance of greenery and open spaces—a perfect harmony. She saw spots of sun soaking the grass beneath the trees and imagined herself spread out on a blanket enjoying a quiet afternoon with a book—or a lover. Sarah longed to sink into the grass as if it were a part of her and she of it. To make this place her home and not a stranger.

"Jean-Pierre, how long have you lived in Marseille?"

"My family moved here when I was a teenager. We lived in Paris until my dad got transferred." He tilted his head to the sky in thought. "I suppose that means I've been here for about twenty years."

"How long did it take to feel like home? Before you didn't feel like a tourist?"

"Hmm, I had a... difficult time in my teenage years. I felt like an outsider everywhere I went, so it took me many years, at least until my twenties, but none of that was Marseille's fault. Should you stay, I doubt it will take you so long."

Their trail ended in an open expanse of concrete across from a short, tree-lined road. Directly ahead was the backside of the fountain and the museums. It felt as if they had burrowed through a tunnel of green and emerged at a cave of treasures. The park side of the fountain was a half-moon shaped complex that connected two museums to the elaborate fountain. Although it looked quite old, as it was built in the mid-1800s, it had to be completely rebuilt after the heavy bombing of World War II.

"Here we are," Jean-Pierre said with outstretched hands. "It is time to make a decision. Natural history or art? Today, we only have time for one."

"Hmm." Sarah thought for a moment. "Let's try the art museum."

"Good choice, *mon ami*. You will like it."

The pair walked through the colonnade that connected the two museums, the park, and the fountain. Sarah couldn't resist snapping photos of the columns and golden roof.

Once inside, Sarah was in love. The building felt like a movie set in the Napoleonic era, but it was real. Everywhere she looked were inlaid arches and bifurcated columns overlaid with the artistic masters of the sixteenth and nineteenth centuries. The museum was small, but the quality was second to none.

The pair paused at a landscape of the French countryside from 1846.

"A lot has changed since then," remarked Jean-Pierre. "We've got some rural areas, but nothing that looks much like that anymore." He pointed to an overturned ox cart with straw that spilled out onto a dirt path, which led into a forest and adjacent to a small stream.

"No, I suppose not. But from what I've seen, it's still a beautiful country."

The two walked the small but splendid museum and took it all in. This was a classically European gallery. No modern art, mostly landscapes, portraits, and still lifes. It felt as if, for the gallery, art had stopped in about 1892. Regardless, to Sarah, it felt like a sacred space or some kind of holy ground. For a moment, part of her wondered what Michael would have said about it, but she shook off the thought as fast as it arose.

"Sarah, can I ask? Why did you come to Marseille, all the way from America? Why Avenir D'or? Why here?"

"Well..." Sarah paused and then chuckled. "They accepted me. Plus, Avenir D'or has everything I want: It's a world-class facility and a growing company. As far as Marseille goes, well, it looked beautiful on the internet, and it hasn't let me down yet."

"You weren't scared off by the stories? The perpetual rumors of crime and violence? Haven't you read those detective stories?" His accent made him sound very serious, though his tone was playful.

"No, a big city is a big city. I can't be afraid all the time. I try not to stay out too late and try to keep out of the more dangerous *arrondissements*."

"Ah, that must be the famous American optimism," Jean-Pierre said with a chuckle. "Seriously, though. You're right, but be careful. This city can get the better of you."

"Well, now you're scaring me. Am I being naive?"

"No, but it has happened to me, so it could happen to you."

"What happened?" she asked.

"I've been pick-pocketed once or twice. And... well, let's sit down." Jean-Pierre motioned to a nearby bench.

They sat on a bench in front of a flowing landscape of a beach with a distant sailing ship. Sarah watched Jean-Pierre's face as he turned serious. His bright cheerfulness had dimmed to a night-light of good humor shadowed by the morose.

"About ten years ago, I was coming home from a club about two in the morning. I'd had a little to drink and took a different way home, down a few roads I didn't know that well. As I walked, I heard shouts in a language I didn't understand. Before I knew it, a group of four men—boys really, probably sixteen or seventeen—had surrounded me." He paused and looked away. Sarah touched his shoulder and gave him a gentle smile.

He dabbed his face with a pocket handkerchief, then continued. "The group kept shouting and carrying-on. I still didn't understand them. They came closer and shouted a word I knew too well—faggot. Apparently, that word is the same in any language. Once I heard that, I knew I was in trouble."

Sarah fidgeted in her seat as Jean-Pierre's cadence hastened.

"They closed in around me. I can still see the grins of delight on their faces. I pushed one away from me and started to run, but the others grabbed me and started to punch and kick me. I fell to the ground, and then it all went black."

"Good lord, I'm so sorry," lamented Sarah.

"It took twenty-three stitches and three days in the hospital, but I became a wiser man. I was lucky they didn't kill me. I still don't know who they were or how I got to the hospital. Don't let this scare you, just remember to be careful."

"Yeah, I will."

"Okay." Jean-Pierre clapped his hands to his thighs and stood up. "Enough of these ghost stories. I promised you a trip to *Saveur Arménienne*, and I intend to deliver. Shall we go?" He raised one eyebrow in a comedic fashion to lighten the mood.

Back into the bustling city, away from the greenery and art, the pair traveled onward. After a few tram stops, they proceeded several blocks on foot. Exotic spices filled their noses, and their ears rang with the pounding rhythms of Moroccan music that blared over distant speakers. As they walked, they passed food stall after food stall of treats and delicacies from around the Mediterranean and northern Africa. Sarah's palate was intrigued and her senses intoxicated as she realized that she had only begun to scratch the surface of the culinary feast that was Marseille. With pleasure, she marched dutifully behind Jean-Pierre as they neared their destination.

A few more twists and turns later and they arrived at *Saveur Arménienne*. It was a modest eatery laid out with a bar and indoor seating on opposites sides of a central hallway with a large outdoor dining area from which one could see the whole restaurant.

They were seated inside with a pleasant view of the outdoors. The room was decorated in light browns, white, and purple, lending it a calming and exotic beauty. They ordered dinners of lentil kufta, lula kabob, rice pilaf, and salad. As they waited, they munched on fresh baked lavash bread and chatted quietly. A short while later, while eating, a robust figure came up behind Jean-Pierre and placed a hand on his shoulder. His face lit up as he turned around and greeted the man.

Sarah could see from the outset that the man had large, bear-like hands and the physicality of a middle-weight boxer who had gently aged into a jovial paunch.

"Sarah, this is my friend, Sarkis. This is his restaurant. Sarkis, this is Sarah."

"Good to meet you. You've got a nice place here. I love this food. How do you find produce so fresh?"

"Thank you, fresh from the market—all day. Please call me Sam. It's easier, plus, I like the brevity."

"Okay, Sam it is then," said Sarah with a smile. There was something commanding and calming about his intense but gregarious demeanor. Sarah warmed as she looked at him and felt at ease, like being in the presence of someone who had everything under control.

Sarah looked Sam over as best as she could in the dim light. He was a short, stocky, handsome man with round, brown eyes and a large, but well proportioned, nose. His hair was a shock of black with slight greying at the temples. Sarah couldn't help but be charmed by his vigorous smile. He looked like a younger, middle eastern Alec Baldwin.

Sarah was impressed. She wanted to say something cute and a little flirty, but as usual, she was at a loss, so she just smiled.

"Can you sit and chat with us for a while?" asked Jean-Pierre.

"That would be lovely, please do," added Sarah.

"I'm sorry, but I just came over to say hello. Unfortunately, I have to run." Sam's accent was unusual, full of harsh, pithy vowel sounds that Sarah found rustic and charming. "I'm on my way to the market to get more supplies. Momma needs me to get some more lettuce—fresh produce. Apparently, the runner didn't pick up enough."

Sam gave Jean-Pierre a hearty handshake and then turned to Sarah. Sam looked directly into Sarah's eyes and shook her hand. His large, paw-like hand completely enveloped hers. "Next time either of you are in, be sure to find me. We'll have a chat. *Au revoir!*" Sam hurried into the street through the loose metal gate that lined the outdoor seating.

"He's a good man. Keeps this place running and is good to his mother," said Jean-Pierre.

"He's handsome too. I'll have to come back and have a chat," replied Sarah with a grin.

"You should," agreed Jean-Pierre with a nod. "From what he tells me, his mother is always trying to fix him up with Armenian women from around town, but he's growing weary of it. Maybe he's looking for something a little different, more foreign?" They both laughed, and Jean-Pierre changed the subject. "By the way, did you hear they took your advice on that cream filling? They changed the formula and added almond extract."

"No, really? No one told me. That's awesome!"

"Yeah, it's great. Keep it up, and they just might offer you a job when this is all said and done."

"Did they say that?" asked Sarah with excitement.

"No one *said* anything," he smirked with a half-shrug. "But you never know."

CHAPTER 26

Sarah gazed up from her literary stack of *The Count of Monte Cristo* and her French-English dictionary and out the restaurant window. She ate inside because, although the sun was shining, the December winds had grown cold. Compared to American midwestern winters, Marseille was positively balmy, but her blood had thinned quickly, and the chill chased her indoors. It was a Sunday afternoon, and Sarah was taking some time to enjoy herself.

With her internship progressing, Sarah had spent the past week and a half rotating through other departments—marketing, warehouse, and quality—while utilizing any spare time in the lab.

Avenir D'or allotted interns discretionary time, and Sarah put it to good use. She had outlined a pair of new flavors: a spicy mushroom, and a red wine and roasted meat flavor. The latter was inspired by her culinary experiences in Marseille; an attempt to capture the intense richness of daube and the creamy feel of ratatouille. It was a work in progress, but the possibilities were intriguing.

Engrossed in the tale of revenge and adventure, Sarah hadn't noticed her near-empty wine glass nor the waiter as he approached.

"Voulez-vous plus de vin, mademoiselle?"

"Oui, un autre verre de vin, s'il vous plait," Sarah responded, a little startled but with proper pronunciation and an unmistakable American accent.

As she waited for wine, she watched the shopkeeper across the street set up his window for the Christmas holiday. Slow and cautious, he strung the lights from hook to hook around the sill and frame. A small tree and a pile of ornaments sat on the floor behind him and waited for their turn. Her thoughts drifted toward home. How many times had she and Loretta decorated the Kettle for the holidays? She wondered what design Loretta was doing this year. What were Bernie and all the regulars up to? It had been weeks since she last spoke with Loretta; the time difference always seemed to get in the way. Sarah missed her—her friendship, kind words, and warm encouragement.

Lost in thought, Sarah didn't hear the footsteps come up behind her. With a jolt, she was shaken out of her daze by the sharp sounds of a familiar voice.

"Sarah? Sarah Hall? Is that you?"

She knew the voice but could not believe it. The deep, rich baritone words coated in a light varnish of pretension; it could only be one person. She hoped she was wrong, but her heart was already beating faster. After a deep breath, she turned around with glacial urgency as she tried to prepare herself.

Her eyes locked with his, and her mouth turned dry in astonishment. Before her stood Michael P. Kensington, stylish as always in a pair of designer Levi's, an untucked DKNY shirt, and a brown leather bomber jacket. Sarah looked him over and realized her hands were sweating.

"Michael Kensington? Of all the gin joints, and you walk into mine. What are you doing here?" Sarah's voice was tinged with a teasing taunt to cover her feelings. She wanted to appear casual and indifferent, but inside she was awash with emotions. On one hand, she was perplexed by the fact that he was even there. On the other, she was still angry with him for leaving. But, damn if he didn't look good.

"That was North Africa, lovely, but I guess we're close enough," Michael responded with a chuckle. "I'm here visiting some friends for Christmas. I saw you in the window and had to stop in. I mean, what are *you* doing here?"

Michael was a shade or two darker than he had been back home. His dirty blond hair seemed brighter as well. Other than that, he appeared to be the same old Michael: cool, handsome, and well aware of it. So far from home, Sarah was overjoyed to see a familiar face but torn because that face belonged to Michael. Uncertain how to proceed, she tried her hand at cool and aloof.

"I live here. I'm doing an internship with Avenir D'or. I hope to stay on after the program is finished, but that remains to be seen. Either way, I'm getting experience and I get to live in France, on the Mediterranean."

Sarah's heart had still not calmed in her chest.

"That's great! Have you been here long—"

A voice from behind distracted Michael as he looked over his shoulder. A group of voices from the vestibule spoke to him. Michael hushed them and turned back to her.

"I have to go. My friends are getting restless. It was really nice to see you." Michael's eyes glowed as they sank into

Sarah's. The look left her disquieted. "I'm in town for a couple more weeks. Want to get together for a cup of coffee or something?"

Stay aloof, stay cool.

"If this were anywhere else in the world or any other time of year, I would say no. But seeing as we're both far from home, and it's the holidays, give me a call. I'll see what I can do."

From the look on his face, the coolness of Sarah's words worked. He seemed to take it as a bellwether of her feelings toward him. Nevertheless, he appeared genuinely excited to see her.

"Great, lovely. I look forward to catching up. See you later," Michael said, his eyes agleam as he hurried out the door.

As Michael disappeared, the waiter brought her wine. Sarah took a large gulp and attempted to turn back to her book but soon discovered it was no use. She'd been knocked through a loop and wasn't sure what to do about it. Despite the resentment that still clung to her innards like plaque, attraction lingered, and curiosity bubbled about his life in Spain. She wondered if it had lived up to his fantasies. On balance, most of her hoped it had not.

CHAPTER 27

Sarah crouched and stared into a black hole chiseled into a rock wall about the size of a small human being. She marveled at the gap and stood up, pacing out the roughhewn jail cell. "It's just like in the book," she said aloud to no one in particular. Sarah stood a mile offshore in the fortress known as the Chateau D'If, in the prison cell of the fictional Edmond Dantes.

The cell and much of the site had been prepared to amuse book lovers and tourists and happily mingled its fake history amongst its real past. This inclination toward schlock didn't bother Sarah in the least; the book had a special place in her heart and so too, then, this rock. After an extended gawk, Sarah headed to find Jean-Pierre.

Outside of the main building, ringed by a series of wide boulders, was a flat landing that served as a meeting place for tour groups and a seating area for the small café. Jean-Pierre stood on the tallest rock in the ring and stared back at the city. In a pair of tan slacks and a white button-up shirt with rolled sleeves, he looked refined but casual, his narrow but noble features awash in oranges and reds from the eventide sun.

"You know, coming here at sunset was a great choice! As long as I've lived here, I've never seen the city from this perspective. It is clear that I've been missing out."

Sarah stood up next to him and caught his view. "The city just emanates with the last wisps of light. It looks like the fading embers of a dying fire."

After they'd had their fill, the pair sat down at a nearby covered table and had a small pour of wine in stemless glasses. Sarah felt relaxed. She enjoyed Jean-Pierre's company; he was both pleasant and innocuous. He made her feel like she wasn't completely alone in a strange city.

"Jean-Pierre, can I ask you a personal question? I'm sure you've had your fair share of lovers, right?"

"Yes, of course," he answered in an amused tone.

"What would you do if an old flame who broke your heart showed up when you were four thousand miles from home?"

Jean-Pierre looked up, his face contorted as he grasped for something to say. He looked like a frog in danger but unable to decide whether to jump or swim. Sarah laughed at his distress and backtracked to explain her recent encounter with Michael.

"Hmm, I'm not sure I like the sound of this man, but clearly you are not sure what the flame in your heart is telling you. Is it out, or is it still smoldering?"

"I... I... don't know. It's complicated," said Sarah hesitantly.

The boatman called from the dock below, and the pair headed toward the last boat to Marseille, each stealing one last look at the city from the ancient fortress.

"Then let him call and hear him out, I suppose. There's no harm to be had. But listen to your heart," Jean-Pierre advised, his face radiating warmth.

They sat on the ship's upper deck and watched the city get closer and closer. A comfortable silence lay between them as the refreshing cool air and mists from the waves breaking on the bow below caressed their faces. Sarah glanced over and noticed Jean-Pierre's brow was furrowed and concerned; he was lost in thought.

"Something wrong? I hope my question about your lovers didn't upset you."

"No, no, I've just been thinking about Ms. Hackingham."

"Theresa? Why? Thinking about switching teams?" Sarah teased.

"Ah, Sarah! No," admonished Jean-Pierre.

"What is it then?"

He sat quietly for a moment. He had the look of a man trying to decide whether to dive off a pier into cold water or just go back to his lounge chair on the beach. "Can I tell you something? I overheard something the other day that has bothered me since, and I need to tell someone."

"Yes, of course."

"You have to promise not to tell anyone."

"I promise."

Jean-Pierre removed his glasses and rubbed his eyes with the palms of his hands. After a deep breath he replaced his glasses and started to speak.

"Okay... so... Ms. Hackingham and I were in the lab on Wednesday, working on a new formula. Marc came in and told her she had a phone call from upstairs. She tried to push it off, but they insisted. Frustrated at the interruption, she took the call in the side room, just off the lab. Before I knew it, her voice was very angry. I tried not to listen, but what could I do, the divider is just that curtain thing. I've never heard her so mad. She was cursing and using words I've never heard. She sounded like... how do you say... a sailor. Even her accent shifted."

"Geez, what happened?"

"From what I could tell, they are pushing her out of her VP role and moving her to a Consultant Director of Sales. Thereby moving her to an outside status, not an actual employee. I assume they're trying to save money. Also, she will no longer have any direct reports."

"Poor Ms. Hackingham. I like her, she's been kind to me."

"That's not all." He paused for a breath. "You were mentioned too."

"Me?"

"She asked about her role supervising your internship. They wanted to give you to Marc, but she fought to keep you. You're her last."

"That's terrible." Sarah shook her head as the sea-breeze blew her curls into her face.

"Yes. They claimed that she can serve the company better in this new role, but I think they're just trying to wax the swine."

"Wait, what?"

"Umm, that's not the expression?" Jean-Pierre asked, confused.

Sarah thought for a moment and started to laugh. "Oh, I think I know what you mean—put lipstick on a pig."

"Yes, that's it. Some of the idioms still get me. You know, there are times when I wonder how long before the corporate types come for us all. Today it's Hackingham, tomorrow, any of us."

"Is this sort of thing common?"

"A little too common. They like to 'restructure' when someone at the top needs more money. Ha."

The boat pulled into Vieux Port, and the pair disembarked.

"Remember, not a word," Jean-Pierre reminded her.

They walked down the dock toward the gate. Sarah was discomfited by the news about Ms. Hackingham and wondered what else the company had up its sleeve. Should she worry? Corporate machinations had always been somewhat of a mystery to her, but she knew enough to be wary.

"Want to grab some dinner?" asked Sarah in an attempt to shift the tone and save an evening.

"How about *Saveur Arménienne*?" responded Jean-Pierre with a grin.

"Sure, my heart is already confused, why not confuse it more? At least my stomach knows what it wants."

Sarah and Jean-Pierre were seated at a small table just beyond the bar, tucked into a corner where the building opened to the outdoor seating. After placing their orders, Sarah excused herself and went to the restroom.

As she returned, she spotted Sam chatting with Jean-Pierre. The words weren't clear, but a slight rumble emitted from their table. Sarah watched Sam's arms flail in convivial chatter. Sweat formed under her arms, and her hands went clammy as her nerves crept up on her. There was something about Sam she liked, definitely a connection, but Sarah was surprised by her reaction.

Sarah pinned herself to the wall and took a few deep breaths in order to calm down before heading back to the table.

"Good evening. It is so good to see you again," Sam said, his voice friendly but rough around the edges, as he reached out his hand.

Their hands touched and, despite the size difference, they connected like a shuttle docking the space station. The strong but gentle touch of his grip impressed Sarah. He had large, broad hands like a gorilla, but they were soft like the pads on a cat's paw. She hoped he hadn't noticed her anxiety-moistened hands.

"Good to see you again. Do you have time to chat with us today?" Sarah fell back to her salesperson-persona to hide her nerves. The server brought their food: two plates of sarma, fried kufta, rice pilaf, and salad.

"Ah, yes, I have a few minutes. The evening rush will be here soon, but until then, I'm all yours." Sam looked directly at Sarah as he spoke with only a slight glance toward Jean-Pierre. "We were just talking about your trip to the Chateau D'If. Jean-Pierre says you're an authority, know all about it, read the book and everything. Sounds like somewhere I need to go."

For Sarah, the rush had already begun. "You definitely should. I'll go with you and give you a personal tour, now that I'm an expert and all," Sarah said with a chuckle. Her nerves eased somewhat.

"I'd like that. He also tells me you're an expert in chemistry too?" Sam wagged his thumb in the direction of Jean-Pierre.

Sarah laughed. "I don't know about that, but I know a few things."

"You know a lot of things about a lot of things," added Jean-Pierre. "You should hear her talk about umami. She's studied it to the hilt. And daube; she analyzes it like it's the cure for cancer and savors it like it's filet mignon and ambrosia rolled into one."

Jean-Pierre laughed and padded her gently on the shoulder.

"What can I say? I like food and I'm a curious person."

"Is that so? What sorts of things are you curious about?" asked Sam in a low voice.

"Oh, you know, this and that. Not just food. I like to know why things work the way they do. Why things taste the way they do. Or how those tastes change when *heat* is applied," she said with a smirk. "But other things too. For example, in the hallway, I saw a bunch of neat, kind of art deco style posters, but what is Near East Relief? I've never heard of it."

Sam turned solemn. His smile trimmed to a small, flat line. Sarah wondered if she'd said something wrong.

"How much do you know about the Armenian people?" asked Sam.

"Not very much, I'm afraid. Most of what I know comes from eating at this restaurant."

"Hmm, that's not unusual. We are a tiny, landlocked country, surrounded by neighbors who would rather we not exist. I don't want to put you off your dinner, but the history is quite ghastly."

Sarah frowned a little and shifted in her seat. This wasn't where she wanted to go.

"During the first World War, the Ottoman-Turks instituted a plan to extinguish us for good. They killed the leaders, intellectuals, and young men and sent the rest—women, children, elderly—to march through the desert to their deaths. Over a million died." Sam's face was dark, his words sharp-edged and quiet as if in confession.

"Holy shit. Didn't anyone do anything about it? Where was the US and everyone else?" Sarah asked incredulously.

"It's more complicated than one would think, unfortunately, and I'll spare you the details. Basically, Near East Relief was created to raise money to help the victims of the genocide—Armenians, Assyrians, Greeks—namely the orphans left behind by the massacre. They distributed those posters to raise awareness and money."

Sarah's eyes widened. She looked over her shoulder and tried to catch a glimpse of the posters in the hallway.

"I have been a collector of original Relief posters my whole life," Sam continued. "I hang them here, along with the other ephemera—family photographs, newspaper clippings, and so on—as a reminder. We must never forget, lest it happen again; to us or anyone else."

Sam's voice grew a little louder, and his eyes lit up as he spoke as if a fire in the pit of his soul had been fed. "That said, we cannot let our past hamper our future. If we bind up our future in collective victimhood, then the perpetrators continue to win. And *that* we cannot allow."

Sarah was astonished. She felt as if someone had handed her a chapter to a book she'd thought she's already read.

"Wow, no one ever taught *me* that in school." As shocked as she was to hear about the fate of his people, she couldn't help but find his passion both impressive and alluring. Though, on the whole, she wished she hadn't broached the subject. In her mind, it was a charming flirt that might lead to a lively art discussion, but instead it turned the conversation somewhere she wished it hadn't gone. Some expert in *chemistry*.

"How did you end up here, Sam?" asked Jean-Pierre.

"My grandparents escaped in 1915, and like many Armenians, came to Marseille. France is our home now. We are French, but we are still Armenian, you know?" added Sam proudly. "I've lived here all my life. Armenia is my ancestral home, but France is *my* home."

The trio sat in silence for a few moments as Sarah and Jean-Pierre caught up on their food. Sarah looked up and noticed the room was suddenly full and crowded with only a single vacant table.

"All right, my friends," Sam said. "The time has come for me to return to my duties. This ship will not sail itself."

"Thanks for joining us," said Sarah sweetly.

"Yes, it was nice," added Jean-Pierre.

"I'm glad we got to talk," Sam said as he stood up and leaned toward Jean-Pierre with an outstretched hand. "It is always nice to see you. Thanks for coming in."

Sam took a few steps around the table and stood directly before Sarah, his stocky frame like a boulder. "Sarah, it was most pleasant to have your company. Please come back soon. We can discuss more pleasant topics: art, music, football, or whatever else you might be curious about. I would like to hear more about your chemistry."

Sam headed to the kitchen as Jean-Pierre and Sarah finished their meal and parted company for the evening.

During the dark walk home, Sarah was buzzed about her time with Sam. She wandered toward her apartment in absentminded glee. After a while, the feeling was quelled as a wave of uneasiness rolled over her. She realized the streets had narrowed and gone quiet. Everything felt still, less crowded, like an air raid drill or the wake of an oncoming storm. A short distance ahead, she saw a small group of teenage boys kicking a ball back and forth. They talked feverishly amongst themselves, but she couldn't hear their words. It all seemed innocuous enough. However, in the pit of her stomach, something didn't feel right.

The group of boys moved toward her. Sarah attempted to move to the side, but it was no use. The ball hit her leg with a soft thud. One of the boys approached with a little, nervous smile and apologized as he retrieved the ball. A moment later, a blur of boys ran past her in a hustle of commotion. They shouted to each other as if in victory and disappeared around the corner. A lightness came across her—her shoulder bag was gone. Her legs pushed off, ready to sprint after them, but it was pointless. They were gone.

Sarah stood in the middle of the sidewalk, shocked, uncertain of what to do next. Instinctively, she checked her front pockets—wallet and phone still there. Thank goodness she wore *those* pants. Gratitude washed over her. At least it was only the bag, which was empty but for the Dumas novel and dictionary. *Maybe the little bastards will learn something.*

The anger hit her first, followed by fear. She felt like a deer grazed by a shot and didn't want to be alone. Sarah backtracked toward the Avenue Alexandre Fleming in hopes of finding crowds and a bus station. Not knowing where else to turn, she called Jean-Pierre. Voicemail. *Shit.*

Sarah quickened her pace and scrolled through her phone—Theresa, Marc, Josephine—all work numbers. Wait, *Sam.* She found the number to *Saveur Arménienne* and called. In near-panic-speak, she explained what happened.

Sam's voice was calm and authoritative. "Don't worry, you will be fine. Where are you?"

She'd made it a few blocks and explained her location. "There's a drugstore a block north; you'll be safe there. I'll catch a cab and be there in ten minutes."

The pharmacy was a small, family run-type of place but was open and welcoming enough. The narrow shelves had all one would expect. In the far corner, Sarah found the coffee and poured a cup. Before long, a grey taxi pulled to the curb, and Sam dashed into the store. After a few pleasantries, he shepherded her into the car, and they settled in for the drive.

"Thanks for coming to get me. I know it's a hassle to—"

"Don't mention it. I always help my friends." Sam waved his hand as if swatting her concern away. His brown eyes shone with warmth.

"I was so scared," Sarah said. "In the first few moments I wasn't, but then as I walked... I got more and more scared. They could have killed me, or worse." A pair of tears cascaded from her eyes. In small sips, the warm coffee calmed her as Sam placed a reassuring hand on her shoulder.

"You're safe now."

Sarah placed her hand over his and smiled solemnly.

For a few moments, they shared a comfortable silence until the cab pulled up to Sarah's apartment and she went in.

Once inside, Sarah felt relieved and grateful. Sam's swift action and warm presence had made her feel safe. She liked it.

CHAPTER 28

Sarah was returning to her desk with a steaming cup of Darjeeling when she noticed Marc was in his office with the door open.

"Hi, do you have a few minutes?"

"Sure," he said with a nod. "What can I do for you?"

"Would it be all right if I came in during break and used the lab? I've been scratching out a few things in my notebook, and I'd like to try them out."

"That's fine." He nodded and seemed indifferent. "Are the holidays making you restless? It can be difficult to be away from home this time of year, huh?"

He rubbed the back of his bald head as he spoke as if smoothing non-existent hair. Sarah had watched him do it in meetings when others were talking, and it seemed like a way to sooth himself.

"A little, I suppose, but there's not much for me at home these days."

"But still, it hits harder this time of year. I remember, ages ago, I was training in Japan and was there over Christmas and… Well, sometimes you'd just rather be home."

"I know what you mean," Sarah said and tried to be agreeable. "But I'm hoping to make my life here, so I'm getting used to it."

"Hmm," Marc said, curling his mouth. Sarah wondered if he doubted her resolve.

She turned to leave but stopped herself.

"Can I ask you something?" Sarah continued without waiting for an answer. "How am I doing here? We're getting to the halfway point, and I want to make sure I'm on the right track."

"You should really talk to Theresa. But I know she's been harder to get ahold of now that she's switched roles." He leaned back in his chair and placed his arms loosely on his desk. "Speaking for myself, I think you're doing well. Theresa sent over your report, and your observations about our product portfolio and future trend predictions were insightful and astute."

"Thanks, I'm glad. I really like it here."

Sarah stood in his small office trying to decide whether to leave or ask what was on her mind.

"Can I ask one more thing? I know it's none of my business, but I've seen a few things about new curry-flavored products, heard a few rumors too, and... Well, this morning, I saw a pair of men who looked... um... very Indian in here speaking with you."

"Sarah... Sarah... Look, I'm not really at liberty to say." He got quiet, nearly a whisper and rubbed the back of his head. "Unofficially, between the two of us, they were from the second-largest distributor in India. We're trying to open up a new market there."

"Oh, I didn't see that coming in my report. That would be huge! That would require expanding several departments—more jobs—possibly a lot more, depending on the size of the deal, including R&D, right?" Her voice was soft but unmistakably excited.

The research for her report focused on the current business. She hadn't even considered market expansion until that moment.

"Yes, if it works out. We've been keeping it quiet until we have something firm. Though, as you've picked up on, we've been doing some tests and preparations internally. The company has put a lot into this, and if it goes well, it would be a sizable expansion. If it doesn't, well..."

Marc's voice trailed off. Sarah barely noticed she was too excited at the prospect of an expansion, especially at R&D. She was so close she could smell it. In this case, like curry.

"Is it too early to apply? I really love it here and—"

"Whoa, whoa, hang on," Marc cut her off. "There is nothing to apply to; there is no deal. If it even happens, it could still be months away."

"Right, of course." Her disappointment was palpable.

"Don't fret. Just keep working hard. We'll see how it goes."

Sarah paced her small living room in excitement with alternated stares between the street below and her little Miró. The conversation with Marc had fired her hopes of landing a job at Avenir D'or, and she needed to share her excitement with someone, so she called Loretta. It was late afternoon back home, and much to Sarah's surprise, Loretta picked up on the second ring.

"Sarah, honey. How's it going? Merry Christmas!" The holidays always brought out the best in Loretta.

"It's going great," Sarah said and filled her in on what had transpired.

"Wonderful! I'm so proud of you. You've worked so hard. You know, I have some news as well. I'm thinking about finding a partner to buy into the Kettle and eventually take it over."

Sarah went quiet. *How could someone else take over the Kettle?* In her mind, it was Loretta's and always would be.

"Wait! Really? Why?"

"Well, I'm getting older—not too old, mind you—but older. I'm starting to think about retiring-retiring and spending more time with my grand-babies."

"That makes sense. Just make sure you get someone good—someone you can trust. The Kettle is too important to go to just anyone."

Sarah didn't like the idea but tried to play along.

"You're right, honey. We've all poured our passion into this place; we've made it something special. That's my New Year's resolution this year. To start looking for a partner. I'll put my feelers out and see what I can find. If I don't find anyone, I'll just keep it running until I simply don't want to do it anymore. We'll see. I'll keep you in the loop."

"I'm sure you'll find someone good. I know I'm way out here, but let me know if I can be of any help."

"I will. I have to go now. I've got some friends coming over for a late Christmas party, and I have to finish glazing the ham. It was nice to hear from you."

"Sounds great. Have fun with them. Happy holidays, again."

When Sarah ended the call, she felt happy but hollowed. It felt good to talk to someone who knew her and who really cared. The fate of the Kettle weighed on her mind; she couldn't imagine it in anyone's hands but Loretta's. For the first time in months, homesickness set in, and it dawned on her that she might have been wrong when she spoke to Marc that afternoon. She did have something at home, and she missed it.

CHAPTER 29

The *La Bouche du Lion* was one of the oldest and best-liked bars in Marseille. Steps away from the Old Port, it was a unique place where the elite, tourists, and regular citizens alike mingled for good drinks and revelry. Even camaraderie if *Olympique de Marseille* was on TV. Aside from its central location and the people watching, the other main attraction of the *La Bouche du Lion* was its patriotic decor. Both splendid and flashy, the bar featured a theme based on the Marseille coat of arms. It had a magnificent and regal silver ceiling—silver leaf over tin—in a repeated pattern of crowns, bulls, and lions; a white marble floor; and a white bar with silver and blue accents. Behind the bar was a cast concrete sculpture of the Marseille coat of arms three meters wide. There was also a spectacular side room, known as *La Chamber de la République*, or the Republic Room, that was decorated with the same marble floor but featured a motif based on the French Tricolor.

Sarah sat at an open-sided booth in the middle of the bar and admired her surroundings. It was open and visible and, most importantly, not too intimate. Initially she'd agreed only to coffee but conceded to drinks when Michael suggested the *La Bouche du Lion*. It had a reputation as a must-see spot in Marseille, and Sarah welcomed the excuse to check it out.

The light from the bar glared off the crystal of her watch in colorful beams of blue and silver as she checked the time: 7:38. Michael was late. Unsurprised, Sarah sat and sipped her pinot noir. She happily relaxed and absorbed the atmosphere. A few minutes later, looking casual and unperturbed by his tardiness, Michael sauntered in wearing a light grey jacket and trousers with a black button-up shirt, partially unbuttoned. *Apparently, he thinks it is a date. He dressed up.* Michael stopped at the bar and ordered a Johnny Walker Black on the rocks and nodded in approval as he surveyed his surroundings. The bartender handed him the glass, and Michael promenaded over to the booth and slid in across from her.

"You look fantastic! Thanks for meeting me." A broad smile bloomed on his lips as he wiped the condensation off his glass with a small napkin square. "I dig this place. My friends suggested I check it out. I certainly regret not doing so sooner."

"Thanks, Michael, but I'm wise to your charms," Sarah said seriously but with a smile. She wore a simple pair of Levi's and a ruffled white blouse. Her long brown curls fell down past her shoulders and covered her semi-open neckline. Backlit by the blue and silver lighting, she looked like a saint—unadorned, plain, but very beautiful.

"Whoa, okay, okay. I'm just glad you agreed to meet me. I've been thinking about you since the other week—before then, really." He paused and took a sip of scotch. "I've been looking forward to catching up."

"It sure was a surprise to see you." Sarah shook her head, still somewhat astonished at running into Michael in Marseille. "I never expected to see anyone from back home, especially you."

"Well, Spain isn't so far away, you know? Now that you're out here, do you talk to the folks back home much? How's your mom doing?

Sarah looked away and repositioned herself in her seat. Her mind drifted to thoughts of Nancy's ashen body in its thin nightgown; her slow, drawn-out words saying "...you're leaving me... am I gonna die alone..." To avoid tears, she shifted her attention back to Michael.

"And what about the lady at the tea shop? What was her name? How is she?"

"Loretta. She's fine," Sarah said, a little testy. "My mother, on the other hand..." Sarah trailed off. She didn't want to talk about Nancy, but she had to tell him. "My mother had an accident and passed away. It's fine, but I really don't want to talk about it."

"Sarah, that's terrible. I'm so sorry. I didn't know." Michael's voice was soft and apologetic. His face showed that he understood the pain of loss and how the nerves lie so close to the surface covered only by shallow scabs. He took a long drink of his Johnny Walker. "How are you enjoying life on the Mediterranean? It's a far cry from the old Midwest, isn't it?" His voice was cheery now, as if he wanted to get onto something light and agreeable and away from the subject of Nancy as fast as possible.

"I love it. I love that the sun shines all year. I love being able to dine al fresco most of the time. I've adapted well." Sarah played casually with her hair as she took a sip of her pinot. "So, how have you been? Still teaching?"

"Yeah, still teaching. I'm in the same village, a little way outside of Barcelona. I still like it. The town is nice and the people are great, but I think it is getting a little stale. I am starting to think about what to do next."

"What does come next? You were so in love with that village, it's hard to think you could replace it with anything." A tinge of bitterness coated her words.

"Honestly, I'm not sure yet. I've just had this feeling for the last six months or so that it may be time for a change. Maybe I'll go to Italy and brush up on my Italian. I have a few friends there; I'm sure I could find a teaching gig. After all, when you speak as many languages as I do, you can usually find something."

"I suppose that's true," Sarah said as she shook her head and rolled her eyes a little. "How many languages do you speak now?"

"Five, or seven if you count the smattering of Polish and Czech I picked up while traveling. Recently, I've been working on my Portuguese. I'm not fluent-fluent, but I could have a pretty decent conversation. Once you know Spanish and Italian, most of Portuguese just kinda falls in line," Michael said light-heartedly. "Have you been working on your French?"

"Yes, it's coming along nicely, or, *Oui, je pense que je vais très bien.* I've been reading Dumas—*The Count of Monte Cristo*—in French. Or, at least, I was. It was a slog, but I got through most of it. I got more out of it in French, but that could just be because I'm reading it again."

The waiter saw that their drinks were running low and politely inserted himself into the conversation. "*Excusez-moi, monsieur et madame, aimeriez-vous un autre verre?*"

"*Oui, s'il vous plaît,*" responded Michael before Sarah had an opportunity to speak. "*La même chose.*"

"Michael, you didn't need to order for me. I really don't need another drink."

"Sorry, I just assumed..." The look on Michael's face was a combination of terror and incredulity.

Sarah could tell that he hadn't meant to cross a line but seemed to want to pick up where they'd left off. She realized she'd over reacted. "It's okay." She waved it off. "Never mind."

"Tell me about your job." Michael leaned back. "Where are you working?" He was back to cool and casual.

"Well, at the moment, I'm interning with Avenir D'or." Sarah told him about the day-to-day of her internship and how much she'd learned.

"Sounds like a great opportunity." Encouragement warmed his words. "I'm glad to hear that you've had such success." He stopped and looked into her face. "You know, Sarah, your eyes have the brightest sparkle, especially when talking about something you care about, like your work. It's really stunning."

Michael's eyes had turned glassy. Either that second drink was hitting him hard, or he'd had a couple before he arrived.

"Thanks, Michael. That is sweet of you to say." Her tone was flat and polite. His flattery still worked, but she didn't want to show it.

"Do you ever miss home?" Michael asked.

"Yeah, I do. Sometimes. I miss the familiarity of knowing where everything is and all of the fun spots, all the memories. But it is also nice to be away. Really, my dad's gone, my mom's gone, not much to miss there." Sarah shrugged. "I miss Loretta and Bernie a lot, though. And the Kettle and those folks. It's strange to think of it, but Loretta is probably my best friend. She's twice my age, but she is truly great and has been there for me through everything, my mother's death especially. You know, I don't think I've said that out loud before."

Her candor surprised her. She'd meant to keep it simple and ended up telling him the truth.

"I understand that," said Michael in a banal fashion. "How long are you going to stay abroad, then?"

"I don't really know. I hope to launch my career and see where it takes me. I think I want to end up back in the States eventually, but who knows? It could be in a few months if things don't go well here or could be a decade or more if my career takes off. How about you? Are you planning on going back?"

"It's funny, I've asked myself the same question lately. I guess if I found the right opportunity, I'd do it. Which is more than I would have said a few months ago. After all, it is a big country. I'm sure there is something I can find."

The crowd had gotten denser and seemed to consist of mostly tourists. Sarah wondered if a cruise ship had decamped. Sarah and Michael looked at each other in silence. For a moment, it felt like the old days: bantering conversation interspersed with punctuated silences. Michael took another drink of scotch and then spoke.

"You know, Sarah, I can't get over how good you look. I can't put my finger on what it is, but you... just... look... stunning. Have you done something different to your hair? It shines."

Sarah thanked him for the compliment. It seemed to mean a lot less when he was drunk. She could tell he was trying to get into her good graces and was suspicious about his motivations. She found herself conflicted. Half of her, the lizard-brain half, was still intensely attracted to him and twitterpated with every compliment. The other half, the thinking-half, remembered how it turned out last time and was wise to his game. She started to look for a way out of the conversation. When the waiter came around again, Sarah found her opportunity.

"*Excusez-moi, monsieur et madame, aimeriez-vous un autre verre?*" asked the waiter for the second time.

"*Non, merci beaucoup.* My friend has had more than enough. *Puis-je avoir l'addition, s'il vous plait?*" Sarah said, not noticing that she had switched to English. She was quick to answer this time.

"I can get this," Michael said as the waiter brought the bill, his voice a little slurred. Michael covered it with his hand to avoid Sarah from taking it first. "You were nice enough to meet me. The least I can do is pay."

"At this point, Michael, I'm not going to argue with you."

Michael paid the bill as they stood up to say their goodbyes. Sarah thanked him and offered a polite hug.

As she left, Sarah felt a pang of uncertainty worm through her. She was simultaneously flattered and repulsed by Michael's behavior and, though she wouldn't say it out loud, she loved compliments from him. Nevertheless, she could not ignore the hurt he had put her through. She tidied it away in her mind that it was nice to see him and that was that. She'd worn her helmet.

CHAPTER 30

Sarah took a big sip of pinot noir and clicked her pen open and closed with obsessive persistence. The previous evening, she'd received an email from Loretta to "set up a call," something they'd never done before. Usually, they just picked up the phone. Loretta's "something important to discuss" had Sarah both intrigued and concerned. Now, all she could do was wait.

The clock on the wall ticked, 6:58 and counting, second-by-second. So close, so curious. The hour turned over and the call came through—exactly on time. Sarah set it to speaker and set the phone on the wood-look coffee table. After a brief flurry of pleasantries, Loretta got straight to it. She was in business mode.

"Do you remember when I said I was looking for a partner to help with the Kettle?" Loretta asked, her voice even but with an undercurrent of excitement.

"Yes. Have you found someone? Who are they? How much is the Kettle going to change?" Sarah clicked open the pen and held it down with her thumb. Her nerves were getting the better of her.

"I found someone, kind of," Loretta answered. "See, I've spent the last few months looking for, and examining, potential partners. I reached out to friends back at Smith and Broderick's as well as folks I know at the Chamber."

Sarah released her thumb from the pen top and examined the imprint mindlessly as she listened to Loretta.

"I've had some serious interviews with several candidates, all with great portfolios and pockets deeper than the Mariana Trench but none of them had passion... no spark for tea or our customers. Savvy businesspeople for sure—all of them would have this place ringing. But they all wanted to make the wrong kinds of changes."

Sarah put down the pen and curled her hair around her finger. The idea of changing the Kettle unsettled her. She fidgeted on the couch.

"All they wanted to talk about was branding, expansion, franchising, and so on, but none talked about customer experience or 'little extras.' It's been eye-opening but also frustrating and stressful. Then, it came to me."

"Who?" asked Sarah, both excited and fearful.

Sarah was sitting up bolt straight and staring in concentration at the blank phone screen. She listened to Loretta's voice and could hear the tension in it as Loretta took a breath before continuing.

"I think it should be you. I think you should be my partner at the Kettle."

"Me?" Sarah asked as if she'd just touched a hot pan. "I don't have any money. I could never afford to buy into something like that. Plus, I'm way over here."

Sarah's mind searched for possibilities about how Loretta's idea might play out. None of it made sense. She silenced her thoughts and just listened.

"Right, well, here's what I was thinking. You've worked with me for a long time. I know I can trust you and that your heart is in the right place. Your hard work has helped make the Kettle what it is today."

Sarah smiled to herself in quiet pride.

"Not a day goes by that I don't get one of the regulars asking after you. You have certainly left your mark on this place. So, in my mind, you've built up some sweat equity. I'll give you credit for that, and the rest will be part of your compensation as we move forward. After a certain amount of time, you'll be a full partner. Your investment is your work, not your money."

That was a revelation to Sarah. It had never occurred to her that she could work toward some kind of ownership.

"I'm not sure what to say, Loretta. I'm flattered and appreciative, but... I mean, I'm in France. My internship is nearly over; I'm hoping for a job offer. It's an open question, but there's a chance." Her speech was fast and spaceless, the words flowing without a breath. "I am really going to have to think about it."

"I know, honey. I wouldn't have it any other way. I know I'm throwing this at you with no warning, and you've got a lot on your plate. So, I'll tell you what."

Sarah grabbed her pen, poised to record Loretta's plan.

"Think about it. Just think about it. Take your time. No decision this big should be entered into on a whim. Take some time to reflect, then let me know."

With a deep exhale, Sarah jotted down *think about it* in a hurried hand.

"I will. This is really exciting. Everything is happening all at once. Things go from simple to complex very quickly."

"Well, if you decide to come home, you have something to come home to. Also, if I may tempt you further, I've been thinking about starting a new line of teas. It would be for new and unusual flavors—stuff outside the norm—and we could brand them 'Select.' I would put you in charge of developing the line—free rein over the flavors and everything."

Sarah's mind kicked into overdrive. She thought about all the success she'd had with her blends. Quickly, she started to imagine what she could do with a whole lineup. She jotted down a few flavor ideas as Loretta continued.

"I don't know if that would scratch your itch or not, but it's available to you."

"That'd be awesome! It's a wonderful idea." Sarah paused. "I think I could serve well in that role. I just need time to think."

"No problem, honey. Finish your internship and consider it. We'll talk soon, okay?"

"Okay."

"Alright, that's settled for now. I'll talk to you soon, goodbye."

Sarah hung up the phone and found herself elated but overwhelmed. Loretta's offer was generous and enticing, but she wasn't sure she was willing to give up on her dream of being a food scientist; not so close to the moment, or so she hoped.

With her eyes closed, she imagined what both lives might be like. On one side, she visualized herself as co-owner of the Kettle, developing a new line of products and learning firsthand how to build a successful business. As her mind felt the metes and bounds of the idea, she began to wonder if joining Loretta at the Kettle would really be a foreclosure of her dream. New blends might only be a start.

Then, her thoughts turned to Avenir D'or, and she saw herself submitting her new flavors and expanding their products to include her ideas. She hoped an opportunity would come.

As she thought, something stuck in the back of her mind: Ms. Hackingham. They pushed her out as VP and into that outside role—and she had thirty years of experience. What could they do to Sarah, an aging newbie just out of school? Her mind churned.

CHAPTER 31

Sarah hustled her way through the packed streets of Marseille. The spectacular morning sun bathed the city in deep oranges and scarlets that reflected off the tiled roofs and made the ancient city sparkle like a jewel in the desert. The blue doors at Avenir D'or swished open as she arrived and hurried through the turnstiles. She flashed her badge at Gunter, who tapped his watch and shook his head in jest. As the elevator zipped up its cable to the fourth floor, Sarah's phone rang with a jittery buzz. *Who would be calling me now?* Sarah fished her phone out of her purse. A local number, but one she didn't recognize.

"*Bonjour*," answered Sarah in a hurried but cheery voice.

"Good morning, lovely. Gone native?"

"Michael? I'm about to start work. What do you want? Is something wrong?" Her voice was quiet, but her words were firm.

"No," he responded, a little taken aback. "Everything is fine. I'm in town; I'd like to see you. I've been thinking about our meeting at the Lion, and I need to see you."

"I really don't have time right now. I've got work due, and I have projects to finish before next week."

"C'mon, lovely. It's Friday! How about this weekend? They're having an art fair downtown." Michael was cheerful and his voice slick.

"I can't, I'm sorry. I've got too much to do."

"I'm only in town until Tuesday. Can we meet up sometime? It's important," Michael pleaded.

Sarah reached her cubicle and set her things on her desk. A quick glance at the clock—two minutes before nine. "Look, Michael, you just picked a really bad time. Everything is happening at once. My internship is almost over, and I've got so much to finish up. I've got to go."

"Wait, wait, wait. It's important, just give me thirty minutes. How about Monday, we'll meet for lunch?"

"I can't, I have a lunch meeting."

"How about Tuesday?"

"Ugh, I have to go. Can we just talk about this later?"

Out of the corner of her eye, she spotted Marc headed in her direction.

"Okay, okay. Lunch on Tuesday, there's a café in the hotel lobby," Michael pleaded.

"Okay, fine, but I have an important meeting with my boss that afternoon that I cannot be late for! So, I only have the lunch hour."

He gave her the name of the hotel, and she hurried off the phone.

Her weekend was a blur of work and preparation. However, in the small gaps, the quiet moments between hustle, her thoughts sometimes jumped to Michael. She couldn't help but be curious about what was so urgent that he'd agree to a hurried lunch. A quick meal wasn't in his vocabulary. On

Sunday night, as she packed her workbag for the following day, she thought about the call from Michael. The fact that she'd brushed him off made her feel terrible. She looked forward to seeing a familiar face, especially of someone who knew her so well. But, after the episode at the Lion, she didn't know what to expect. She wondered where her relationship with Michael really stood. Were they friends? Acquaintances? Or simply ex-lovers?

The week ahead worried her. Would her meeting with Ms. Hackingham bring an offer or would it be thanks but no thanks? There had been no more news about the India deal, and Sarah feared that Theresa would simply praise her work and wish her well. In her year with the company, Sarah had learned that the inner workings of large corporations were often opaque and mysterious or, more cynically, cruel and fickle. All she could do now was prepare the best she could and leave it at that. The rest was out of her hands.

Her stomach grumbled and forced her to think about more immediate concerns. It had been a busy day, so she decided to reward herself with dinner at *Saveur Arménienne*. She had a craving for their beef kebab and rice pilaf—with a side of seeing Sam.

A benefit to life in southern France was an amiable climate that made outdoor dining a way of life, a habit Sarah assimilated readily. Her table was of black iron shaded by a red, blue, and orange umbrella. It was the perfect place to watch the world go by and sip a cold Kotayk lager as the Sunday evening slipped into dusk. As the people passed, the shoppers, the tourists, the right-angled old ladies, Sarah wondered what their lives were like. Who and what did they love? From her outdoor vantage point, she had an equally good view of the restaurant and liked to alternate between her imaginings about the lives of passersby and the hustle and bustle of the inner workings of the restaurant. This kept her entertained as she awaited her food and kept an eye out for Sam.

Though uncertain about her status with Michael, she knew that she found Sam's passion and rustic, casual demeanor charming. Plus, after her mugging, she knew he was reliable. Without a doubt, he was someone she wanted to know better; a friend if not a lover, but she discounted no possibilities. If what Jean-Pierre said were true, then Sarah wanted to get in the mix before it was too late and one of his mother's matches actually clicked. The thought revved her competitive engine.

By the time her steaming hot plate of rice pilaf and beef kabab arrived, Sarah was famished. The tender morsels of meat melted in her mouth as she savored every bite and washed it down with a second cold Kotayk. With only the last bits of salad and pilaf on her fork tines, she spied a familiar silhouette as it moved down the hallway. The silhouette emerged into the glowing evening sunlight like an entertainer into the spotlight and began to work the room. It was Sam.

Sarah's heart pulsed a little faster as she watched Sam walk up and down the tight rows of outdoor tables. One at a time, he worked each table with a quick chat and a handshake. The diners smiled and laughed readily at his quick jokes and convivial compliments. A few tables in, Sam noticed Sarah on the far end and motioned that he would stop over. As he squeezed his way across the seating area, sucking in his little paunch, Sarah thought he looked like a cute bear on an obstacle course. The thought made her laugh to herself and steadied her nerves. When he finally reached Sarah, he shook her hand with a mighty heave. She felt her hand tingle and his strength course through her palm as they touched. It felt electric.

"Sarah! Good to see you. I kept hoping I'd see you again soon."

"You too," Sarah said with a smile. "I missed you last time I was here. Must have been your day off." She acted casual and at ease, but inside her heart beat a solid cadence, like a bass drummer in the last performance of a Fourth of July parade. She hoped the beer would fortify her courage.

"Day off?" Sam laughed. "What's that? I was probably in the office."

"Can you stay and chat?" Sarah waved her hand toward the empty chair across from her in as nonchalant of a fashion as she could muster.

Sam looked around and checked his watch. "Yes, I think I can." He pulled out the heavy iron chair and made himself comfortable. "So, let's talk about something pleasant this time. Jean-Pierre tells me you like art, so how about that?"

Sarah's face lit up. "Yes, let's. Do you have any favorite artists?"

"In fact, I do, but it really depends on my mood." Sam leaned forward in his chair and rested his arms on the table, his hands only several inches from Sarah's. "When I'm happy, I love Monet. I know it's a little cliché—but I can't help it." Sam laughed a solid, deep rumble as he continued. "When I'm a little more down, I'm partial to Jean Jansem or Arshile Gorky. Both beautiful artists but even when portraying happy things, their work is still morose. How about you? Who are your favorites?"

"My absolute favorite painting is by Miró, but—"

Sarah was interrupted by the hustle of a busboy who clanged noisily to Sam's side before whispering in his ear. Sam listened, nodded, and then turned to her.

"I'm sorry," Sam said with a frown. "I wish I could stay and chat further, but unfortunately, there is a small situation I have to attend to which will take some time. I will have to see you next time. We'll chat then, for real. Until then, *au revoir.*"

Sarah shook her head in understanding as Sam hurried and disappeared into the back. A few moments later, as Sarah prepared to leave, she swore she heard a roar emanate from the back of the kitchen, like a lion on the savannah a mile out of camp. She took that as her cue, paid her bill, and headed home.

Though disappointed, she was pleased that the conversation was thwarted by circumstance rather than her own lack of courage or chemistry.

As she walked to the bus stop, Sarah's disappointment gave way to relief. It came on as a realization. One less thing to weigh on her mind. As interested in Sam as she was, she knew she had to figure out her own future first—back home at the Kettle; or, presumably, here at Avenir D'or. A decision like that needed to be made on her own and could not be swayed based on potential romantic entanglements.

CHAPTER 32

Tuesday came fast, and Sarah's fate with Avenir D'or hung in the balance. The meeting with Ms. Hackingham was in the afternoon and left her with plenty of time to worry. Her stomach knotted and churned as she busied herself with emails and a deep clean of the lab. She hoped that if it were her last days with the company, at least she'd be remembered as conscientious. A pleasant coincidence was that the labs were closer to the exit and bought her additional time for lunch. After their last phone call, Sarah felt that she owed Michael whatever time she could spare. When lunch approached, Sarah headed to Michael's hotel.

The place was typical Michael. Located in an old, historic area in a Renaissance-style building updated to the latest trendy styles. The brick facade gave way to a large marble hall that served as the lobby. An elaborate winding staircase and fresco paintings inset into the plaster molding on the ceiling lent Old World charm while the purple and green colored up-lights gave the room a modern feel. Something closer to a nightclub than a hotel. The room was furnished with simple, Scandinavian furniture in bright colored fabrics and beautiful natural woods.

Sarah entered through the large glass lobby doors and looked for the café. Clots of people cluttered the broad room. The lobby was crowded, heavy with midday traffic—guests checking out, people milling about, and sightseers in for the decor. The far corner of the lobby had what could possibly be termed a café, but, to Sarah, it looked like a coffee cart and a display case of sandwiches. There were small tables and chairs in front of a bank of booths built into the wall in rounded alcoves. The arched openings had elaborate molding that matched the ceiling, a majestic look amongst the modern decor.

A voice called from an alcove across the room. "Sarah! Sarah, over here!"

Sarah turned and saw Michael's waving hand. As she approached the table, he slid out of the booth and stood in front of her in a stylish Hugo Boss tuxedo. In his hands he held a bouquet of long-stem red roses, and his face beamed with an ear-to-ear smile.

"These are for you, lovely," Michael said and handed her the flowers. "I know time is short, so please sit down." He gestured toward the booth.

Taken aback, Sarah took the flowers and sniffed them. The sweet smell of the roses intoxicated her nose. Her eyes opened and she raised her head to look at Michael. *What is his plan? What is he thinking?* On one hand, Michael looked as handsome and debonair in his tailored tuxedo as Sarah had ever seen him. On the other hand, he looked almost foolish dressed up as he was in this quasi-café at midday. He looked as out of place as he did attractive. Sarah sat down across from Michael. In front of her was a plastic-wrapped sandwich and what appeared to be a side salad in a clamshell take-out container.

"Not exactly what I'd call a café," remarked Sarah.

"It's a few notches below normal, I grant you, but I knew you were tight on time, so I took the liberty. I hope it's okay," Michael said in a timid voice just above a whisper. His face was soft like a newborn kitten.

"It's fine, very considerate."

Sarah began to eat and waited for Michael to speak. After a few delicate stabs at his salad, Michael put down his fork and turned all of his attention to Sarah.

"Lovely, thanks for meeting me today. You've got a lot going on, so I'll just cut to the chase." Michael paused to take a breath. "I want you back. I've been thinking about you for a long time, and seeing you at Christmas reignited something that I thought I'd lost."

Michael's hands were more animated than usual. *He must really be nervous.*

"I've wanted to say this to you for these past few months but was never sure how. I was worried about what you'd say, but with all you have going on, I figured it's now or never. So, it's now. I made a big mistake leaving you back in the States. I want you with me from here on out." His voice was hurried but soft.

Sarah's eyes widened a little and astonishment filled her. "I'm not... How... Would this work? I..."

"I've got a job lined up back home," Michael interjected before she could finish. "And I want you to come back with me. I'm ready to make a commitment. I've been wandering around Europe long enough. I think it's time to go home and make a life." He poked the top of the table as he spoke, his voice growing louder.

"Michael... I mean, I *have* a life, here. I thought you did too. Why are you going back to the States? You said no one there knew how to live; everything was drab and boring." She shook her shoulders and parodied his movements from years ago.

"Hear me out. I used to think that way, and honestly, back home could use a little more spark, but that's not the point. I realized I had gone away to find a home, maybe a future, but it's really just back there waiting for me. The longer I've been gone, the more I've learned to appreciate what I've left behind. But it would never be the same, never be right, without you." Michael's voice was sweet; his words dripped off of his lips like delicate dabs of honey.

Sarah stared at him for a moment, her eyes widened. There was a time she would have killed to hear something like that from Michael. Now, she was mostly confused.

"I don't know. We've been through a lot. You hurt me badly. I'll admit, our time together was amazing. You taught me a lot about the world and how to look at things, at life, but it's different now. I'm piloting my own ship; I don't need someone to show me how to steer."

Sarah was proud of the person she'd become. She'd finally learned to value her own worth.

"What you taught me, what we had together was special. What you did to me pushed me to follow what I wanted, and that's what brought me here."

"Sarah, I get that, but we'd still be great together." Michael's hands spread open as he spoke and leaned toward her. "We have a house waiting for us; it's up to us to make it a home. We—you and me—can make Uncle Geoffrey's old place a home again. Our home. We can make it live. We can make it our place, make the ties that bind us more than just people in a place together, but a family. We can make our own little world, right there."

As he spoke, Michael overflowed with enthusiasm. His piercing blue eyes grew intense and focused. It was clear he believed everything he said. Sarah was cautious not to get caught up in the excitement.

"You make it sound so good, but I'm not sure if it would play out that way. I've started my own life. What would I do back home?" Sarah asked rhetorically. Her voice was questioning but pleasant; she'd ruled out nothing.

Sarah's mind flashed to her conversations with Loretta from the past weeks. She paused and considered what it *might* look like. If she accepted Loretta's offer, she'd be home again amongst old friends and people who cared about her. The pieces moved and arranged themselves in her mind, and they fit. It was easy to envision herself as a partner in a successful business, fashioning her own line of products, and redecorating Uncle Geoffrey's house. She imagined fresh coats of paint on the wainscoting and walls, new art and furniture to make it their own. She thought about being with all of the people she cared about, who cared about her, all in one place.

But there was one question left unanswered: What about *her* future? The one she had spent the last few years building. The one she'd been dreaming of for so long. What happened to that? Then there was Marseille and *that* unknown future. If she left, she'd never get to know her full potential in food science and would leave any prospect of getting to know Sam on the table.

Soon, other questions bombarded her. *What if there's no job? What if Hackingham says, "Well, done. Good show," and sends me on my way? Why does everything always happen at once?*

Welcome to the real world.

Sarah glanced at her watch. She was already late. The conversation was not over; she didn't want to leave it unfinished. She did not even know what job he was taking, but she had to make the meeting with Ms. Hackingham. She had to leave.

"Michael, I have to go. I'm sorry to leave you like this, but I have to get to that meeting. I can't miss it; I can't be late."

"Lovely, I understand. Go, get to that meeting. I leave tonight, but I'm going to be back in town Monday. You can give me your answer then. I'll be on pins and needles, but I'll live. Now go."

Sarah shimmied out of the booth and stood up as Michael followed. She looked at her watch and shook her head.

"Okay, I *really* have to go," Sarah said as she kissed him on the cheek and dashed toward the lobby door.

Sarah stood on the bus and fingered her keys with impatience as she moved toward the front in eager anticipation of her stop. The pneumatic brakes hissed and brought the bus to a halt. Almost before the driver opened the doors, Sarah hurried down the steps in a mad sprint toward Avenir D'or. She still remembered to shout a frantic *"merci"* to the driver.

Sarah made it back to her cubicle and dropped her bags. Not knowing what else to do with the stack of flowers in her hand, she shrugged and set them on the desk. A glance at her pocket mirror revealed wind-blown brown curls frizzed out as if attending a 1970s disco. After a hasty smooth down, and with only minutes to spare, Sarah grabbed her pen and notebook and headed to Ms. Hackingham's office.

Ms. Hackingham was seated at her desk. With a small wave, she gestured Sarah into her office and asked her to sit down. This was her new office, which corresponded with her new position, and was much smaller than her old one—it was clear she was still adjusting. The walls were bare except for a small portrait of the Queen. Full moving boxes were stacked in the corner with the topmost one torn open, oozing packing material. After a quick British-style-apology for the mess, the meeting began.

"Sarah, thanks for coming. I've said it before: I think you've done a great job. To tell you the truth, the members of the team forgot you were an intern and considered you one of them."

"Thanks. They really made me feel like I belonged. I'm grateful. Did you read the final report I sent you?" Sarah asked in a sober, business-like tone.

"Yes, I did. It was good." Ms. Hackingham paused for a moment and readjusted the paperwork in front of her. Sarah tried to get a glimpse of the contents without being observed. The office may have been small, but the desk was not; she couldn't read a thing.

"So, Sarah. As you know, the internship is only for experience and does not guarantee you a position with us or any other entity within our organization."

Sarah's heart sank. She was afraid of what Ms. Hackingham was going to say next. She always knew there was a chance that despite her best efforts, the Fates could conspire against her, and she could get a "thanks but no thanks" from Avenir D'or. She sat quietly and waited for the ax to drop.

"However," continued Ms. Hackingham, "it also does not preclude us from extending offers to interns who have shown exceptional skill and value in their time here. Provided we have an appropriate position available, of course."

"Of course," parroted Sarah in sober business-speak.

"You have shown yourself to be a true asset to the team." Theresa's voice was stiff and formal as she looked more at the paper on her desk then at Sarah. "Your time here has been marked with achievements that surpass your role. It is clear you committed yourself one hundred and fifty percent. You should be very proud of what you've accomplished," Ms. Hackingham said, her Leeds accent leaking through her practiced diction.

"I am, ma'am," said Sarah. "I really love it here and am grateful for the opportunities I've had. I only hope there is a place for me." Sarah's tone stayed even and did not betray her growing anxiety.

Ms. Hackingham grabbed a plain manila folder on the top of a pile near her left hand and set it in front of her. Sarah, uncertain about what was coming next, could feel herself holding her breath and then breathing in quick bursts. Her chest felt like a car engine on its last fumes, sputtering to its destination. Ms. Hackingham, in her usual stiff-upper-lip manner, opened the file and began to read a letter to Sarah. "Dear Ms. Hall, we wish to thank you for all of your hard work with us during your internship year. Your work has been top rate."

Sarah let out her breath and smiled.

"Unfortunately, at this time we are unable to extend you an offer of employment. We wish you the best in your future endeavors and career search."

Sarah fought back the tears that pooled in her eyes. This was her shot. She'd put in everything and was left with nothing more than a "thank you." She'd known it was a possibility, but it stung.

 Ms. Hackingham noticed the pained look on her face and was quick to add, "I'm sorry, Sarah. I pushed for you as hard as I could—after all, you are my legacy, in a way. But, unfortunately, my influence doesn't extend very far these days. I truly am sorry."

 "Thanks." Sarah's voice was barely above a whisper. The pain of disappointment was evident even in that one word. "I was hoping for something different."

 "It isn't as bad as it seems." Ms. Hackingham's voice turned uncharacteristically soft.

 "It is from where I'm sitting. This was my chance."

 Sarah hadn't finished her sentence when Ms. Hackingham walked to the door and closed it with a muted thud. The disappointment on Sarah's face was now joined with confusion.

 "I want to talk to you about something, but I'd like to keep it quiet, okay?"

 "Um, okay."

 "So, you know about the India deal, right?"

 "Yeah, why? Did it go through?"

 "No, it's crashing and burning as we speak. The company poured tens of millions of Euros into developing the project, and it failed. Personally, I think we forgot to bribe the right people, but what do I know? Anyway, this company was counting on it. We've been spending with the expectation of closing the deal. Now, since that isn't happening, I can assure you, layoffs are imminent."

 "Oh, my gosh."

 "Yes, it is quite sad. This company had amazing growth but never shored itself for the rough times. Executives came in, took their bonuses, and moved on. But that's a story for another time. Here's the deal. As they've already pushed me out the door, or at least to the threshold, I'm leaving to start my own enterprise, and I need a food scientist."

"What? Yes, I'd love that! It would be an honor." Sarah's mind was shifting gears like an F1 race car.

"Don't get too excited. You haven't heard all the details yet."

"Oh," Sarah sighed and slouched slightly in her chair. *Always a catch.*

"The good news is, Jean-Pierre is coming with me, and I've got a space leased." Theresa closed the folders in front of her and leaned a little toward Sarah. "It's going to be tight quarters. A tiny lab and a few desks. The bad news is that I've only scraped together enough funding for about six months. Unless we get rolling, the compensation will be dismal and, overall, our chances of success are low."

The enthusiasm sank from Sarah's face. *From one sinking ship to another.*

"But if I've pegged the market right, we have an opportunity. Frankly, I need someone like you; someone who is smart as a whip and knows how to work."

And comes cheap. Sarah chided herself for the cynicism.

"You're asking me to take a heck of a risk," said Sarah. "I don't have much savings, and Marseille isn't cheap."

Sarah thought about her fast-dwindling bank account and the emails she'd received from the lawyers about Nancy's estate. How that was all going to end up was still an open question.

"I know. Like many things in life, it's high-risk, high-reward." Ms. Hackingham rose from her chair and opened the door a little. "Now listen, I want you to think on this. You're here until next Wednesday, and I'm headed out of town. I'll be out through the weekend. I shall return on Monday. Please give me your response at that time. If you choose to accept, we should be able to start in a fortnight or so. Have a good rest of your week and a good weekend. I will see you Monday."

With that, Sarah was released to her cubical.

She headed to her desk and felt as if she'd been put through a spin cycle. She was disappointed by the kiss off she'd received from Avenir D'or. What she hadn't expected was an offer from Ms. Hackingham herself.

As she settled down in front of her computer and reflexively checked her email, a shy knock came from the top of her cubicle wall.

"So, Theresa asked you to join our little experiment?"

Sarah turned around. It was Jean-Pierre.

"From one sinking ship to a dinghy. It will be all arms aboard wood." His voice only a shade above a whisper.

"That's what I was thinking. Wait, what?" Sarah shrugged, confused by Jean-Pierre's turn of phrase.

"That's not the saying?"

Sarah thought for a moment and started to laugh. "Did you mean, all hands on deck?"

"Yes, yes, that's it. Damned idioms. Are you going to take it?"

"I don't know. It's exciting but really scary. If it fails, I'm destitute. I have so much coming at me at once." Sarah explained the situation with Michael and Loretta.

"Oh, wow, looks like you have some big decisions to make. Personally, I hope you come with us, even though you'll be my boss. It'll be an adventure. Let me know if I can help."

"I will, Jean-Pierre. Thanks for listening."

An hour or so later, Sarah was called into Marc's office. As she sat down, she noticed the spots on his bald head looked darker than normal and his countenance looked soured.

"Sarah, I want to talk to you about a few things." He spoke quicker and quieter than usual. "First, let me say I'm sorry that things didn't work out with you here. It wasn't the plan. I had always expected to bring you onboard, but regretfully, that's not an option right now."

"I was disappointed, to say the least," Sarah said. Uncertain where the conversation was going, she waited to let Marc speak.

"Well, thing is, the India deal we spoke about fell through, and there just isn't room... or budget."

"Yeah, I heard."

"Oh? From Hackingham?"

"Um..." Sarah hesitated. "Yes."

"I see." Marc paused and brushed a few crumbs from his brown sweater. He leaned back in his chair and crossed his arms over his chest.

"Did she ask you to join her little organization?" The contempt in his voice was obvious. "It's okay, you can answer. I've heard all about it. It's hard to keep secrets in this place."

"Well, yes, she did." Marc had always been kind to her, and she needed all the advice she could get. Sarah told him about what happened in Theresa's office and the situation with Loretta but kept light on the details about Michael.

Marc listened and nodded his head as though listening to a sermon, arms still crossed. When Sarah finished, he was silent a moment and then asked, "Do you want to know what I think?"

"Of course. I'd love your input."

"Go home. You've had a nice period abroad; take what you've learned and apply it. You've got friends, people who care about you, and what sounds like a good opportunity."

"But I've always wanted to be a food scientist," Sarah pressed, almost a whine.

"Look, let me be honest." Marc grew stern and leaned into his desk. "Theresa is nuts. There's a reason they've pushed her out. And that 'opportunity' she thinks she sees, well, Valhalla foods is already moving to fill that gap. By the time Hackingham gets up and running, it'll already be gone."

"But Jean-Pierre is going with her. He thinks this is worth a try."

"Jean-Pierre is a nice guy and really looks up to Theresa, but he doesn't understand the industry. Josephine is staying put, turned her down flat, because she knows there's nothing there."

"Ms. Hackingham asked Ms. Blasier too?"

"Of course. D you think she started with you? Oh, my dear girl." The exasperation in his voice was unmistakable. "Take my advice. Go home."

Sarah left Marc's office and trundled back to her cube. The gravity of her situation and the decision that lay ahead of her became clear. Life once again presented her with two divergent options—one with Michael in her future and one without—both with far-ranging consequences.

CHAPTER 33

Five days. Sarah had five days to decide in what direction to pivot her life.

Her week was slow-motion agony. As the internship faded, Sarah had time and time and time to fret and agonize over her decision. Time enough to repeatedly play the options against each other in her head, but a resolution never came. She found herself of two minds: Her intellectual side wanted to stay and take the opportunity with Ms. Hackingham wherever it led, consequences be damned; her emotional side longed for comfort and security, to be with people she knew thoroughly and trusted, in familiar surroundings. The strain of being pulled in two directions at once wearied her.

At fleeting moments, she wondered what her mother—or even Henry—would have said. Would they have had some perspective or pull to influence her decision? Probably not. It didn't matter—they were gone. Side-by-side, the wounds they'd inflicted, and the pain of their losses, still ached in Sarah, dulled by time but not forgotten.

By Sunday morning, Sarah was thoroughly stuck. She was inclined to accept the offer—she was so close to her dream—but the risk and uncertainty left her feeling that it wasn't quite right. The refrain of voices—Loretta, Michael, Marc, and Jean-Pierre—echoed through her mind, casting doubt upon doubt to every choice. Each voice pleaded its case; each gave her pause. Sarah held them at bay and tried to weigh the pros and cons to her dilemma.

The offer from Hackingham was both an exceptional opportunity and an exceptional risk. If all went well, Sarah would be a food scientist on the ground floor of a new company and well-situated to influence its direction. She would also have an outlet for the flavors she'd been developing. If it failed, she'd be out of money and out of options in a foreign land with a fast-expiring visa.

Moreover, Loretta wouldn't wait around forever. And Michael? He seemed to have turned a new leaf, but one could never be too sure. Sarah figured if Hackingham's company failed in six months flat, the window at the Kettle just might still be open. That said, if it lurched and lingered into failure, the window would certainly be closed. Sarah would find herself back home, jobless, and with minimal opportunities. Sarah knew Loretta well enough to know that contingency plans were in the wings. A refusal from her would spring those plans into action. Loretta had given her time to think, not to dither.

Sarah then wondered what would happen if she went home. What would she gain? A chance to own her own business (or at least part of it) and work with someone she loved, cared about, and could trust. Unlike the mysterious and vapid corporate world, there would be no business subterfuge at the Kettle. In time, control of the business would be hers, and it would be up to her to grow it into something more than just a little tea shop. Product development would be vital to that growth and to her future.

Of course, outside of that scenario, things were much bleaker. What if things turned sour and the Kettle had to close? The other prospects back home were dismal.

Then there was Michael. Trying to pin down her feelings on him was like trying to pin down a politician on a straight answer: Every time you think you have an answer, you really just have a different question. Sarah knew she cared about Michael, despite how he treated her. She felt, in a way, that she owed some of her success to him. He opened her eyes to new things, and when he left, it forced her to take control of her success. In a strange way, she was grateful for that. They also had a deep connection between them due to Uncle Geoffrey's death; a closeness that comes only through the crucible of tragedy. Feelings of love and nostalgia were intricately intertwined like a cluster of nerves. Sarah wondered if time and distance had colored her perception of their relationship and now exerted a force on both the past and her potential future.

The idea of living with Michael, especially in Uncle Geoffrey's house, had appeal. Not only was the house big and beautiful, but Michael's lifestyle also appealed to her. Michael was not afraid to savor and seize the beautiful essences of life. To Michael, the boundaries to his desires and expectations came from within, not without. However, Sarah had experienced firsthand the pitfalls that stemmed from his mode of thinking. Sarah couldn't bear to get hurt again. In a way, the offer from Michael was much like the offer from Hackingham—high-risk, high-reward.

Sarah reflected on the problems they'd faced the first time around—mostly Michael's lack of commitment and how he looked at other women. It remained an open question if anything else had ever transpired. Now, Michael insisted that that part of his life was over, but was that really be true? Would he get bored after a time and move on again? Would she be left behind a second time? Too many questions, too few answers.

With a sudden jolt, her cycle of questions and doubt were interrupted by the pulsating ring of her phone. To her shock, the screen read *Bernie,* and she answered in hurry and surprise. After a quick adjustment of Bernie's hearing aids, he began.

"Good morning, sweetheart; or, I guess I should say afternoon?" Bernie's warmth resonated even over the thousands of miles.

"Oh, Bernie, it's great to hear from you. How are you doing?"

"Me? I'm fine, just old." He let out a laugh under his breath. "I'm calling about you. See, Loretta tells me you've got quite the decision in front of you. How are you holding up?"

"Honestly? I'm a mess. I feel like I'm being pulled in two directions at once. I can't make up my mind." Sarah sighed and filled him in on everything that had been swirling around in her head.

"Sweetheart, you're doing great. You will make the right decision; you're a smart kid."

"Thanks, Bernie." Sarah blushed with pride. "I've missed you."

"And I've missed you too. But don't let that sway you. You've worked hard, and you need to do what's right for you. You've spent your life looking after other people's interests. This one has to be for you."

"Hearing you say that makes me want to go home even more. I mean, I have a lot to stay for, but there's an awful lot to go home to, even with Mom gone."

"Look, Loretta, the gang, and of course, me..." Bernie paused a moment as if to emphasize his point. "We all love and miss you, but we all understand that it isn't about us. If you think the Kettle is the right move, take it. If you want to try your hand with that Ms. Hackingham, do it. Just don't let your past cloud your future. I have my opinions about Mr. Michael, but that isn't important. You need to do what your heart tells you. Either way, you already make us all proud."

Sarah could tell he was squinting, even over the phone.

"Aw, Bernie. That means so much coming from you, thank you."

The conversation shifted to life at the senior center and the Kettle, followed by an update on Bernie's health. After a few more minutes, it was over, and Sarah was alone again with her mind and her dilemma.

The call was a sweet and lovely distraction, but moments after the call ended, the ceaseless back-and-forth in Sarah's head recommenced. For the ensuing days, all her questions hung from the ceiling like a spider's web and waited to ensnare Sarah's every thought. She stalked her apartment and turned it over in her mind, almost to madness. Stress and frustration almost got the better of her. She sought out fresh air and food to try to turn the tide.

The sun laid low in the western sky and painted the world with sharp jabs of scarlet hues, nestled closely by tangerine highlights. Sarah had finished a dinner of daube from a restaurant a few blocks from her apartment. In hopes of clearing her head, she decided to take a walk through a nearby park. It was small with a short, winding, asphalt path lined with enormous trees and skirted by tracts of green grass. Sarah gazed at the old wooden behemoths and wondered how they managed to reach such heights. What perseverance and tenacity—as well as good luck—the trees must possess to survive so long in an urban climate. Many triumphs and injustices had come and gone under their sentinel-like gaze: industrial revolutions, world wars, occupations, pollution, climate change, and so on. Yet there they stood, probably for centuries. Sarah lingered for a few more minutes, her head craned skyward, and then continued to wander along the path. The clarity or epiphany she'd hoped for did not arrive. Her decision weighed heavily on her mind. As the sky darkened, she headed for home.

Coteaux d'Aix-en-Provence Cabernet Sauvignon flowed into her glass in a deep aubergine shade. Her time in France had expanded her wine palate; she relished the breadth and depth of the local wines. Glass in hand, she slouched on the green couch and sipped. The skin around the base of her neck crinkled and bunched, huddled together in ridges like thin rows of cording on a vintage chair. She sat still for a few minutes as she rolled sip after sip around on her tongue and savored the subtle hints of peppercorns and limestone. In the gentle calm, she let the wine sink in.

After a while, Sarah stood up and paced the room, back and forth across her little apartment living room. Slowly, she began to notice, and then examine, items in the room. She realized how much these things—simple items—reflected both her life as well as the people within it.

Her morning teapot and cup sat on the coffee table, part of a partial set Loretta had given her just before she left. The pattern was a collection of blue chevrons and shields intertwined with blue vines, an homage to France. It felt regal and projected strength but was still refined and delicate. In some ways, it was a reflection of what Loretta had been to her. Strength and comfort; an unceasing friend.

Sarah looked at the wine glass in her hand and thought about her mother and father. About how drink and drugs had been such an integral part of their, and her, lives. Alcohol had been her father's drug of choice, and, to him, it was a shield against the pains of life, a way to dull an existence too intense. Drugs, so many drugs, of all types and assortments had aided her mother in her battle with her mental demons but ultimately led her to an early end. Sarah was struck by how this simple beverage, grapes plus yeast plus time, and others like it were a paradoxical symbol of the highest peaks and the deepest valleys of her and her family's lives. It represented all of those bad moments and conflicts but also the good times, the celebratory times, the times that life worked out. And, to Sarah, a constant source of sapid inspiration and growth.

The cream-colored walls of her apartment had a subtle, fabric-like texture as she ran her hand along it. Nearly barren, except for her little Miró. Sarah squared herself to the small still life and lost herself in it. The more she looked, the more it resonated and reflected her. In it, she saw her own search for strength, independence, and love. In it, she saw something about herself, something she'd never be able to articulate. A revelation that would be unexplainable to others. She now knew why this painting meant so much to her. In her heart, in the dark-red depths of her chest, she understood.

The painting showed both her past and her future. The bold parallel lines spoke to her of both stability and modernity. The foundation she had built for herself: an education, a small but loyal group of friends, and a willingness to face hard truths.

The beautifully sculpted flowers outlined in black lines that accented both their beauty and their form—to Sarah, these were like her looks and her brains. A woman of deep, personal beauty but void of the heightened, superficial attractiveness of the glossy magazines. She had moved past the labels of men and editors and was comfortable in her own skin. The world had to reckon with her as she was, not how it wanted her to be.

To Sarah, that little painting was the same way. Miró had pushed beyond realism into the realms of impressionism and cubism. Further, it was a transitionary work. Miró had not yet reached peak form, just as she was still climbing. The work was beautiful and complete but not a summation of his talents, just as she was still in her ascendancy but was nevertheless whole and complete.

Sarah refilled her glass and sunk deeper into reflection. The whole painting was stalked by a brown, tonal, and undefined background which, to Sarah, represented the future—uncertain and ill-defined, like shadows that blurred and twisted and demanded that we create cognizable shapes of our future or face madness. Truly unknown, the future may be nothing more than a play of shadows upon the wall. Unknowable until it becomes the present, the future is promised to no one and may never come to pass. That reality, that realization, was now etched into Sarah's mind. *I have my helmet.*

Sarah now understood what she must do, what path she must take. Her life had led to this moment, and a decision had been made. This life was her own, and she owed it to herself to live it on her terms, her way. To dare in the face of the unknown, to mold shapes from the shadows and to push for her dreams.

Her mind made, Sarah collapsed onto the couch in exhaustion and relief and slept.

CHAPTER 34

Sleep held Sarah until the rays of the morning sun kissed her cheeks, and the alarm on her phone tore her from its blissful embrace. With an automatic thrust of her arm, the tone was silenced. Sarah laid face down on the green Scandinavian couch, her eyelids like sandbags. Wisps of hair curled around her face and stuck to her lips. Her mouth tasted of gravel. The previous night's revelation, or possibly the wine, had sapped her energy and left her with a lack of strength to overcome the inertia of her sleepy state. The minutes passed as the sleep evaporated from her body. The weight of the day pressed against the surface tension of her mind, and she realized it was Monday morning—her future was now.

After a quick shower and a cup of steaming Irish Breakfast, she was off to see Ms. Hackingham. Sarah beamed at Gunter as she passed through the turnstile and caught the elevator. Ms. Hackingham's door was half-open when Sarah arrived. She watched Theresa's eyes dart back and forth between a large file folder, balanced precariously on the top of her keyboard, and her monitor as her right hand automatically raised and lowered her glasses.

Sarah knocked on the door frame with a gentle motion and waited with patient anxiety. Ms. Hackingham set her glasses on her desk as she looked up and saw Sarah.

"Oh, Ms. Hall. Very good to see you. Please, come in and sit down." She smiled and motioned toward the small chairs that faced her desk. Sarah took her seat and waited. "I take it that your presence in my office indicates your intention to join me on my little venture?"

Sarah's heart pounded in her chest as she heard the blood rush through her ears. *This is it.* Like in death, bits of her life flashed through her mind—all of the classrooms, the studying, Henry, Nancy, Loretta... Michael. It all culminated in her mind, and she was certain. *This is the moment.*

"Yes, I want to be a food scientist. I've worked too hard and dreamed too long not to try," Sarah said, her voice resolute.

"Atta girl, that's the kind of drive we're going to need."

"So what do I do now? I mean, do I need to sign something? Or—"

"All of that will be taken care of later. You have to finish out your term and I mine." Ms. Hackingham reached down into her bag, pulled out a small manila folder, and slid it across the desk to Sarah. "For now, everything you need to know is in there. Report to that address two weeks from Wednesday. I suggest you finish out your time here in good form and then spend the next couple of weeks looking for a new apartment."

"I will," Sarah said and thanked her. As she drifted her way back to her desk, she glanced over the paperwork.

Back in her cubicle, she phoned Michael. She'd promised him an answer.

"Hello, lovely, good to hear from you," Michael said, ebullient and assured.

"Hi, Michael. We should talk. Are you back in town today?" Sarah asked cheerfully but serious.

"Yeah, I just got in last night. I'm available when you are." Michael remained positive and upbeat, though Sarah could tell he sensed that he wasn't going to like what she had to say. She knew he would work to change her mind if he could. The pair arranged to meet at *La Bouche du Lion* that evening.

After work, it was time to give Loretta the news. While disappointed, Loretta was happy for her and praised Sarah's hard work and determination. "You know, Sarah, I feel like I'm marrying off my daughter. I'm losing you for myself, but the world is gaining your talent and will benefit from it. Plus," Loretta began to laugh, "now, I've got an excuse to visit France." The booming laughter made Sarah smile. She felt good about her decision and proud of herself. Loretta always had that effect on her.

Calls finished, Sarah pulled out her laptop and began to search for a new apartment and waited until it was time to meet Michael.

Sarah arrived at *La Bouche du Lion* early, and it was quiet. Plenty of people mingled and talked in the main bar, but the tables were mostly empty. Sarah secured a back booth; she wanted a quiet spot. It was going to be a hard conversation, and she wanted some semblance of privacy.

The waiter approached, and she ordered a Bordeaux. At precisely seven o'clock, Michael walked through the door in a grey Ralph Lauren suit with a blue and white striped tie. He looked as though he had just stepped from a business meeting. *Maybe he has changed. He's on time and dressed for business.*

These changes surprised her, but she was undeterred. Michael sat down at the table, and the waiter approached. He ordered a dirty dry martini and turned his attention to Sarah.

"Hello, lovely. Thanks for meeting me. You look beautiful tonight," Michael said as he grinned ear to ear like the cat in a Lewis Carroll novel.

"No problem." Sarah ignored his compliment. "Why are you so smiley? What's with the business suit? What are you up to?"

"This suit?" Michael said, feigning surprise. He flapped his lapels as he spoke. "Oh, nothing. I'm just feeling good and want my clothes to match. I am seeing you, after all." His grin sharpened.

"That's it, huh?"

"Well, that and the fact that you're looking at the new International Sales Manager at New Tech Corp." Michael clapped his hands and rubbed them together in excitement. "I'm trying to get used to wearing a proper suit."

"Congratulations. Where does that gig put you? Are you staying in Europe?"

"No, not exactly. I will be based in an office back home with the occasional trips around Europe and sometimes Dubai, China, and Japan. I told you that knowing five languages would help me land somewhere." Michael nodded in satisfaction.

"Sounds like you have a few more to learn now. Good luck with your Mandarin," Sarah said with a wry smile. "How did you end up with such a high-profile gig? I mean, don't take this the wrong way, but you've been an English teacher. What do you know about international sales?"

Sarah leaned back in the booth and sipped her wine.

"Ah, ah, ah, ye of little faith. I worked at the school store in college." Michael placed his hands behind his head, fingers locked, and leaned back. "Plus, I've got a degree from Georgetown and a pretty silver tongue in any language. I told them what they wanted to hear and did it in French, Spanish, Italian, Czech, and Polish. Everyone there only spoke English, so they were suitably impressed." He was clearly proud of his little linguistic showoff.

"You're really heading home, then? I never thought I'd see the day." Sarah's shoulders drooped as she shook her head.

"I start in two weeks. I fly home on Thursday so I can try to put the house in order and make it livable again." Michael paused. "The big question is whether you'll be coming with me."

Sarah's smile diminished as she folded her hands on the table. The time had come. She hadn't planned her exact words but knew she had to be direct. Michael seemed to sense the change in her demeanor and winced.

"I'm sorry, Michael, I can't. I'm not going back with you." Sarah explained the situation with Avenir D'or and Ms. Hackingham. "I've been working toward this for a very long time, well before we were together. I have to try. I've got a few flavors I've been working on, and who knows, I might have a hit on my hands!"

Sarah's words were warm, but her tone stern. She didn't want to give any appearance of equivocating. Any sign of weakness would only make the conversation more difficult. Worse still, too much reflection might cause her to doubt herself.

"I had a feeling you were going to say something like that," Michael said and swallowed hard. "Congratulations on the new job. I hope it all works out. You've always had a good palate. I'm sure it will serve you well. You'll be great."

"Thanks, Michael," Sarah said, slightly surprised at his good grace.

"The thing is, I *need* you back home! We have to make Uncle Geoffrey's house *our* home. It can't possibly be complete without you."

A deep sigh emanated from Sarah's lips as she rubbed her face with her hands. She assumed he was going to press the point, but not like this.

"There will always be a void unless you are there. The place will be filled with a huge, churning black hole," Michael said in a plead, nearly a beg. "You were the one who made that city bearable, that made it a home for me. When I think of it, I think of it with you. I *need* you there."

Sarah cast her eyes downward as if studying the far corner of the booth. She struggled to look at him. "I'm sorry, Michael."

"That's it? I'm sorry? Sarah, please. I need you. Come back with me." He was almost whining.

"Where was this passion, this zest, for me when you broke my heart three years ago? I needed you, and you dropped me. Now, suddenly, you can't live without me? What is that?" Sarah began to get upset and stared him in the eyes.

"You know the old cliché—you don't know what you have until it's gone? Well, that's exactly what has happened. I came back to Spain and settled into the old routine, but over time, its luster started to fade."

Michael ran his hands through his hair and took a long sip of his martini before continuing.

"I started to think about you more and more. I'd find myself wondering where you were and what you were doing.

When I ran into you last Christmas, it seemed like it was meant to be. Since then, I've missed you even more. Every day, I wonder if there will ever be a 'you and I' again. I hoped desperately for it to be so. Now, I have my answer." Michael's face was grey and defeated. He looked like a man who had bet it all on a horse that didn't come in.

The waiter made his way back to the table, and Sarah ordered another drink. Michael stared, stunned and sullen. Sarah ordered one for Michael as well. *He looks like he could use another.*

"I hate to say it, Michael, but you had your chance. I would have done anything you asked me to. I would have followed you anywhere. I was so in love, I thought you were the one. It would have been a grand and splendid life, but then you chose to leave me behind." Sarah became edgy, almost angry. Her hands clenched a little as the words coursed from her lips.

"It can still be that way. You know we'll have great times together; we always did. Look, I made a mistake. I can only say 'I'm sorry' so many times. I don't want to pay for that mistake my whole life. More importantly, I don't want you to regret this moment for the rest of yours." Michael spoke in soft but emphatic tones.

Sarah resisted the urge to roll her eyes and instead enjoyed a hearty sip of her wine. "Don't make this any harder than it needs to be. We had our chance—you and I—but that window has closed. We cannot go home again. We can't go back. The spell has been broken." Sarah rubbed her neck and pulled her hair into a ponytail before continuing. "I'm a new person. I'm wiser, I'm more focused, and I'm more comfortable being me, just me. I don't need anyone else to make me whole. In a strange way, I have you to thank for it."

"Oh? How so?" Michael asked, his face screwed up in confusion.

"Because if you hadn't broken my heart, I wouldn't be here today." Sarah's voice softened to normal. "After you left me, I had a realization that I was responsible for my own happiness, and if I wanted something out of life, I had to get it for myself. I had to live it on my terms and not on anyone else's. Not my mother's, and not yours. For that, I thank you. It was a brutal lesson to learn, the fire burned deep and left scars, but I came through stronger."

Sarah finished her drink. A small grin grew on Michael's face, the look both surprised and gratified. As if his disappointment was tempered slightly by satisfaction. But it didn't last. The grin melted to a frown.

"Oh, Sarah, I'm sorry I put you through so much. I didn't mean to hurt you. I was so selfish."

"Yes, you were, but I think it worked out just fine. Once I learned that lesson, I pushed myself to be better than I was. Now, with luck and arduous work, I just might get what I wanted."

Sarah sat back for a moment as the waiter set the next round of drinks on the table and cleared away the empty glasses. "You need to understand that I loved you, I still love you in many ways, and I've thought long and hard about this—about you. I've come to the conclusion that this is something I have to do."

"It's funny," Michael said as he sipped his new drink. "I have changed because of all of this too. I wanted you back, and I knew that the same old Michael wasn't going to cut it. That's what got me thinking about getting back to the States and trying to do something different with my life."

Michael rubbed his face with his hands and let out a sigh. "That said, I'm very disappointed and heartbroken. For the last few months, I would sit and dream about what our life could be like. I imagined us transforming Uncle Geoffrey's house, adding little tidbits and accessories from our travels, making it our own. I imagined going to dinner and plumbing the region for any culinary exceptions we could find."

He became a little more animated and excited. "I envisioned enjoying whatever new flavors you'd cooked up and so on. However, now I see that will not happen. I am not happy about it, but I understand. I am happy for you but not for myself. I recognize this is the world I must inhabit. I must follow the path I chose years ago."

Michael tilted his head back, far back, and took a long drink of his martini. He raised his glass high in the air like a stage actor overplaying his movements for the back seats. Bits of condensation dripped off the glass and splattered on the wooden tabletop. As he pulled the glass from his lips, he held it in front of his eyes as if to inspect it in closer detail. From her vantage point, Sarah saw his eye, enlarged and distorted by the wet glass, and he appeared to be hiding a tear. He continued to look through the glass a few more moments and then placed it on the table. In a slow, deliberate fashion, Michael rose from the table, pulled a pair of twenty Euro bills out of his right trouser pocket, and tossed them gently onto the table. He returned his hands to his pockets and looked to Sarah.

"Well, I guess that is all there is to it." He pushed his hand forward through his pockets as he spoke. With a slight bow, he turned to walk away from the table, his eyes downward.

"Michael!" He stopped in his tracks and pivoted. "Don't go like that."

Sarah stood up, walked a few paces, and put her arms around him. He leaned into her, burying his face in her shoulder, and began to cry. She tightened her grasp and held him as she whispered softly in his ear.

"It's okay. This is not the end. You can call me any time you want. I am still your friend; I still love you. We're just on different paths."

Michael nodded as she spoke, his head still implanted in her shoulder. As he pulled away, Sarah held his hand gently by the fingertips. Michael cleared the tears from his red, worn eyes and stared into her face, as if trying to memorize every last curve and contour. When he was finished, he smiled.

"Thank you, Sarah," he said in a whisper. "I needed that. I hope to see you around."

Michael walked down the row of booths, past the bar and dancing patrons, and out the door. Sarah went back to her seat and finished her drink. She had never felt more confident in any decision in her entire life. Deep in her soul, she knew that she'd done the right thing. Pity and love for Michael flowed out of her in equal measure. She knew she had hurt him and lanced his soul. After a few minutes, her glass empty and her heart full, she paid the waiter and went home.

CHAPTER 35

To experience the birth of a new company is a stressful and exciting affair. Much like a new child, the process is fraught with risk, nerves, and lack of sleep. For Sarah, the transition from the large, expansive corporate campus of Avenir D'or to the rusted, dingy, rented space off *Avenue de Londres* was jarring but exhilarating. Sarah found herself on a bright edge of promise ringed with deep valleys and sharp pitfalls. Everything was new, and the potential felt limitless but tinged with danger.

As the new company got on its feet, Sarah introduced her new flavors to Ms. Hackingham, who was eager to take up their potential.

On her home front, Sarah found an apartment in *Cours-Julien* that was pleasant and reasonable. It was close to nightlife and shops. She enjoyed the vibrant atmosphere of the sixth *arrondissement*.

The process of decorating her new apartment was one of rejuvenation and self-affirmation. She enjoyed picking out new pieces of furniture and decorations but was cautious to select only what she needed. She knew all was tenuous and that her future with Hackingham could implode at any moment, so all of her choices echoed that reality.

Aside from her clothes, toiletries, and small personal effects, the only thing that carried over with her was her beloved Miró. She chose the wall and placement with great care and settled on a wall in the living room just above the couch. The print was too small for the room so, in her one extravagance, she had it reframed with a large matte. It looked like an overgrown version of photos one would see in fancy museums. Sarah loved it.

Ms. Vartanian greeted Sarah on sight and showed her to her favorite outdoor table. Sarah's heart pulsated, and her mouth was dry and chalky. She took her seat, anxious to soothe her parched tongue with a refreshing gulp of water. Today was the day she would finally ask Sam for a date. For many weeks she had tried in vain, but a suitable opportunity never presented itself. Today was different. She had a plan; she was determined.

Sarah had learned she was most likely to catch Sam in the late evenings after the rush had slowed when he often hung around the dining room as service finished up. Sarah planned to eat late and casually read a book until Sam came out of the office.

She started with a Lahmajune and yogurt and ordered a full meal of lamb stuffed grape leaves with sides of hummus, grilled vegetables, and a green salad. As usual, she complemented it with a fresh, crisp Armenian lager that paired perfectly with the char on the vegetables and the creamy, oily hummus. She devoured it with glee.

Sarah finished her meal and ordered baklava and coffee for dessert. She sat back and enjoyed the cool evening breeze as she cracked open the Asimov trilogy she'd received from Bernie and began to read and sip. After many attempts, she had finally acquired a taste for Armenian coffee. The potent brew was served unfiltered in a small cup, like a shot glass with a handle. She once described it to Loretta as an espresso with dirty grounds at the bottom. Engrossed in her book, Sarah was startled to hear a familiar voice approach from behind.

"Sarah, how are you? I've missed you."

Sarah knew it was Sam but turned in a slow, deliberate fashion and tried to act a little surprised. "Oh, hi, Sam. I was just lost in my book. Looks like the crowd is thinning out a little. How's it going today?"

"It's good. Business is good. I heard from Jean-Pierre about your new job. He said you guys are running yourselves clothed. I think he meant ragged; he's funny. So, I've seen him but not you. Too busy to stop in to see me?" Sam's arms moved in large gesticulating circles as he spoke. His movements were as exuberant as his personality.

"I've missed you the last few times I've been in. We must be on different schedules or something." Sarah spoke with open palms. "Work has been crazy busy. We're making a go of it, but it is exhausting. I don't think Theresa has slept more than three hours a night since we started. It's a little scary to think we're putting in all this work, and it could collapse at any moment."

"Sounds like you might be working too hard. You need to come here and relax more often. It's good for you." Sam's smile filled his face as he laughed a little. "Anyway, how are you liking France now that you're no longer a tourist, so to speak?"

"I find that it suits me, particularly the climate. Of course, now I'm trying to settle in and get better acquainted with the locals." Her eyes sparkled.

As she spoke, Sarah noticed that the other tables had cleared out, with only a few people around. Now was her chance. Her heart raced and kicked so hard in her chest that she feared she might faint.

"Do you have time to join me?" She motioned toward the chair next to her. The words came out calm despite the jackhammer throbbing in her chest.

Sam looked around the patio and glanced toward the bar and kitchen. All of his employees were busy and engaged in their work. "Sure, it looks like they have everything under control. How about a brandy while we talk, no?"

"That would be lovely."

Sam signaled that he would be right back and disappeared into the restaurant. Sarah placed a bookmark in her book, then stacked her dirty plates together and set them at the edge of the table. A couple of deep breaths calmed her as she leaned back in her chair.

Two minutes later, Sam emerged from the bar with a bottle and two snifter glasses. He sat down next to her with an exuberant thud. "What do you think of this?" he asked as he handed her a bottle with a golden label and writing she did not understand.

"I have no idea, but it looks great."

"The label says 'Ararat' in Armenian. This is Armenian cognac!" Sam raised his shoulders and looked around back and forth rapidly as if he expected to get hit with mortar fire at any moment.

Confusion was evident on Sarah's face.

"I shouldn't say that too loudly," Sam whispered. "Everyone gets real pissed when you call something cognac that's not from France. We have to call it brandy." Sam threw back his head and laughed straight from his belly.

Sarah looked at his face. He looked less than youthful but not old. It was clear that middle age had set in—the lines on his face were deeper and more plentiful than a young man—but Sarah didn't mind. The extra cracks and creases enhanced his rugged, handsome appearance and gave him an experienced, commanding air.

"Oh, yeah, of course." Sarah nodded, well aware of the *appellation d'origine contrôlée* designation but felt no need to comment.

"Anyway, in Armenia it is cognac; in France it is brandy." Sam pulled the stopper from the bottle and dropped a generous pour into each of the waiting glasses. He raised his glass and said, "*Genatzut!*"

"*Genatzut*," replied Sarah. "Or as we say in America, cheers!"

"Cheers!" Sam replied.

They both took lingering sips of their brandies. The opulent, golden spirit tasted slightly sweet on Sarah's tongue; notes of vanilla and oak danced on her palate. While not a frequent brandy drinker, she knew what she liked, and she liked this. The pair sat in silence as they each enjoyed a few more sips. Sarah felt like she had gathered all of the courage, liquid or otherwise, she could muster. The timing would get no better.

"You know, Sam, I really enjoy talking with you. But I feel like we only barely know each other. That seems like a shame." Sarah's words were soft and silky.

"It is," Sam agreed. "I always look forward to seeing you. Any time you show up, the whole day gets better." He smiled earnestly.

Sarah, encouraged by his words and smile, pushed herself to continue. "I was wondering if you'd be interested in going out together sometime? I have tickets for a play called *Beast on the Moon* for next Sunday. I've never seen it, but I'm told it's very powerful and that it has an Armenian connection."

"I would love to, yes," Sam answered enthusiastically. His accent added charm to his words.

"It won't interfere with running this place, will it?"

"No, no. I can arrange for someone else to manage that night. Sundays are usually slow anyway." Sam paused and rubbed the back of his neck. "It's funny, I've been meaning to ask you out, but I've always been too nervous. Imagine, me, too nervous."

They both laughed, and their eyes exuded warmth.

"I'm so glad you beat me to it," Sam said.

The last remaining customers had dwindled. Sarah and Sam found themselves alone at the wrought iron table with the colorful umbrella. They talked, laughed, and drank until it became apparent that the staff had cleaned up around them and were waiting to leave. Sam dismissed them, but the moment had gone. With joy in their hearts, the pair said their goodbyes. As Sarah walked home, she felt something unfamiliar to her. A warm upwelling from deep inside, like a circle being completed: satisfaction.

CHAPTER 36

The ancient trees welcomed Sarah back as she eased her way down the narrow path and basked in the warm rays of the Marseilles sun. Her heart was full, afloat in a deep well of warmth and satisfaction she'd thought unobtainable. She felt satiated, like a tigress sprawled on the savannah after a gorge on fresh-caught deer. Sarah's life had become full; rarely a moment without work, a date, or an errand to run.

In a bid to help Hackingham's new company along, she'd submitted the flavors she'd begun at Avenir D'or: a spicy mushroom sauce—a huge hit of umami followed by a slow cayenne burn—and a red wine and roasted meat flavor—rich like daube but creamy and intense.

A few days earlier, a call had come through from the lawyer. The house had been sold and the estate was basically settled. He'd sent over some paperwork for her to sign and wired her the modest remainder of her family's net worth. With that, it was all gone. Her childhood, her mom, her dad, all reduced to an unimpressive number on a bank statement. She couldn't help but chuckle when she thought about what her parents might have said about her current situation. Which choice aphorism would Henry have applied? Would Nancy have been proud? She hoped so.

Sarah's thoughts turned to Sam. Their relationship had bloomed into a healthy, loving romance. Their first date was a resounding success, despite *Beast on the Moon* having been a poor choice for such an occasion. The performance was superb, but the play was heavy; the characters were pained and tormented as survivors of the Armenian Genocide. It was about as upbeat as *Schindler's List* on a January night, outside, naked... in sleet. Nevertheless, they enjoyed the performance and cried together. After the show, it took a couple of brandies to realign their spirits.

Sarah was continually impressed by Sam's adorable demeanor and soft touch. At the restaurant, he was a lion, or a king, who commanded the kitchen staff with a firm hand and only on occasion let his gentler nature show. In everyday life, Sam led with his heart. Sarah learned to love the little things about him—the way he held her hand and caressed it as they walked down the street, or the softness of his kisses as they lay on her couch and watched the world go by.

A favorite thing about her relationship with Sam was that they were both a part of it because they wanted to be. In the past, Sarah had always felt like she needed somebody, never just wanted them. This time was different. Sarah and Sam were independent, self-sustaining organisms.

However, every now and then, in the late hours when things were calm and her mind was still, thoughts of home would creep in like a cat in the mists. The images came through like a portal to another lifetime—another world. Sarah would wonder what everyone back home was doing at that very instant. Were they happy, lonely, satisfied? She wondered if anyone ever thought of her the way she thought of them now. She missed Bernie's advice and good humor. Her compassion overflowed as she thought about Richard and Phyllis and Bea. She hoped they were all well and happy. Sometimes, in the dark, she would even think about Michael. Had he been able to make Uncle Geoffrey's house a home? Did he find someone? Usually, just as she was drifting off on the river of sleep, she would resolve herself to return one day and check in on him.

More than anyone else from back home, Sarah missed Loretta. Not a day went by when Sarah did not miss her friendship, wit, and advice. While she had become close with both Jean-Pierre and Theresa, neither compared with Loretta. Even thousands of miles away, Sarah still regularly called her and basked in the glow of their friendship. Loretta's tireless support and good humor had helped Sarah through dark times and added even more joy to her new, brighter days.

A gentle wind blew the limbs of the mammoth trees that swayed in a soft murmur. Sarah sat on a small, wooden bench and breathed deep. The fresh air felt good; the bold afternoon sun warmed her face. As she exhaled, she let go of the worry and uncertainty that followed her like a shadow—*will I have a job in six months? If not, what then?* Instead, she reflected at how far she'd come and the boundlessness of her future. No longer was she what someone else wanted her to be; she was what she needed herself to be. Come what may, she was reaching for her potential. For once, she felt fortunate and happy, unafraid to dare, risk, and hope.

In her mind, Sarah tried to freeze it all, so she could take it all in full. She wished to gaze at her present life in a snapshot, like a painting, and observe and feel it. But, of course, she could not and relented to the physical universe. With a sigh, she acknowledged that the arrow of time moves only in one direction and cannot be stopped. It was a happy sigh, a relief, as if she had let it all out—the past, the future, all of it. For that moment, that one fleeting moment, she sat still and was present.

ACKNOWLEDGMENTS

I wish to acknowledge and thank Ani Saryan Kopf, David Kopf, and Kristine Nieman for their early and continued support, without which this book would never have come to life. Thank you for believing in me.

With a humble mind and a grateful heart, I want to thank all the supporters who helped make this book possible:

Zach Abramowski,
Karlla Albertini,
Faye Analla,
Kevin and Ann Anundson,
Diana and Diran Balekian,
Alex Bargamian,
Brett Bargamian,
Jordan Bouikidis,
Daniel Budziszewski,
Bryan Conti,
Donna R. Crnovich,
Alex Crowe,
See Delaney,
Brad Dezek,
Lara Dilanjian,
Linda and Jerry Doran,
Jace Dowd,
Connie Ellingson,
Karen and Hal Francisco,
Jason Gierl,

Elizabeth Gramz,
Cheri Griffin,
Lisa A. Groh,
John Grochowski,
Rick Hagopian,
Mary Kay Hajinian,
Melanie Haroian,
Patrick Hessling,
Jessica Horning,
Benjamin Hoyt,
Susan Jackson-Afong and Roger Afong,
Jeremiah Johnson,
Judith Kalajian,
Michael Kalajian,
Laura Kee,
Nicholas Kee,
Scott Kietzmann,
Eric Koester,
Dave Kopf,
Evelyn Kopf,
Gerhard Kopf,
Susan Kopf,
Michelle Kosalka,
Carla Lemminger,
Susie Lietz,
Lance Lippincott,
Shae Maclin,
Vahan Mahdasian,
John Marszalkowski,
Amanda McGinness,
Ally Miller,
Kristine Nieman,
Shane Olivo,
Lisa Marie Parker,
Cassie Patterson,
Linda Paul,
Donald K. Petersen,
Beth Riffe,
Carolyn Rowland,
Clare and Darlene Sampley,
Brian Sampley,
Ani Saryan Kopf,
Arlene Saryan and Christian Alexander,
Armen Saryan,
John and Debra Saryan,
Judith Saryan and Victor Zarougian,
Shirley and Levon Saryan,
Rebecca Scheller,
Karen Scofield,
Lynnewood Jeff Shafer II,
Kenneth Siegel,
Reh Starks-Harling,
Chuck Tolentino,
Kenneth Uzquiano,
Tamar Vartanian,
Victoria Vuletich Kane,
Jennifer Watson, and
Laura Zarougian

I would also like to thank Joanna Hatzikazakis, my editor, for her guidance and excellent suggestions. This novel is a much better book thanks to you.

An additional thank you to Eric Koester for putting me in touch with New Degree Press.

Made in the USA
Middletown, DE
11 May 2022